50-17

# TO HOMER
# THROUGH POPE

An Introduction to Homer's *Iliad* and
Pope's Translation

*By*

## H. A. MASON

**BOOKS**
10 East 53d St., New York 10022
*(a division of Harper & Row Publishers, Inc.)*

Published in the U.S.A 1972 by
HARPER & ROW PUBLISHERS, INC.
BARNES & NOBLE IMPORT DIVISION

ISBN 06 4946347

© H. A. Mason 1972

Printed in Great Britain

# Contents

# Acknowledgments

THIS book is substantially based on lectures as delivered under the terms of the F. R. Leavis Lectureship Trust during the Hilary Term of 1969. I have to thank the Faculties of *Literae Humaniores* and of English Literature in the University of Oxford for including me on their lecture lists and providing an excellent time and place for delivering the lectures. Similar facilities and privileges were granted to me at Cambridge in the previous term.

I also have to thank the Rector and Fellows of Lincoln College, Oxford, for allowing me to be their guest while I was giving the lectures.

The task of providing the best texts for quotation was made easier by the kindness of the Master and Fellows of Trinity College, Cambridge, who made available to me some of the treasures of the Wren library for consultation and transcription.

Acknowledgment is also made to the following publishers and copyright holders for permission to quote from published work:— Ezra Pound, Faber & Faber Ltd. and New Direction Inc.: *The Cantos of Ezra Pound* and *Collected Shorter Poems*; Thomas Nelson & Sons Ltd.: W. H. D. Rouse's translation of *The Iliad*; Penguin Books Ltd.: E. V. Rieu's translation of *The Odyssey*, Copyright E. V. Rieu, 1946, and of *The Iliad*, Copyright E. V. Rieu, 1966.

*It is always a fortunate moment in the literary life of a country when masterpieces from the past unthaw and once again become matters of urgent contemporary interest, for they then produce on us a completely fresh effect. The Sun of Homer dawned for us afresh, very much in keeping with the spirit of the times, which strongly favoured his reappearance. For after a long period of continuing emphasis on Nature, we eventually learned how to look at the Classics from this angle.*

GOETHE
*Aus meinem Leben. Dichtung und Wahrheit.*
Part Three, Book XII.

*A very interesting chat with Wordsworth about his poetry. He repeated emphatically what he had said before to me, that he did not expect or desire from posterity any other fame than that which would be given him for the way in which his poems exhibit man in his essentially human character and relations as child, parent, husband, the qualities which are common to all men as opposed to those which distinguish one man from another.*

H. C. ROBINSON
Aug. 17, 1837

# ONE

# Introductory: Inevitable Ignorance?

'To Homer through Pope' is all very well as a general title since it sums up my theme fairly adequately, but it could easily prove misleading if it were thought to contain a suggestion that Pope's version of the *Iliad* was the equivalent of the original. Just think what a claim that would be! It would amount to placing Pope on a level with Shakespeare. I have not fallen into such an absurdity, though I may soon be thought to have become the victim of a notion quite as absurd when I declare that we need the help of translations, however good our Greek, if we are in any real sense to possess the *Iliad*. If my aim had merely been to assess the merits of Pope's translation, I could have spread myself in various directions and taken in a number of features which would show Pope's work to greater advantage and more poetically successful than it will be allowed to appear in any part of this book. But my aim is to say persuasively something central about the *Iliad*, and to show how useful Pope's version and Pope's Notes can become if we want to be brought into the right frame of mind for appreciating the lasting value of the epic.

Each chapter is offered as 'a wholly new start' in that in each some part of the *Iliad* or of Pope's translation is taken as an excuse for raising one of the questions that ought to engage us first, whether we are comparative beginners or seasoned fellow-travellers with both Homer and Pope. For my design is to do more than hand out a few critical tips on selected portions of Homer. I hope it will be found that I have presented a coherent set of hypotheses which can be tried out at leisure on all the forty-eight books and on all the translations of Homer published under Pope's name.

If I am willing to leave the emphasis here, with the remark that half the travel for the beginner consists in making the right *premier pas*, my reason was to redress a wrong that occurred when I was myself an undergraduate and tackling the Homeric epics seriously for the first time. For I imbibed from my teachers several ideas about both Homer and Pope that proved wrong, and limited my enjoyment of both through the prime of my life down to what Henry James politely called the middle years. There is very little that is overtly polemical in these chapters, but they were brought into being in part as a criticism of contemporary views of Homer and of the contemporary estimate of Pope, if the word 'contemporary' may be allowed to extend backward to the 1930s, when, as far as I am concerned, the trouble began.

Such presumption cannot be expressed too modestly, for it is of such a kind that if I fail to justify it I fall very flat indeed. It will not take the form of claiming that my views on Homer and Pope are worthy to replace those that have been current in the last thirty or forty years because they are *new*, even though they came to *me* rather late in life as new and unexpected experiences. I prefer to say that I shall be doing with Homer something like what I tried to do with Juvenal,[1] i.e. returning to views that had a long and respectable history which had become obscured by the pedantry of scholars without critical ability. In helping to bury the immediate past I hope at the same time to be exhuming and releasing the imperishable current of ideas that once ran freely in the great world about Homer's epics and in England about Pope's translations.

The first question I should like to ask is, what kind of opinion is worth having on Homer, and who has it? At one time I was sure of the answer, and would have maintained that it was embodied in the following anecdote. Alexander Pope is said to have gone up to Bentley one day at Dr Mead's and to have addressed him in these words:

'Dr. Bentley, I ordered my bookseller to send you your books; I hope you received them.' Bentley, who had purposely avoided saying any thing about Homer, pretended not to understand him, and asked, 'Books! books! what books?' 'My Homer,' replied Pope, 'which you did me the honour to subscribe for.'—'Oh,' said Bentley, 'ay, now I recollect—your translation:—it is a pretty poem, Mr. Pope; but you must not call it Homer.'[2]

---

[1] In articles first published in *Arion*, Vol. I, Nos. 1-2 (1962), under the title 'Is Juvenal a Classic?' and reprinted in *Critical Essays on Roman Literature: Satire*, (1963), ed. J. P. Sullivan.

[2] Taken from *The Works of Samuel Johnson, LL.D.*, Vol. IV (1787), p. 126n. This is the popular version, but a more probable, and certainly a juster, account was given in the *Gentleman's Magazine*, first in October 1773 and again in June 1781, where the 'pay-off' line runs, 'Why, . . . the lines are good lines, the translation is a good translation, but you must not call it Homer, it is a good translation of Spondanus.'

When I was an undergraduate, that seemed to be that: the question was disposed of once and for all, since I supposed that, because Bentley was the greatest living classical scholar of the day, he *knew* Homer in a way a half-educated poet could not hope to rival. But now I am inclined to ask, what in fact did Bentley know? Let the discovery of the digamma (F) be taken as representative of that knowledge. My question would now be whether the possession of that kind of knowledge has any bearing on our search for the poetical merits of the *Iliad*, and whether the passage from classical scholar to literary critic is not as enormous and unthinkable as that from the category of *is* to that of *ought*? In fact, I wonder whether Pope did not have the last laugh, and settle the question, when he wrote:

> As many quit the streams that murm'ring fall
> To lull the sons of Marg'ret and Clare-hall,
> Where Bentley late tempestuous wont to sport
> In troubled waters, but now sleeps in Port.
> Before them march'd that awful Aristarch;
> Plow'd was his front with many a deep Remark:
> His Hat, which never vail'd to human pride,
> Walker with rev'rence took, and lay'd aside.
> Low bow'd the rest: He, kingly, did but nod;
> So upright Quakers please both Man and God.
> Mistress! dismiss that rabble from your throne:
> Avaunt——is Aristarchus yet unknown?
> Thy mighty Scholiast, whose unweary'd pains
> Made Horace dull, and humbled Milton's strains.
> Turn what they will to Verse, their toil is vain,
> Critics like me shall make it Prose again.
> Roman and Greek Grammarians! know your Better:
> Author of something yet more great than Letter;
> While tow'ring o'er your Alphabet, like Saul,
> Stands our Digamma, and o'er-tops them all.[1]

So powerfully had I prejudged the issue on general grounds—I return again to my undergraduate days—that this particular case, the claims of Pope's translation to reproduce the essential spirit of Homer, went completely by the board. But what was a personal prejudice can easily be seen to be almost universal. How many editions of Pope's Poems

---

[1] *The Dunciad, in Four Books.* Printed according to the complete Copy found in the Year 1742. (1743.) Book IV, lines 199-218.

contain his Homeric translations? How many editions of Pope's Homeric translations contain his Notes? Even now, when those notes have been at last made available, the Twickenham Edition[1] gives us Pope's Homer as a poor relation of the rest of the Works—of less importance than a trivial collection of Minor Poems!

Now, in my old age, I say: before we can answer our particular question, we must answer the general question: what sort of critical opinion, if any, has *authority*, and how much? I have spent my adult life considering this question and yet I don't think I could answer it. The world at large has not answered it, and, generally speaking, the answers it has accepted were foolish answers. For instance, there is no such thing as the verdict of Time, or, if you can make the phrase stand for something real, that something has no authority. Nor is number any criterion: fifty million Frenchmen can be wrong. What is so maddening for me is that I can't shrug the whole thing off as an antiquarian delusion. Even though I can't say what true judgement is, I am sure it stands for something that both has existed, exists and will come into existence. Yet I have academic colleagues who continue to lecture on the merits of authors while firmly believing that any one opinion about merits is as valuable and as worthless as any other. This is what makes the question so lively: everybody is to some extent inconsistent in dealing with it. Although the question is obviously too big for me or for our immediate concern, I am sure that we ought not to let it drop because it is, as it were, too hot, or too unwieldy to manage.

The question that therefore remains is: who is fit to pronounce on the merits of Homer? Two extremes can be ruled out at once. It is possible to know a great deal about Homer's words and syntax and to be quite incompetent when it comes to Homer's poetry. On the other hand, it is hard to see how a man with all the competence in the world as a judge of poetry can have anything valuable to say about Homer unless in a real sense he knows Homer's words and syntax. But has anybody capable of grasping textual problems as well as those of lexicography ever said anything even mildly impressive about the poetry? If we find it hard to name names, this is an astonishing fact; something so unnatural that we ought not to accept it without asking questions. Must the blame for it lie exclusively on schools and universities? I wish I were not so ignorant, for it seems to me that if we

---

[1] See Epilogue, p. 196.

could find out how it all began, we might be able to recover what seems to me the natural combination of skill in scholarship and skill in literary judgement. I take it that in the heyday of Humanism schoolmasters were not pedants, professors were not merely scholars. That Humanist heyday does not seem to have lasted long. Is it true that the effective life of the Classics has consequently had to run outside the universities ever since Shakespeare's day?

Perhaps I could advance our enquiry by asking an easier question and giving a particular answer. If we want to know who is fit to comment on Homer, we might ask: what are the qualities of mind that make a successful reader of Homer, and what sort of response must you have to Homer before you have anything material to go on as a critic? Shall I be knocking on an open door if I require that before I can listen to criticism I must believe that the critic has been an enthusiast? That cool judgments are born in the fire? Cold judgments tell us only about the critic, not about the poem? Let me give an answer in concrete form. It is taken from a letter written by a young man aged twenty, who was, on religious grounds, refused entry into a university:

> [I value] the Authority of one true Poet above that of twenty Critics or Commentatours. But tho' I speak thus of Commentators, I will continue to read carefully all I can procure, to make up, that way, for my own want of a Critical understanding in the original Beauties of Homer. Though the greatest of them are certainly those of the Invention and Design, which are not at all confin'd to the Language: For the distinguishing Excellencies of Homer are, (by the consent of the best Criticks of all nations) first in the Manners, (which include all the speeches, as being no other than the Representations of each Person's Manners by his words:) and then in that Rapture and Fire, which carries you away with him, with that wonderfull Force, that no man who has a true Poetical spirit is Master of himself, while he reads him. Homer makes you interested and concern'd before you are aware, all at once; whereas Virgill does it by soft degrees. This, I believe, is what a Translator of Homer ought principally to imitate: and it is very hard for any Translator to come up to it, because the chief reason why all Translations fall short of their

Originals, is, that the very Constraint they are obliged to, renders 'em heavy and dispirited. The great Beauty of Homer's Language, as I take it, consists in that noble simplicity, which runs through all his works; (and yet his diction, contrary to what one would imagine consistent with simplicity, is at the same time very Copious.) . . .[1]

If I had known this letter of Pope's when I first heard the Bentley anecdote, I might at once have opened what was then a closed case. As it was, I trifled with Bentley's *Dissertation upon the Epistles of Phalaris*, etc., and stuck to the *Iliad* in Greek.

But a disagreeable personal question cannot be put off: am I, in the first place, too *ignorant* to qualify as a reader of Homer? If we take the word 'know' strictly and seriously, I do not know through what stages, if any, our Homeric text has gone, harking back to the time before it was a text and continuing to the time when it was finally fixed. The whole notion of this development lacks plausibility for me, just as all the suggested parallels with folk or primitive epics only serve to convince me that if you mean know, really know, then I do not know anything of the *Entstehungsgeschichte*, and would recommend a beginner to turn his attention rather to what is solidly there in the poems. But how much is there, solidly there? Somebody has said that of all genuine Christians Samuel Johnson managed to believe the least. Among enthusiasts for Homer I may be the one to whom the smallest amount of Homer has got through. I have no absolute conviction that the *Iliad* is a whole composed of our twenty-four books, no more and no less. I don't possess either epic in such a way that would enable me to dispute much about architectonics. I can go a little way but I lack real assurance. Worse still, I cannot get interested in long stretches of the epics, and this boredom arises in part because I cannot see why certain things that are there have to be there. So, although I have one advantage—a strong feeling that the best bits cannot be surpassed—I cannot enter on several topics that are happily treated in some other literary appreciations of Homer's epics.

How far is ignorance of this kind general and inevitable? Can it be shown that some of those who proclaim that they know more are living in a fool's paradise? Each man should make his own self-confession. It may lead to an inevitable parting of the ways, for the

---

[1] Alexander Pope to Ralph Bridges, April 5th, 1708. (*The Correspondence of Alexander Pope* (1956), ed. G. Sherburn, Vol. I, p. 44.)

reader who does not feel that the price of having a complete Homer is that we fill in huge blank spaces from our imagination won't have patience with me when I urge that we all need translations, however good our Greek. One of the things Pope's version is useful for, I shall be arguing, is to show us how to fill in and fill out the areas where Homer is not a solid fact. We can't fill our blanks with Pope's imagination, but we can imitate him and try something analogous ourselves.

The only great fact about the *Iliad* I feel sure of is that what we read is poetry and very much meditated art. I might go on and fall into the temptation of saying that it is obviously older than any art we know in the sense that it has more directly behind it than our Dante and Shakespeare had behind them in epic or drama, but that would not be what my knowledge tells me. I am happy enough to see that Homer is not separated from later poets, and that what he has in common with Virgil is more important than what separates them. Yet, in saying all this, I am aware that I have gone too far with one extreme, and it is time to do justice to the other. We cannot put our nineteenth-century inheritance to sleep. Time and Western Man can never now be parted. Consequently, to be modern for us is to be something quite different from what it meant to Virgil or Pope. If I claim that bits of Homer can become modern, I am saying something that strains credibility. I am certainly nauseated by those translations into modern English that part with everything that could have commended Homer to the great men of the past. I find it very hard, though, to say what I really want. I may be longing for an impossible co-presence of the present and the past; yet something of what I want occurs to us all when we read the original and forget ourselves and remember ourselves, immerse ourselves and re-emerge into the modern world still taking our Achilles or Odysseus with us. The experiences we have then make it plausible to hope that even fuller experience could be had if there were great contemporary translators, translators willing to absorb every scrap of knowledge that makes us see Homer as both like and unlike us.

The most awkward criticism of my pretensions I know of is one that I find it much easier to make by imagining it as coming from a very friendly voice: 'I can quite sympathize with your desire to be useful in introducing the *Iliad* to beginners, but wasn't the introduction made perfectly once and for all by *Matthew Arnold*?' My

admiration for Arnold's lectures[1] on translating Homer is very great:
I would place the book among his own best things, and it is the best
introduction to the *Iliad* that I have met with. I shall simply assume
that anyone reading this book will have made himself familiar with it
or will take my tip and give it a fair trial.

In the first place, on the charge of ignorance, you will find in his
fourth lecture, *Last Words*,[2] a reply to his victim's self-defence,[3] the
test by which I must stand or fall, be finally exposed or, if not vindi-
cated, at least let off for the time being. For Arnold there admits that
he himself, compared with the scholar, was an ignorant man:

> And yet, perverse as it seems to say so, I sometimes find myself
> wishing, when dealing with these matters of poetical criticism,
> that my ignorance were even greater than it is. To handle these
> matters properly there is needed a poise so perfect, that the least
> overweight in any direction tends to destroy the balance. Temper
> destroys it, a crotchet destroys it, even erudition may destroy it.
> To press to the sense of the thing itself with which one is dealing,
> not to go off on some collateral issue about the thing, is the
> hardest matter in the world. The 'thing itself' with which one is
> here dealing,—the critical perception of poetic truth,—is of all
> things the most volatile, elusive, and evanescent; by even pressing
> too impetuously after it, one runs the risk of losing it. The critic
> of poetry should have the finest tact, the nicest moderation, the
> most free, flexible, and elastic spirit imaginable; he should be
> indeed the 'ondoyant et divers,' the *undulating and diverse* being
> of Montaigne. The less he can deal with his object simply and
> freely, the more things he has to take into account in dealing
> with it,—the more, in short, he has to encumber himself,—so
> much the greater force of spirit he needs to retain his elasticity.
> But one cannot exactly have this greater force by wishing for it;
> so, for the force of spirit one has, the load put upon it is often
> heavier than it will well bear. The late Duke of Wellington
> said of a certain peer that 'it was a great pity his education had
> been so far too much for his abilities.' In like manner, one often

---

[1] *On Translating Homer: Three Lectures Given at Oxford* (1861).

[2] *Last Words: A Lecture given at Oxford* (1862).

[3] *Homeric Translation in Theory and Practice* (1861). A Reply to Matthew
Arnold, Esq., Professor of Poetry, Oxford. By Francis W. Newman, A Translator
of the *Iliad*.

sees erudition out of all proportion to its owner's critical faculty. Little as I know, therefore, I am always apprehensive, in dealing with poetry, lest even that little should prove 'too much for my abilities.'[1]

Arnold's genius was to make clear to us what are the permanent issues that everybody must consider who takes up Homer. These permanent issues can then be discussed, once properly isolated and freed from trivial collateral issues, without further reference to Arnold. What makes his work unique is that it is the only one I know to escape Pope's sweeping condemnation of the books on Homer written by the learned:

> It is something strange that of all the Commentators upon *Homer*, there is hardly one whose principal Design is to illustrate the Poetical Beauties of the Author. They are voluminous in explaining those Sciences which he made but subservient to his Poetry, and sparing only upon that Art which constitutes his Character. This has been occasion'd by the Ostentation of Men who had more Reading than Taste, and were fonder of shewing their Variety of Learning in all Kinds, than their single Understanding in Poetry. Hence it comes to pass that their Remarks are rather Philosophical, Historical, Geographical, Allegorical, or in short rather any thing than Critical and Poetical.'[2]

Arnold is especially valuable to us here because he virtually says: 'Let us not talk about anything until we have told ourselves what in a general way we take Homer to be.' He suggests that we must occupy a position somewhere between two extremes. The question, put shortly, amounts to this: is Homer the world's greatest poet, who has never been surpassed, or does he belong in the *Beowulf* class, a gifted, primitive child, whose central ideas have all been left behind? Both extremes have been seriously held, for both are securely based on selected facts. Which perhaps gives us a hint of the way to answer the dilemma. We can also learn something from noting that one view incorporates the tradition from antiquity down to the eighteenth century, while the other represents the triumph of the German ideas on which modern classical scholarship is based.

Some might make it a charge against Arnold that he was deaf to

---

[1] *Op. cit.*, pp. 10-11.
[2] *Observations on the First Book* (1715), p. 3.

what the eighteenth century had to teach him, and too eager to listen to what his contemporaries who wrote in the early part of his life and those writing just before he was born were telling him of the modern European spirit. Yet this is a charge I am unwilling to push, for I don't find it easy to tap the wisdom of either Dryden or Pope. I shall have to struggle much harder to get fair play for Pope than to get recognition for the best parts of Homer. But if I may for a moment glance ahead to my central theme, I am quite confident that to try to see why and how Pope took Homer as he did will help us when we are trying to see how *we* ought to take Homer. For Pope seems to me to have been looking in the right direction. Which is only a way of confessing that my mind is made up. I am committed to Pope's view that Homer is interesting because he has something to tell us about Man. So I don't mind archaeologists and others using Homer to fill out their meagre pictures of the civilization or civilizations in the Aegean during and before Homer's day, if I am allowed to put as my main question to the epics: are they great poetry and can they perform poetry's greatest office, to make us, in a good sense, more knowing about Man?

Yet all the same it would be cant if I said I thought that Arnold's introduction would do. Although I shall go back to it again with a sure expectation of finding further illumination, I must pronounce a verdict on it that for me is final, but may make the opposite impression on many modern readers. The side of Arnold I cannot stomach is the Victorian. Now that many to-day are so stuck on the Victorians or so stuck in the Victorian age that every other seems without interest; now that every third-rate Victorian novelist seems to compete with Shakespeare if not to surpass him, it may sound hopelessly old-fashioned to declare that some Victorian values have not lasted very well. Let me at any rate single out one *trait* in Arnold's lectures that makes me put the book down and try to approach Homer on my own. It is the wilful attempt to see Homer as an example of Victorian *nobility*. I call it wilful, since the attempt could not be made without deliberately ignoring what was visible to all Victorians in Homer's text. (For this reason alone F. W. Newman's reply to Arnold should be bound up with every copy of Arnold's lectures.) Homer, I shall hope to show, is not noble in the way Tennyson was noble, and Arnold was canting when he persevered in the face of the facts in setting up our author on a false pedestal.

Severe as this verdict sounds, I should prefer to begin to make it good by starting with further tribute to the merits of his lectures. For Arnold raised his own mind to its highest pitch to match Homer's. He rightly saw that we cannot hope to relish Homer's true greatness unless we place him alongside 'the five or six supreme poets of the world'. But how can we do this effectively? People who try to balance and play off the world's greatest poems usually end in the Higher Waffle. Arnold had the tact and ability to select passages from great poets which bring back the telling contexts in which they are immortal. So far so good. But what is this *nobility* that he considers characteristic of great poetry and of Homer? Could this be one of the blind spots of the Victorians?

Arnold introduces the epithet 'noble' as one of four defining qualities. Homer, he says, is eminently noble. From the beginning Arnold thinks of this quality as one of manner and style:

> . . . in spite of this perfect plainness and directness of his ideas, he is eminently *noble*; he works as entirely in the grand style, he is as grandiose, as Phidias, or Dante, or Michael Angelo.[1]

Arnold, therefore, quite properly devotes his second lecture to the task of defining the grand style, and admirably approaches it by contrasting it with the ballad style:

> Homer's manner and movement are always both noble and powerful: the ballad-manner and movement are often either jaunty and smart, so not noble; or jog-trot and humdrum, so not powerful.[2]

I shall therefore attack Arnold where he is at the height of his argument, illustrating what he calls *the* grand style. For this is the place where he attempts to give us the essential note, a great part of what he calls the general effect Homer makes on a qualified reader. But as soon as I allow myself to say 'attack', my sense of things reminds me that although I am going to invite you to look at a very different Homer from Arnold's, it is, I hope, the same Homer, *minus* the Victorian eccentricity. Even in Arnold's parting summary there is much that I gladly take over:

> Well, then, the ballad-manner and the ballad-measure, whether in the hands of the old ballad poets, or arranged by

---

[1] *On Translating Homer* (1861), p. 29.
[2] *Op. cit.*, p. 47.

Chapman, or arranged by Mr. Newman, or, even, arranged by Sir Walter Scott, cannot worthily render Homer. And for one reason: Homer is plain, so are they; Homer is natural, so are they; Homer is spirited, so are they; but Homer is sustainedly noble, and they are not. Homer and they are both of them natural, and therefore touching and stirring; but the grand style, which is Homer's, is something more than touching and stirring; it can form the character, it is edifying. The old English balladist may stir Sir Philip Sidney's heart like a trumpet, and this is much: but Homer, but the few artists in the grand style, can do more; they can refine the raw natural man, they can transmute him. So it is not without cause that I say, and say again, to the translator of Homer: 'Never for a moment suffer yourself to forget our fourth fundamental proposition, *Homer is noble.*' For it is seen how large a share this nobleness has in producing that general effect of his, which it is the main business of a translator to *re*produce.[1]

I wish that nowadays one could count on all readers having freshly present in their minds the contents of the last book of Virgil's *Aeneid*, since I feel fairly confident that if anybody placed one of Arnold's 'touchstones' for determining the grand style in its context, his inevitable report would be in terms of distaste ranging from mild to repulsive:

> disce, puer, uirtutem ex me uerumque laborem,
> fortunam ex aliis. . . .          (*Aeneid* XII, 435-36)

which Arnold rendered:

> From me, young man, learn nobleness of soul and true effort;
> learn success from others.[2]

The priggish-melancholy note of Aeneas, oh so conscious in his modesty of the nobility of the example he is setting his son, is exactly what the Victorians found 'edifying'. They are welcome to it, but not to confounding it with the quite different note sounded by *Achilles* in a situation where he is behaving like a cad and a brute and is violating one of the most sacred laws of Greek religion. Arnold does his best to get away with the *supercherie* by rendering the Greek of his other touchstone as if it were from the 'soppiest' part of Virgil:

[1] *Op. cit.*, pp. 60-61.   [2] *Op. cit.*, p. 58.

Be content, good friend, die also thou!
why lamentest thou thyself on this wise?
Patroclus, too, died, who was a far better than thou.[1]

When we see how Newman taunted Arnold with his inability to
admit the word 'bitch' into the *Iliad*,[2] we know we are up against a
deep defensive scheme. Newman was, of course, right in insisting that
Homer was continually lapsing from the Victorian standard of noble
decorum. But just as Arnold failed to appreciate these 'lapses', he also
failed to see what was Homer's true dignity. Homer's dignity is quite
another thing than Victorian dignity. Like Shakespeare's and Dante's,
it is compatible with a great deal of low-level coarseness. For failure
to see that it is not a blemish in the highest poetry to use expressions
which are in everyday life vulgar or coarse, Arnold's Homer resembles
Bowdler's Shakespeare. So let us place Arnold's touchstone in its
context. A mere glance will suffice at the Twenty-First Book of the
*Iliad*, where Achilles in his rage at the death of his friend, Patroclus,
kills an unarmed suppliant, named Lycaon:

He was an intelligent youth, and the speech he made a
Model of supplication: but all the same the
Voice that replied had no mercy in it for the son of Priam:
  'You were a fool to try that on me. There was a time, no
  Doubt, when, given the choice, I preferred on the whole to
  Let Trojans off; and most of those I caught alive I
  Returned for a ransom. But Patroclus had not then come to
  The hour of his reckoning. Now not a single one of
  The Trojans, and especially not one of Priam's sons, shall
  Get away with it, if god's doing plays them into my hands
  Between here and Ilium. So you, boy, come quietly, and
  Go the way of Patroclus, a better man than
  You are any day. Take a look at me, son,
  See what a fine chap I am. My father was one of
  The best; my mother from heaven. Yet my turn is coming,
  Sure as fate; maybe morning, maybe evening, or it could
  Even be mid-day, when my life will be taken
  From me. I don't know who from or when I
  Shall feel the final touch of a spear or hear the
  Last whistle from the bow-string.'

[1] *Op. cit.*, p. 58.   [2] *Op. cit.*, p. 57.

When the other
Got the message, his heart and his knees went flabby,
And he let go of his spear, and flopped down stretching
Out his arms. Achilles drew his sharp sword and
Plunged the blade in up to the hilt near the collar-
Bone. There the young man lay face down and his black blood
Ran into the earth. Achilles took him by the foot and
Slung him to drift down the river, and he chose this
Occasion to make a taunting speech:

'Go and sleep in
The river's bed. Cold fish will soon be along to lick the
Blood from your wound. I'm afraid you will have to do without
your
Mother's lament as she tucks you into your last good night. The
Wide sea instead will offer an ample bosom
When Scamander whirls you down there. Then some
Fish will shudder up on the black wave to nibble the white fat
Of Lycaon.

Die, damn you, the whole lot
Of you! Run all the way back to your sacred
City, and I'll get each one of you death in
Your backs. It'll be no good looking to the silvery
River for protection. I know you've killed any number
Of bulls and you've thrown in live horses to win the
God over. But that won't help you. You're all going to die
Like dogs till you've paid, the last man jack of
You, for getting Patroclus and raiding our ships, when
I was not there to save the Achaeans.'          (97-135)

Homer's episode is, in the original Greek, a fine study of the point
where the hero turns into a brute. There is no overt comment:
Homer's point is made by the dramatic speech which accompanies the
brutal act: the unashamed nakedness of the language of Achilles'
blood-lust. Homer is humanity gazing on and seeking to comprehend
inhumanity.

Arnold could easily have found a parallel to this in Dante, for
another of his famous 'touchstones' is taken from an episode which
opens in the thirty-second Canto of the *Inferno*, where the hero visits

the frozen region of the lowest hell reserved for traitors. Earlier in
this Canto Dante uses Homer's method of making the unspeakable
reveal itself by speech:

> And next I saw a thousand livid faces,
> Wizened by the cold: cold so intense that I
> Shudder as I recall the ice-bound waters,
> And always I must think of them with horror.
>
> As we moved towards the centre of all gravity,
> I shivered in the everlasting chill. Whether
> It was an act of will or chance or fate, I
> Cannot tell, but as we made our way between
> The frozen heads, my foot struck one in the face.
>
> Tears came, and it bawled: 'What are you treading
> On me for? Is this a fresh instalment of
> The punishment I suffer for my treachery?'
> I turned to Virgil. 'Wait for me here awhile,
> Master, till I find out who this is. You may
> Hurry me on at your good will hereafter.'
>
> Virgil halted, and I said to the mouth that
> Was still cursing hard, 'What do you think you are
> Doing, swearing like that? Who are you?' 'Who are
> *You*?' it replied, and what do you think you are
> Doing in this region of the Trojan trai-
> tor, kicking people in the chaps? It felt like
> A blow from a living foot.' 'That's what it was,
> And you ought to be glad that I'm alive. I
> Could enter your name in my travel-notes, if
> You want publicity.' 'That's just what I *don't*
> Want,' it said, 'Take yourself off. We're not exactly
> Keen to be interviewed in this part of Hell.'
>
> So I took him by the hair at the scruff of
> His neck. 'You had better give me your name,' I
> Said, 'or you've seen the last of this little lot of
> Hair.' 'You can have every hair on my head,' it
> Replied, 'but you won't hear my name or see my
> Face, no, not if you give it a thousand kicks.'

I got a good grip on his hair and pulled out
Several chunks, but he only screamed and kept
His eyes turned to the ground. Then another trai-
tor began to shout: 'What's all this, Bocca? Curse
If you must, but why the devil d'you have to scream?'

'So that's your name, is it? Bocca!' I said, 'You
Needn't bother to talk now, you dirty trai-
tor. I'll make a full report and tell the world . . .'
'Tell them what you like,' he said, 'but get out of
Here, and if you do manage to return from
Hell, don't forget to mention what this fellow
Who couldn't keep his foul mouth shut is here for.'

'Put down this in your report: "among the trai-
tors kept in cold storage", you can say, "I saw
Buso of Dovera, known to all my read-
ers as the man who took bribes from the French." And
If they ask you who else was there, I can give you
A few more names.'

(70-118)

I must apologise for the translation and ask you to take on trust that
the qualities it seeks to bring out in Dante are really there in the Italian.
The chief thing I wanted to get across was what I called the *naked*
way of speaking. I mean by this that the speakers are not thinking about
the impression that they are making as they speak. They are not keeping up appearances. They express themselves with crude vigour. They
are not bothered about epic *decorum*. This, at any rate, is how I can't
help reading Homer's *Iliad*. Achilles seems to be speaking frankly
without airs. Just *what* is the right equivalent in modern English we
shall never know. But I am sure it is nothing like Arnold's:

> Be content, good friend, die also thou! why
> lamentest thou thyself on this wise?

We are not, however, driven back on to third-rate translations if
we seek through English to get closer to Homer's note in these
passages. The problem of presenting the hero as he merges into the
brute was solved by one of our own authors. I shall give the passage
in full to clinch my whole objection to Arnold's conception of the
grand style. What I wish to get rid of is all that is Victorian in the

word 'noble'. The note of nobility does not, I contend, involve removing action or speech from the centre of life and diverting it towards the 'edifying'. Certainly, we must be made to feel above the brutality presented: we must be allowed to see it through the eyes of humanity. The modern sickened fascination with brutality is not noble. But enough of generalization. Here is a passage that should help us to define true nobility in the context of brutality:

> *Macbeth.* Why should I play the Roman Foole, and dye
> On mine owne sword? whiles I see lives, the gashes
> Do better upon them.
> *Enter Macduffe.*
> *Macd.* Turne Hell-hound, turne.
> *Macb.* Of all men else I have avoyded thee:
> But get thee backe, my soule is too much charg'd
> With blood of thine already.
> *Macd.* I have no words,
> My voice is in my Sword, thou bloodier Villaine
> Then tearmes can give thee out.          *Fight: Alarum*
> *Macb.* Thou loosest labour,
> As easie may'st thou the intrenchant Ayre
> With thy keene Sword impresse, as make me bleed:
> Let fall thy blade on vulnerable Crests,
> I beare a charmed Life, which must not yeeld
> To one of woman borne.
> *Macd.* Dispaire thy Charme,
> And let the Angell whom thou still hast serv'd
> Tell thee, *Macduffe* was from his Mothers womb
> Untimely ript.
> *Macb.* Accursed be that tongue that tels mee so,
> For it hath Cow'd my better part of man:
> And be these Iugling Fiends no more beleev'd,
> That palter with us in a double sence,
> That keepe the word of promise to our eare,
> And breake it to our hope. Ile not fight with thee.
> *Macd.* Then yeeld thee Coward,
> And live to be the shew, and gaze o'th'time.
> Wee'l have thee, as our rarer Monsters are
> Painted upon a pole, and under-writ,
> Heere may you see the Tyrant.

*Macb.* I will not yeeld
To kisse the ground before young *Malcolmes* feet,
And to be baited with the Rabbles curse.
Though Byrnane wood be come to Dunsinane,
And thou oppos'd, being of no woman borne,
Yet I will try the last. Before my body,
I throw my warlike Shield: Lay on *Macduffe*,
And damn'd be him, that first cries hold, enough.
                              *Exeunt fighting. Alarums.*[1]

The humanity of Shakespeare is present in more complex ways here
than in the Greek or the Italian. Consider, for example, how much
else beside naked dramatic speech there is in the line

          And to be baited with the Rabbles curse . . .

But this is not the time or place to develop these arguments further.
I am aware that a reader must have leisure to try the passages over for
himself, to read them again and again until their local and temporal
peculiarities recede into the background and the foreground is occupied
by the note of true nobility.

    In the meantime I shall draw only one conclusion: that I now have
the reader's permission to emerge from under Arnold's blanket and
try for something simpler *de mon cru*.[2]

---

[1] *The Tragedie of Macbeth* (1623), Act V, vii.

[2] In offering this mellower account of Arnold's lectures on Homer, I do not
repudiate two earlier expressions of opinion, in *Arion*, Vol. I, No. 3, autumn 1962,
and in *Delta*, autumn 1963. The *Arion* review, entitled 'Arnold and the Classical
Tradition' has been reprinted in a collection of articles contributed to *Arion*, edited
by Professor W. J. N. Rudd. If the accent in Arnold's book were laid on the word
*translation*—which is, after all, the ostensible subject—my account would have to
be almost wholly adverse.

# TWO

# Basic Structures of
# the First Book of the *Iliad*

I T may sound astonishing to say that a man, after carefully going through all the main things that have been written on the *Iliad* since Greek times, might reasonably conclude that Homer's reputation has not yet been properly founded, and that his future reputation may well be greater even than anything he has enjoyed in the long centuries during which he was regarded as *princeps poetarum*, the chief of poets. Speaking for myself, I must be put in the class of those who believe with Pope that Homer's honours will grow with increase of ages, for I am convinced that Homer's *Iliad* is a much greater poem than it has so far appeared to me. Quite specifically, I regard the poem as potentially revelatory: Homer is a Sphinx from whom an Oedipus could obtain an answer: Homer, I feel, has something to reply about Man that is not now generally available. If we could get into the poem, we should find there something that would alter in a corrective way the stock of slumbering ideas on which we draw when measuring our actuality and potential as human beings. Homer has certainly despaired of Man but he has also affirmed, and, I have a sort of hunch, affirmed gloriously.

The poem, however, is hard to enter if it is a revelation of this kind. To return to Matthew Arnold, I should say that he was misleading in assuming that we immediately possess the poetry, and can engage in serious discussion about its quiddity, just as if we were tackling Milton. My Greek does not allow this, nor, I suspect, did Arnold's. So I advocate a very wary approach.

We ought rather to be happy to follow Arnold in searching first for the broadest, simplest truths about the poem, such as those he went for with his short slogans, 'Homer is rapid', etc. Now that Arnold has shown the way, I have come to think that you don't have to be an Arnold to do better than he did, particularly if you can be a great deal simpler and less pretentious than he was and go for matters that crop up in a naïve reading long before it is possible to say anything telling about poetic style. Recent experience has encouraged me to believe that a profitable meeting of minds can occur at this level, and that, provided that reference to words and phrases in the original is allowed, those who are approaching the poem for the first time and through English versions can engage with those who have been for years as familiar with the Greek as any modern can hope to be.

If we measure how slow to come actual enlightenment is on the central question: what is Man? when we use every channel of access, we know before we start that any introduction to the revelations in the *Iliad* is going to be a very slow process, and we can guess that many different kinds of approach will be needed. This chapter is merely a challenge to the sceptical who doubt whether *anything* can be made of the poem at this late date. I have supposed that the sceptic has said, 'Can you even start reading it, let alone finish?', and I have noted some things which I hope will be found to occur to anyone taking up the First Book and using a text with a facing translation, reading it, in fact, as it was read in bygone days by most people, including Chapman, Dryden and Pope.

The predominating impression left on me by a reading of such a kind was of a *complex unity* or of unity in complexity, and at the same time I was made aware of some of the artistic means used to obtain it. In particular, this impression of complex unity seems to derive its strength from the combination of two elements in the composition of the book: on the one hand, there is the artist's deliberate self-restriction to *one* aspect in his treatment of the history, on the other, there is the deliberate parallelism and contrast and interplay between Troy and Olympus, between man and the gods. The second impression is also mixed. While we are from the beginning made aware of the artist, of a mind behind the story, his point of view does not appear to be simple and the artistic means he adopts appear occasionally contradictory. Consequently, whereas some things seem right and inevitable even at a first reading, others jar and puzzle no matter how many times we return to them. When, for instance, we note the laconic manner in which we are told how the epidemic afflicts the troops—all Camus' *La Peste* in three lines—we think we have understood the author's manner, his love of economy; we think we see what Arnold meant by 'Homer is rapid'. But then we come upon lengthy, detailed accounts—and, as we discover later, *stereotyped*, detailed accounts—telling us how a ship is launched or how a sacrifice is prepared, and our sense of proportion is shocked.

There are, moreover, contradictions more internal than this. In the manner in which the heroes speak there is a contrast between elaborate rhetorical structure, elaborate diction, and the most brutal directness, such as

τὴν δ' ἐγὼ οὐ λύσω

('Let her go? Not me')

or

τείσειαν Δαναοὶ ἐμὰ δάκρυα σοῖσι βέλεσσιν

('give them a bullet for every teardrop')

phrases in which we cannot imagine that the words themselves or their order were chosen to suit the metre, for they are as short and brutal as in real life. All the speakers—yes, even Nestor—sooner or later come to the point in pithy, direct language: yet always the ringing phrase emerges from a deal of oratory and stereotyped phrasing. So often is this so that we must suppose that not only did the author intend, he *admired* the contrast. So that if we continue to say 'Homer is rapid' we must also say 'Homer is leisurely'. Consider, for example, in this book the number of repetitions of what we have been told once. If you notice how closely they follow each other, it is hard to maintain that they are *functional* in the sense that a hearer as distinct from a reader would need to be reminded of them. Once again it looks as though the author, like the authors of the Bible, enjoyed this form of narrative, enjoyed telling us once more what we already know. Lastly, there is the puzzle that though we feel that the author is standing back and judging his puppets—gods as well as men—it is hard to make out what he thinks of them and whether his attitude to them is consistent, the result of systematic meditation on all their actions.

But let us first turn to the overwhelming impression of unity: that the book is firmly restricted to one subject. If our first reply to the question: what is the subject? is, 'look at the first word of the poem, clearly it is μῆνις, something more elemental and more brutal than a filthy temper, though something a good deal less dignified than the *wrath* of the deity of the Old Testament, the μῆνις which is exhibited in dramatic speech and in narrative action', surely on reflection we must substitute the answer: 'Homer's subject is the *cause* of μῆνις'—for the cause is made plain throughout. What started it, the author

asks rhetorically, and proceeds at once to give his answer: it began
with a god. Thus what I have called the parallelism, that which
makes the unity complex, is brought out at the very beginning of
the book. Achilles has μῆνις, Achilles and Agamemnon have ἔρις
because Apollo had χόλος. And what made Apollo's liver secrete
bile? What caused him gall and bitterness of soul? It was because he
had *lost face, his honour was assailed, his prestige was damaged*—in a
word, because of τιμή. *The subject of the book is the rôle of τιμή in
earth and heaven.* The difficulty of making out all that this word
involves and finding equivalents in modern English epitomizes the
whole problem of the entry into this book.

Although, by the alternative translations I offered a sentence or
so back, drawn from the societies of Old China, mediaeval Europe
and modern America, I show that, if the Greeks had their word for it,
we have ours, I think we should first study the τιμή code as it displays
itself in this book. Let us take the first chain of events working back-
wards in time. There is an epidemic in the army. What caused it?
Apollo. Why? Because he was angry with Agamemnon. Why was he
angry? Because Agamemnon had taken away or destroyed the τιμή of
Apollo's own priest (cf. the verb ἀτιμάζω in line 11). Why should
Apollo kill people, on behalf of his priest? Because the priest paid τιμή
to him. The material acts of the cult, setting up altars and sacrific-
ing are the concrete, necessary constituents. We may say, then, that
though τιμή be an abstract notion, a man or a god knows very clearly
what acts show that he is getting it paid to him and what acts show that
he is losing or has lost it. Let us consider how the priest lost it. Not,
as you might have thought, through the loss of his daughter. She was a
legitimate prize and war-casualty which fell to the victors when
Chryse was raided by the people the author calls Achaeans or Danaans
and whom we may for convenience call the Greeks. But just as the
capture and enslavement of women were legitimate, part of the order
of things, so was ransom. The priest had gone through all the proper
forms to ransom his daughter, and the Greek army thought he should
have thereby got his daughter back. Nobody in the story seems to have
felt that Agamemnon's feelings about the girl mattered. (They only
matter to us who know what the consequences are going to be when
Agamemnon returns home!) No, the feelings that count are not
connected with Agamemnon's *love*, but those that arise from his τιμή.
For that was how he got the girl in the first place: she was allotted to
him when the captive females were distributed among the 'top brass'.

She was given to him because his τιμή required it: she was not his girl, she was his γέρας.

It is often overlooked that before we come to the μῆνις of Achilles, we get the μῆνις of Agamemnon. And why was he in a filthy temper? Partly, no doubt, at being forced to lose the girl, but the *indignity* of it strikes him equally. What will have happened to his τιμή if he loses his first prize and all his subordinates keep their prizes? The girl for him is finally his γέρας—the outward specific act required from the whole army, 'the sons of the Achaeans', to affirm publicly and manifestly his supreme military position. The importance of τιμή in the Homeric world—I mean in the epic—can be measured by what you had to pay for slighting it (τιμὴν τίνειν), what you had to do to 'satisfy' it. As we saw, Apollo requited the priest's loss of τιμή by the death of many soldiers, to say nothing of the mules, etc. One explanation of the length of the account of the expedition to Chryse may be that it was given to emphasize what it cost to satisfy the injured feelings of Apollo and to restore him his full measure of τιμή.

But the chief measurement of the importance of τιμή is the fierceness and the filthiness of temper of the man or god who has lost it or feels that he is threatened with loss of it. And when the dishonoured hero is in a temper it is no longer a question of paying back the 'just price'—all sense of measure is lost. Agamemnon is no longer to be satisfied by a *promise* of three- or fourfold compensation: he must have, and at once, the prize of the man who brought this indignity upon him. This throws *Achilles* into a paroxysm of τιμή-consciousness. In this state of mind he sees the whole Trojan campaign as a dirty device for providing the sons of Atreus with τιμή (line 159). His grievance is twofold:

(a) by giving up *his* girl he will be placed in the disadvantageous position rejected by Agamemnon;

(b) his τιμή has never been properly paid him.

Grievance (b), is shown by the others to be baseless. Nevertheless we can easily imagine that it represented a painful stage in the evolution of Greek civilization, I mean the moment when the chief fighter ceased to be (automatically) the chief leader, the moment when the lion's share no longer was given without question to the lion-killer. This distinction, the passing away of this phase in culture, is marked in the *Iliad* by two words: καρτερός (the stronger) for Achilles, φέρτερος (superior) for Agamemnon. Agamemnon declares that he does not require the τιμή he would get from Achilles accepting his orders as long as the other Greeks pay it to him and—μάλιστα δε μητίετα Ζεύς! ('and above all Zeus of the counsels') [Lattimore]. This last remark is meant to suggest to Achilles that the prestige position of Agamemnon among the Greek soldiers resembles that of Zeus among the Olympians. The author does (as we shall see) go a long way towards justifying this suggestion, though never to the extent Agamemnon would like.

Agamemnon's claim to be the most powerful provokes Achilles to the extreme position. Just as it had led him to contract out of the war, so it might lead him to contract out of the recognized laws of society and to return to the earlier stage of culture that we often refer to as a state of *nature*, where the καρτερός was φέρτερος. He fingers his sword: but in a flash his opposite number from Olympus intervenes. But instead of lecturing him on the foundations of social order, she offers him more or less what *he* had offered to satisfy the τιμή of Agamemnon. So Achilles refrains from murder and takes his μῆνις out ἀταρτηροῖς ἐπέεσσιν ('in words of derision') [Lattimore]— and here, incidentally, he puts a great strain on the modern translator. For his foul abuse could not be swallowed by a European knight or gentlemen of the eighteenth century without provoking a duel. But in the Greek they do not seem either to ruffle Agamemnon (at least his μῆνις is speechless, see line 247) or to interfere with the flow of elaborate hexameters in which Achilles vows to pay the Greeks out for not paying him the τιμή he claims he deserves.

While these two are raging, Nestor gives us the verdict of society: Agamemnon has no right to Achilles' prize: Achilles has no right to lord it over Agamemnon:

> ἐπεὶ οὔ ποθ' ὁμοίης ἔμμορε τιμῆς
> σκηπτοῦχος βασιλεύς, ᾧ τε Ζεὺς κῦδος ἔδωκεν.
> εἰ δὲ σὺ καρτερός ἐσσι, θεὰ δέ σε γείνατο μήτηρ,
> ἀλλ' ὅ γε φέρτερός ἐστιν, ἐπεὶ πλεόνεσσιν ἀνάσσει.

(278-81)

> ('. . . since never equal with the rest is the portion of honour
> of the sceptred king to whom Zeus gives magnificence. Even
> though you are the stronger man, and the mother who bore you
> was immortal,
> yet is this man greater who is lord over more than you rule.')
> [Lattimore]

The relative and absolute claims to τιμή, he says, are based on the dispositions of Zeus. Zeus made Achilles a good soldier and so gave him certain claims, but he gave the *sceptre* and with it κῦδος—which here seems to mean supreme τιμή—to Agamemnon. Nestor adds the rider that Agamemnon is also recognized as chieftain by the greatest number of vassal chiefs.

In Nestor's view, then, the relation of Agamemnon to Zeus seems the nearer. Achilles, however, is not satisfied. Surely, he thinks, Zeus owes him τιμή via his mother (lines 352 ff.), and will not allow him to be robbed of it by Agamemnon. His mother seems to agree with him: at any rate she puts their joint case to Zeus in a form similar to that used by the priest to Apollo: i.e., entirely in terms of τιμή: τίμησόν μοι υἱόν...' Ἀγαμέμνων/ἠτίμησεν ... σύ ... μιν τεῖσον ... ὄφρ' ἂν Ἀχαιοὶ/υἱὸν ἐμὸν τείσωσιν ὀφέλλωσίν τέ ἑ τιμῇ ... and she adds, 'if you refuse I shall be getting the lowest rate of τιμή among the goddesses'. And, to conclude this first point with a glance at the second, the rest of the book is taken up with the power and prestige relations among the Olympians.

Before considering the deliberate parallelism (as it seems to me) of gods and men in this book, I should like to return to the beginning to see what we are given about the power and nature of the gods. Nothing better illustrates the author's freedom and variety of approach to his deities than the first treatment of one of them, in Apollo's visitation. Apollo first seems like the God of the Old Testament who is angry and sends a plague upon the Egyptians, who hears the prayers of his prophet and ... action follows! But there is a difference: in the Greek a *person* comes into action. We are even given a 'close up' of the killer's weapons. The priest invokes Apollo by his silver bow, just as the prophet calls on the God of Jacob, etc. But we hear the terrible twang, the frightening noise of the gun. And yet Apollo comes *like night*: he is both a force and a person. So Thetis comes like a mist on the sea, but 'materializes' into a very human mother. Two things are then brought out at once: that gods interfere with and are bound up with men, and that when they interfere, they are no joke. For, as we have seen, they insist on their prestige rights and exact the last penny, just like the leaders of the Achaeans.

Here I must change my tactics and instead of trying to make the relation between man and god seem nearer to our ways of thinking

c

than it can ever be, I should instead like to deepen the chasm between Homer and us by reminding you of the very great differences caused by the development of Christianity. The next episode in Book I of importance to us is the dramatic intervention by Athene, which, by averting murder, enables the epic to take its proper course. What I invite you to do is to consider how Dante handled a similar piece of his epic machinery. For our purposes we do not need more than a broad outline, for the critical intervention of the divine occurs, as in the *Iliad*, almost at the beginning of the epic.

The hero of the *Commedia*, like Achilles, threatens to go wrong in the first crisis of which we hear. There is a right way and a wrong way, there is darkness and light, there is death and salvation. As in the *Iliad*, the hero is brought to a point where his own unaided efforts can only result in disaster. Unless help comes from the supernatural the hero is doomed. Nothing is more striking than to contrast the sudden appearance of Athene and the slow preparation of Dante, the gradual revelation to the hero through a series of intermediaries, since the final remedy for his plight and predicament is not found until the very last lines of the long work, when the hero is given a sight not normally vouchsafed to mortals of the source from which his help has come.

But to focus the difference between the pagan and the Christian epic, let me take a narrower span, the gradual revelation to Dante's hero of the news that help is forthcoming. It is from the beginning shrouded in mystery. Virgil suddenly offers himself as guide and conductor through Hell and Purgatory, and when the hero exclaims that such a proposal strikes him as folly, in the line Eliot has made familiar to us all, 'Io non Enea, io non Paulo sono,' Virgil reveals the chain of causation by which the will of heaven stretches down to the sinner on earth. In the *Inferno* he says (II, 52):

'I was living among those who long for paradise without hope of attaining it, when a lady called to me, a lady from heaven and of such heavenly beauty that without prompting I asked her to command me to do her will. Her eyes were brighter than the stars and her voice as she spoke in her own tongue, the tongue of angels, was both soft and smooth. 'Gentle son of Mantua, still famous in the world after a thousand years, your fame will last as long as this world shall last. I have a friend on earth, who has no other friend. In his solitary journey through the world he has found his road barred and he has turned back in utter panic. I am afraid that he has lost his way for ever. If what I hear about him in heaven is true, I may have left it too late to help him. Go to him, with your gift of elaborate language and all else he needs to make his escape, help him and so comfort me. I, Beatrice, order you to go. I have come from where I am impatient to return. Love makes me speak which made me come to you. When I am once again in my sovereign's presence, I shall often speak well of you.'

Since she said no more, I replied: 'Lady, that excellence in you which puts mankind above all else between earth and moon makes your commands sweet. I feel that had I completed in this instant the task you set me I should still have been laggard in serving you. You need say no more: I understand what you wish. Yet tell me why you were not afraid to come down to this deep narrow place, so far from the vast open region to which you long to return.' 'If you wish to know so much of my motives,' she replied, 'I will tell you as shortly as I can why I am not afraid to come down here. Only things which can hurt one are to be feared: what cannot hurt cannot cause fear. God gave me grace and made me so that your torments do not touch me, the flame of this fire cannot burn me. As for this barrier I ask you to remove, there is grief over it in heaven great enough to infringe the just law of damnation. A Lady I dare not name went to Saint Lucy and said to her: "Your help is needed now. I bid you save one who has always loved and worshipped you." St Lucy, who cannot endure undue severity in any form, got up from her place, crossed to where I sat by Rachel, and said: "Beatrice, as God is praised in your creation, why are you not helping the man who loved you so much that for your sake he left the company of ordinary men? Can't you hear how pitifully he cries? Can't you see that Death is fighting him on a river far stormier than any sea?" Men on earth are quick to fly what hurts and run after what seems good. But I was quicker, when I heard her use such language, to leave my seat in heaven and come down here to you. I put all my trust in your command of words. They are an honour to speak and an honour to hear.'

'Her eyes were bright with tears and she turned them away. This made me more eager to obey her, and I have come to you in obedience to her will. Now that I have saved you from the beast that barred the short cut to the lovely mountain, what is

the matter with you? Why do you stand still? Why do you hug
your cowardice to your heart?'

As many steps as Dante puts between heaven and earth, so many
are the removes between our conceptions and Homer's. Yet, after
due realization of what worlds away Olympus lies from us now,
there may come, on returning to Book I of the *Iliad*, the opposite
reflection, that Dante by his elaboration has lost the true drama,
which is after all *psychological*, an awakening in the soul of the hero.
We may miss the great structure of thought Christianity has erected
round the divine, but Homer gives us, however simplified, the
essential features of the reality, the real dilemma Achilles stands in
as he makes his lightning decision which impulse is to have the
mastery. The two common 'explanations' of this event seem to
contradict the facts. As we shall eventually see (if we do not see at
once), the author appears to be highly sophisticated about, or well
outside, his figures, whether mortal or immortal. Yet, however
sophisticated he may be, he is not sophisticated in a modern way.
That is to say, I do not think that the intervention of Athene is a
way of describing merely what went on inside Achilles' head. Nor, on
the other hand, do I think that Athene is merely what the French
used to call a 'machine'. For, firstly, she does not say the kind of things
that a restraining impulse in the mind might suggest to an angry
man. There is, after all, a great difference between thinking, 'perhaps
my fellow-generals will compensate me for my present loss if I put a
good face on it now', and the formal assurance from the goddess that
he *will get* compensation. Nevertheless, the explanation I reject could
never have been given if the intervention had been thought of as
mechanical and entirely external. Achilles was about to entertain
thoughts similar to those of Macbeth, thoughts that shake the single
state of man, and to find himself divided, as the author explicitly
states:

$$\text{ἐν δέ οἱ ἦτορ}$$
$$\text{στήθεσσιν λασίοισι διάνδιχα μερμήριξεν} \dots \quad (188\text{-}89)$$
[the heart in his hairy chest felt two-way division]

So we have here the same phenomenon as with Apollo: the goddess is
both in and outside.

The 'outsideness' causes the greatest difficulty in the poem. Though
we are still on the periphery, we cannot shirk a question that goes to

the heart of the matter: how far do we meet with truly responsible individuals in the *Iliad*, individuals who act from their own centre? It is a fair counter to answer: how far can we say we meet such individuals in ordinary life? And we might let this answer serve for the accounts of motives in the poem which seem to be in a reasonable convention in that they express what we loosely call irrational forces in the psyche. But this answer will not cover the instances where what we should consider integral parts of the conscious personal self are attributed to the influence of the gods. There is no glaring instance in Book I, but the germs of uneasiness are present when we find treated as equally 'gifts of Zeus' the authority of Agamemnon and Achilles' talents as a fighter.

The difficulty is whether Homer's suppleness and multiplicity of approach, his sophistication about the relations of gods and men, make it impossible to see the human and divine figures as *seriously involving us*. We can easily darken counsel if we call Homer's poem *tragic*, for nothing is more certain than that Homer's attitude differs from that of the Greek tragedians. The other extreme is equally unhelpful: to see the author as a superior Boy Scout leader, identified with a primitive account of behaviour such as boys might like to fancy a true account of what happens in life. Nor is the middle road very comfortable, the view that Homer is a neutral reporter, an earlier Isherwood or Hemingway, putting down the facts without commenting on the confusing muddle of our actual behaviour.

Since the answer to this puzzling question will have far-reaching consequences for our estimate of the worth of the epic as a whole, we might break off here before pursuing the theme of the second part of the book, where the gods are seen as in some respects a *mirror* for the actions of men, and give ourselves time to glance at Book III, and to the notorious passage involving Helen. For here there is a strong suggestion that the moral impulses of men are doomed to be nullified by the gods' indifference to morality.

Homer begins by offering us Paris volunteering to do the right thing, i.e., to step out and 'take first knock'. But his heart fails him when he sees that his opponent is going to be Menelaus, and he withdraws into the mass of fighting men. He is afraid. This makes Hector angry and he taunts Paris, not by regarding him as a congenital coward but by reminding him of his bravery in the rape of Helen,

and Hector does not suggest that Paris succeeded there by his good
looks alone. Incidentally, he then raises what might be called the
theme of this book: *the power of love in human affairs*. But Aphrodite
is first mentioned in an external way. Hector *did* suppose that the gifts
of Aphrodite played some part in the success of Paris with Helen, and
he contrasts them scornfully with the gifts required now that the
Greeks have come to take Helen back. Paris admits the justice of this
charge, but makes this significant reply:

> μή μοι δῶρ' ἐρατὰ πρόφερε χρυσέης Ἀφροδίτης·
> οὔ τοι ἀπόβλητ' ἐστὶ θεῶν ἐρικυδέα δῶρα,
> ὅσσα κεν αὐτοὶ δῶσιν, ἑκὼν δ' οὐκ ἄν τις ἕλοιτο·

(64-66)

(Do not bring up against me the lovely gifts of golden Aphrodite.
The glorious gifts that the gods of their own free will bestow on
Men are not to be flung aside, though no one would of his own
Free will choose to have them.)

But Homer does not push this remark to the tragic extreme. To
judge how far he was here from wishing to extract the utmost from
this human fatality, we have only to glance at the sequel, for Paris
himself at once brings us back to the most primitive level. But to see
what depth can be extracted from the view that love comes from
outside, against the lovers' will, so that they feel themselves doomed,
and yet, paradoxically, they also feel guilty, i.e., responsible for
loving, let us postpone the drop into the banal and once again turn
to Dante, who is perfectly adequate to both sides of the paradox,
and so both involves us deeply in the lovers' plight and also allows
us to stand back and measure the power of love as an external force.
Dante's example will also serve a further purpose, for it will help us
to decide whether Homer's *detachment* from his theme is altogether
admirable.

To feel the full significance of sinful Love, as Dante presents it,
we need every word of the fifth Canto of his *Inferno*, for he has taken
great pains to set the episode in which he crystallizes his values. I can
at least enumerate the elements of the setting. We must imagine
ourselves in pitchblack darkness and in a raging storm of wind. This
storm not only blows the damned lovers about the sky, but tortures
them as it blows, so that they shriek, groan and curse God as they
fly round. Yet, insensibly, Dante allows sympathy for these carnal
sinners to creep in. They are compared to beautiful birds, storks and

cranes, and the examples Dante names are of great souls, however damnable, Semiramis, Dido, Cleopatra, Helen, Achilles, Paris and Tristan: bloody lovers, who died for love and caused others to die. Dante confesses that, at the sight of them, he felt pity and was near fainting. But he expresses no curiosity, no desire to speak with these illustrious figures. Instead he is drawn by secret sympathy to an obscure couple, who are likened to doves, and instead of being battered by the wind, find in it their proper element as though they stretched out their wings to co-operate with the wind and let it bear them to their nest. So great is Dante's affinity with them that, when he calls, his call has magic power to draw the lovers out of the storm. Indeed the wind appears to calm down for a moment and allow them—or rather, Francesca alone—to show in dramatic speech that she is *amour courtois* personified; that love which came, in a mysterious combination with heretical religion, into Italy from Provence.

Here, however, I must allow Dante to speak directly to us, or rather, as directly as I can make him speak in prose translation:

'You are gracious, you are kind, strange visitor in this dark-blue air. We, who once dyed the whole world blood red, if the king of the world were our friend, we would ask him to give you his peace, since, though seeing our wickedness, your feeling is all pity. Whatever you wish to say and wish us to say we will listen and speak while the wind keeps still here. I was born in the city by the sea-shore where the river Po goes down to its tributaries to be at peace with them. But Love—the well-born heart learns fast!—captured him who is with me here through my beauty. That beauty was taken away from me: the manner of the undoing still hurts. Love never allows the lover to love in vain; it captured me, so that in him who is with me here I found such pleasure that, as you see, Love still has me in hold. Love led us both to death in the same place. The depth of hell is waiting for the one who choked the life out of us.'

When I felt in these words the hurt they had suffered, and knew who they were, I looked down and stared at the ground for so long that the poet said, 'What are you thinking of?' 'What loving thoughts they must have had,' I replied, 'oh, how immense must have been the desire that took them to the place of everlasting pain.' Then I turned again to the pair and said, 'Francesca, I feel so full of sorrow, so full of pity for your sufferings that I am in tears. But tell me this: at the time when you were still only sighing, by what sign and in what circumstances did Love permit you to know desire that trembles between doubt and certainty?'

'Pain has no greater pain than to remember what it was to be happy when happiness is past recall. Ask Virgil, he knows. But since you long so much to hear the first beginnings of our love, I shall tell it to you through my tears.

'One day we were reading together for pleasure in *Lancelot du lac*. No servants or friends were round us, yet, though we were alone, we were not alarmed. As we read how Love caught Lancelot, our eyes met more than once and the colour went from our cheeks. But not till we came to a certain page were we beaten. When we read that the knightly lover kissed the smile on the queen's mouth, he who now can never be parted from me, all trembling, kissed my lips. So was the book and he who writ it Love's go-between, like Gallehault in the story. We read no further all that day.'

While the one spirit was saying this, the other was crying, crying, so that for very pity I fell into a deathly faint and dropped to the ground like a corpse.

We shall be needing this touchstone again soon, when we come to the scene between Aphrodite and Helen. But to return to its opposite: after speaking in such *potentially* tragic fashion of the gifts of Aphrodite, Paris brings his love affair with Helen down to the most primitive level. 'Let force decide', he says in effect, 'and let us settle the accounts on a commercial basis.' Indeed one line:

$$\text{ἀμφ' Ἑλένῃ καὶ κτήμασι πᾶσι μάχεσθαι} \qquad (70)$$
('to fight together for the sake of Helen and all her possessions')
[Lattimore]

suggests that the prize of the victor is not so much Helen herself as the valuable property she took with her when she left Menelaus! On the other hand, on this primitive level, it is an honourable offer: it means peace at once, and the fight was to be to the death. The Greeks, too, accept it as a bargain to be sanctioned by Zeus himself.

It is at this point that we are switched over to Helen, from the male to the female partner. And what do we find her doing? Like the Lady of Shalott, she is filling her childless leisure by weaving in a tapestry the fighting of which she has been the cause. We are not told what she thought as she wove, but we might suppose her to have been peculiarly blank about everything and neutral in her sympathies, for when she hears that she is to be fought over by her two men, she doesn't think anything herself but, says Homer:

θεὰ γλυκὺν ἵμερον ἔμβαλε θυμῷ
ἀνδρός τε προτέρου καὶ ἄστεος ἠδὲ τοκήων·    (139-40)

(—the goddess *put into her mind* sweet longing for her first husband,—their palace in the walled town and her parents.)

The point I am trying to make is obscured by E. V. Rieu, the Penguin translator, when he says 'This *news* . . . filled Helen's heart with tender longing', as though the Greek contained no suggestion of *external action* by the goddess.

So far, Homer has been non-committal. He now introduces a piece of choric commentary as the veterans pay an involuntary tribute to Helen's good looks:

αἰνῶς ἀθανάτῃσι θεῇς εἰς ὦπα ἔοικεν·
ἀλλὰ καὶ ὧς τοίη περ ἐοῦσ' ἐν νηυσὶ νεέσθω,
μηδ' ἡμῖν τεκέεσσί τ' ὀπίσσω πῆμα λίποιτο."

(158-60)

(She is horribly like an immortal goddess if you consider her face,
yes,
Like an immortal. But all the same, let her go home with
The fleet, for, if she stays, it will be the ruin of us and
Our children.)

This is remarkably far from a *moral* stance. But the extreme of moral detachment is reached in a second comment, this time by Priam, who supposes Helen might *enjoy* the chance to inspect her first husband and her old friends and compatriots from the top of a Trojan wall. He even goes so far as to give her a complete moral discharge from all blame:

οὔ τί μοι αἰτίη ἐσσί, θεοί νύ μοι αἴτιοί εἰσιν,    (164)

('I don't blame you for what has happened, I blame the gods')

But though this seems to be correct, as we shall see, Helen herself does not accept this view of her behaviour. 'I wish I had died before I left my home in Greece. But I didn't, and I now weep for it.' Yet

nothing of this prevents her from joining Priam in discussing the
Greek heroes as if the two of them were sitting in a press box watching
an England *v.* Australia test match. There is, however, one human
touch: Helen misses two eminent players from her own family, not
knowing that they had died before they could sail over.

The scene is again switched to the gods. Zeus and all the gods are
appealed to in order that right may be done. But Zeus does not
intend to respond. The author has no comment, he leaves us to feel
whatever we wish. But he himself clearly feels no call to excuse the
god for his detachment from morality. Instead the duel proceeds
according to form. Here we should note that when Menelaus appeals
to Zeus to avenge him, it is not in the sacred names of love or marriage,
but on the grounds that Paris committed . . . a breach of hospitality.
Clearly, a primitive scale of values. Zeus grants him, however, the
κῦδος, the ἄσπετον κῦδος (unspeakably great glory) of killing his
opponent in single combat. But at this point Aphrodite intervenes.
This is not in itself shocking—other heroes whose death day had not
come were saved by being whisked away in a mist. But mark what
follows: Aphrodite whisks Paris off to his *bedroom* and herself calls to
Helen to join him there. (We must suppose that, just as Athene
appeared to Achilles without anyone else noticing it, so the extraordinary language of Aphrodite was not overheard.)

But is it proper to use the word 'extraordinary'? Aphrodite is
after all merely making good *one of her gifts*. Helen is her *present* to
Paris and she gave her to him to *enjoy*. But, if she is doing what
might seem natural to Paris, must it not be extraordinary to Helen
to find that,

    (*a*)  she is *not* after all to be the victor's prize;
    (*b*)  she is *not* called on to comfort a blood-stained warrior;
    (*c*)  but she *is* summoned to a concentrated scene of luxurious love,
        where Paris waits for her as if he had just left the dance.

Helen responds just as Achilles had responded to Athene. First she
θάμβησεν (was amazed), then, like Achilles, she recovered herself, and
then replied to the goddess with some force. Her irony is biting and
insulting. Here, for a change, I offer the translation of a classical
scholar who was intelligent enough to know that he could profit by
consulting Ezra Pound—W. H. D. Rouse:[1]

    [1] *The Story of Achilles* (1938), pp. 60-62.

. . . but Aphroditê carried him off in a thick mist, as a god can easily do, and put him down in Helen's sweet-scented chamber.

Now she took the shape of an old woman who used to comb wool for Helen in her old home before she left Lacedaimon, one whom she dearly loved. In this shape she went in search of Helen. She found her on the battlements with a crowd of women, and plucked her by the skirt. 'Come here!' she said, 'thi man wants tha at home. He is in thi room, on the bed, all finery and shinery! Tha'st never think he's fresh from fighten a man! More like just come from a dance, or just goen maybe!'

These words stirred Helen's temper. Now she knew the goddess by her beautiful throat and lovely breast and shining eyes! She was amazed, and cried out:

'This is strange indeed! Why do you wish to befool me? Will you carry me away somewhere still farther off, to some city of Phrygia or Meionia, where you have another friend among the sons of men! I suppose Menelaos has killed him, and wants to take me home, the woman whom he hates. I suppose that's why you are here with more of your tricks and schemes. Go and sit by him yourself. Forget the way to Olympos, and never let your feet feel it again! Fuss about the man, take good care of him, and perhaps he will make you his wife one day, or his slave at least. To that place I will not go — it would be a shame. I will not make his bed! What will the Trojan women say? and I have troubles enough already.'

The goddess flew into a rage and said:

'Don't try me too far, hard-hearted woman! or I may be angry and leave you, and hate you as much as I love you desperately now! I may make Trojans and Danaäns hate each other like death, so that you will have a cruel fate between them!'

Helen was terrified, and followed her in silence, wrapping her robe close about her; the other women saw nothing. When they reached the house, her attendants turned to their work and she went up to her room. Aphroditê all smiles, put a chair for her in front of Alexandros; and there Helen sat down. But she turned her eyes away, and said with contempt:

'You have come back from the battle. I wish you had died there, and a strong man had killed you — he that was my husband before you! It was your boast once that you were the better man

in fair fight. Then go and challenge Menelaos to fight again!—
But no, I advise you not to try. Fight no duel with Menelaos; leave
him alone, don't be a fool, or perhaps you may go down before
his spear.'

Paris answered:

'You need not scold me, my dear. This time Menelaos has
won because Athena helped him. Next time it will be my turn;
for I have my gods too. Let us love and be happy! I was never so
much in love before, not even when I carried you off in my ship
from Lacedaimon, and we shared our first love in that island. I
am more in love with you now than ever, and I want you more!'

So saying, he lay down on the bed, and she came to him.

I hope this passage makes a commentary superfluous. Perhaps
some of the comedy evaporates in a prose version, for instance that
Aphrodite becomes maid-of-all-work to secure her ends. It is also
worth noting that the language of Paris anticipates that of Zeus
himself (in Book XIV) when in a similar situation—also engineered
by Aphrodite—he makes the tactless avowal to his wife, 'Never have
I felt such love for a goddess or even for a mortal woman', and he
gives her a short extract from the catalogue of his human *amours*.

But this is to stray from the point. This passage makes us ask:
what has become of the Trojan war and of human dignity? The
goddess is not interested in Helen as a person. The vividness of
Helen's protest serves only to underline her subservience. The
incident receives its comment in the final phrase—ἄμα δ᾽ εἵπετ᾽
ἄκοιτις ('and his wife went along too'). It is all very well to embroider
on the phrase and project on to Helen either unprincipled lubricity
or fear of Aphrodite overcoming apparent loathing. Homer makes
absolutely no comment. As a human being Helen is extinguished.

So much then for the difficulties that arise when the gods are con-
trasted with men. But in Book I the predominant impression, as I have
said, is that the author is deliberately creating a parallel, not a contrast,
between gods and men. I wish now to consider the way in which
prestige relations on Olympus resemble those before Troy. It is beyond doubt that Homer designed the quarrel between Zeus and his
wife to resemble that between Achilles and Agamemnon. And, just as
we supposed that behind the quarrel of the humans there was a crucial

evolution in human society, so behind the dispute in heaven we may glimpse the difficult transition in primitive Greek religion which shifted the balance of power from a female to a male principle. But, as Homer is out to present the ancient history of Greek religious evolution in human terms, we may as well follow his example.

'Human', you may be thinking, 'surely, "all-too-human", is the word, and a great deal less than heroic.' Homer is indeed very *familiar* in his tone and presents Zeus in particular as a comic figure. But at the same time as portentous. This incongruous treatment can be found concentrated at the end of Zeus' private (as he hoped) interview with Thetis. He begins like a husband in a comedy and ends like the Old Testament God. This passage is a crucial one for translators, since all depends on your sense of humour. The Loeb translator[1] has tried to be solemn throughout. He begins:

> Then, greatly troubled, Zeus, the cloud-gatherer spake to her:
> 'Verily here will be sorry work, seeing thou wilt set me on to engage in strife with Hera, whenso she shall anger me with taunting words.'

Rouse is inclined to the other extreme:

> Zeus answered in great vexation:
> 'Here's a bad business! You'll set me curry-worrying with Hera and make her scold me again! She is always at me as it is before them all, . . .'[2]

But even if you disguise the phrase in the impossible English of the Loeb:

> 'Even now is she wont ever to upbraid me among the immortal gods, and to declare that I give aid to the Trojans in battle.'

an impression of petty whining, as of a much-suffering husband on earth, peeps through. Reference to the Greek (at least to my mind) suggests the nakedness if not the full familiarity of Rouse:

> ἡ δὲ καὶ αὔτως μ' αἰεὶ ἐν ἀθανάτοισι θεοῖσι
> νεικεῖ,

---

[1] *Homer: The Iliad.* With an English Translation (1924), by A. T. Murray, p. 43.
[2] *Op. cit.*, pp. 17-18.

but Rouse, to my mind, has lost the cream of the joke by ignoring the incongruity of the phrase 'she is always at me' with the co-presence in the same phrase of *the immortal gods*. The effect is to belittle the immortals as well as himself. (We might well think that Aristophanes could have found models in Homer.) If there is a joke of this type here, then it is present a few lines further on, when, in a desperate effort to get rid of Thetis before Hera catches them together, Zeus, who knows that his mere word is worthless, since he is notoriously not a man of honour, promises to give Thetis the only solid assurance left to him. Here I cannot believe that, if these lines had survived only on a papyrus, anyone would have thought them 'noble' or anything but a parody on the gods:

> Now look here, Thetis, I'll nod my head and then you *can* trust me. For, you know, when I do that it's a sure sign among us immortals. When I bow my head, why, then what I say is irrevocable, undeceivable, infallible.

The naïve way in which he rolls out those long words—οὐ ... παλινάγρετον . . . οὐδ᾿ ἀπατηλὸν οὐδ᾿ ἀτελεύτητον—needs only the slightest push to be pure Aristophanes. Yet, the next three lines sound as solemn as if Homer had invested Zeus with all the dignity of his stock-epithets. The language is formidably epic, and—what is more—the huge mountain shook as he nodded.

Our uncertainty—which is almost as great as would be that of a company of atheists who had been publicly defying God to blast them, were a voice from the skies to rumble, 'think again, little men', followed by complete silence from the heavens—is deliciously mirrored in the behaviour of the other Olympians who *reluctantly* (I think) get to their feet to pay outward respect as their father enters the council chamber. Homer says explicitly

οὐδέ τις ἔτλη

μεῖναι ἐπερχόμενον,                    (534-35)

('not one of them *dared* keep his seat')

At this point Zeus appears less majestic, less sure of his authority, than Agamemnon himself. Certainly he has to put up with some humiliatingly plain speech from his wife:

> 'Who is it this time?' she began, 'who has been confabulating with you now, you deceiver? You always like to go behind my

back and make secret plans, and lay down the law! You never would tell me a word of your notions if you could help it!'[1]

The husband's reply is very domestic:

My dear Hera, you mustn't expect to be told *everything*, even though you *are* my wife. Whatever it is right and proper for you to be told I shall tell *you* before I tell anybody else. But what I choose to keep to myself, I keep to myself. Don't be so inquisitive.

To which Hera:

Me inquisitive! I never heard such a thing, I never did such a thing all my born days. Why, I always let *you* decide just as you choose.

Is there a word here that would be out of place in a comedy? And even when his wife triumphantly informs Zeus that his secret is no secret to her, he replies at first in the same tone:

Eh, what a one you are for catching me out!

But then, without warning, the gloves are off, and Zeus, like Agamemnon, reveals his mailed fist. He is, after all, the strongest in heaven, and not afraid to let them all see it. What could be more direct and brutal than:

Sit down and shut up and do what I tell you. If I once lay a hand on you, all the gods on Olympus won't be able to save you from a beating.

Hera knows she has gone too far; but comedy intervenes, and, at the same time, provides the commentary. Hephaistos is the perfect lightning conductor in the home, the son who knows how to handle his mother and avert a painful brawl. At the same time he throws a comic light back on the similar efforts by Nestor on earth. For Homer insists that everything end in farce: the bowl goes round, unquenchable laughter arises, and at bed time we find Hera, like Helen, sleeping beside Zeus as if nothing had happened.

We cannot help reflecting on the different consequences of the two outbursts of μῆνις. Whereas when Hera suffered what she considered a serious loss of τιμή, she forgot it over a drink, Achilles

[1] Rouse, *op. cit.*, p. 18.

withdraws from the war, a great number of people die because of it, and he himself suffers irreparable loss. And as we dwell on this contrast, after an initial shock—for we are used to gods who are more serious in character than men—we may reflect that Homer's account of life is more frightening than ours. His heroes clearly have nothing solid to fall back upon. They have no glorious future to aspire to after death, and no assurance of fair play from heaven while they are alive. Instead they are faced with gods who are both fearsome powers and figures of fun. Homer forces us to see life as an indissoluble unity between men governed by the desire for prestige and gods who are equally subject to the code while at bottom not being deeply engaged in the human conflict. There is no 'for God so loved the world'. If we ask what the gods in Homer love, the only certain answer is, wonderful parties in Abyssinia.        (423-24)

This is not the whole story. Even in this First Book there are other quite different impressions that occur during a first reading. But to tease them out properly I need my second line of help, the English translations of Pope and Dryden. For this First Book Dryden is the more important: indeed without him I could not have come out so confidently with all that now convinces me that the *Iliad* is *inter alia* a highly disreputable and profoundly ambiguous work. Thanks to Dryden I can now see that Plato was not being a cheap moralist in expressing his disapproval. But I hope the beginner will also salute in Plato the literary critic who was frightened of Homer's power to draw the reader in.

# THREE

# Pope's and Dryden's Translations of Book I

NOBODY who dabbles with the *Iliad* can avoid the question why some works 'date' very much more than others, and, of course, why this work, above all, seems to defy the years. To account for the fact that we can still get on to any extent with Homer, we must posit some continuity of human nature; so much in fact that we may say without paradox that what binds us to Homer links us to Pope, or, that if the Age of Pope and the Age of Johnson had not elaborated a doctrine of Nature with a special relation to Human Nature, it would have been necessary to invent it both to state the claims for regarding the *Iliad* as a classic and to explain why it is still enjoyable to-day.

A corollary of this view is that both Homer and Pope must have been more than modern from the start. For it is only because, beside describing Man worthily as he appeared on the day of composition, the authors have given us glimpses of what Man might become that their works have an indefinite future before them. (I suppose I must confess to belonging to two opposed schools of thought here. For I feel just as strongly convinced of the proposition that human nature does not change essentially as that its possibilities have not been and perhaps cannot be exhausted. Homer, I believe, saw more in Man than we do. The human race, I trust, may survive to see more and be more than we can yet imagine.)

If so, we can say something about the kind of modernity Homer can have and should be made to have to-day. And we can perhaps see it more clearly by considering in what sense Pope was making Homer *modern*. Perhaps, when we see the consequence for Pope of succeeding in being modern, we may begin to wonder whether this is what finding human nature in the epic ought to result in. For what was modernity for Pope is what now strikes us as the parochial Augustanism that we have no use for.

Some people who notice this draw a conclusion different from mine.

D

They say that Pope was right to make Homer into an Augustan gentleman, since in no other guise could he have entered the Augustan world. And they conclude: of course Pope's translation, because of this, soon began to date. All translations must date: and each new translator must try all over again to make the original modern and up-to-date.

My conclusion is different. I would argue that we should regard those places where all we can find in Pope is a fossilized modernity as the places where he failed, and where he failed to do what he had set out to do as a highly conscious artist. For when Pope raised himself to the height of his task he was asserting the timeless nature which bound him to Homer and links him to us. He expressed this in the line:

> *Nature* and *Homer* were, he found, the *same*.[1]    (135)

To make out the meaning of Nature here is a tricky business, and it is especially difficult to go on from there and discuss a meaning of the word that would link us with both Pope and Homer. This book will have as its object to enrich the meaning of these words as they apply to Pope and Homer. Yet so rich is their meaning that I need not blush to own that by the time I reach my last chapter I shall still be merely sketching a definition. For this reason I need not be too delicate here about offering some crude formulae. In doing so, I feel like the theology lecturer who sets out the proofs of the existence of God in three handy paragraphs. So long as for all his theological students God is an eternal mystery, the wonder of the universe, no harm is done. So, too, with a reader willing to exercise his tact, so long as he recalls that for Pope there was no more sacred name than Nature. Certainly God was a poor synonym.

Just as I earlier revealed my ambition to be helpful in a general way to a beginner taking up Homer seriously for the first time, so I should like to think of myself as creating a longing to get to know and love Pope in a reader who had hitherto found him cold. To such a beginner, who has been reading incredulously what I have written about the importance of Nature, I would recommend some lines in Pope's *Essay on Criticism*, an essay on which I shall be drawing as I expound the theory behind Pope's poetical practice. And I would recommend the beginner to read the *Essay* in the Twickenham

[1] *An Essay on Criticism* (1711), p. 10.

edition,[1] for there he can find in a few pages an admirable summary doing all that a summary can to expound the meaning of Nature for Pope. The passage I especially recommend begins on page 219, where there is this comment on Pope's line,

> '*True Wit* is *Nature* to Advantage drest . . .'

This 'Nature' is the ultimate authority in the *Essay*.

After their summary the editors conclude:

> It is against this background that one may best comprehend the reverence for Nature which is so visible in the writings of Pope and others, and understand too their conviction that, in 'following Nature', they were giving expression to all that gave the universe and human life its meaning and dignity.

The primary, though not the only, meaning of 'Nature' as the term appears in the *Essay on Criticism* can best be seen in these famous lines:

> First follow N A T U R E, and your Judgment frame
> By her just Standard, which is still the same:
> *Unerring Nature*, still divinely bright,
> One *clear*, *unchang'd*, and *Universal* Light,
> Life, Force, and Beauty, must to all impart,
> At once the *Source*, and *End*, and *Test* of *Art*.

The scarcely veiled analogy here is one between Nature and God: the attributions and formulae used are those traditionally reserved for the First Cause. Nature is one, eternal, immutable, and the source and end of all things. There is of course no suggestion of pantheism here. Instead, this is Pope's statement of the old idea that as God gives being to beings, so He makes causes to be causes, and thus grants to them the ability to participate in His power. That Nature which from one point of view may seem to have merely *received* the laws and order of its being, may from another be seen, by its participation in causality, as *conferring* these qualities. Pope is here concerned with a Nature which has a mysterious analogy to its Source in all its functioning.

---

[1] The Twickenham Edition of the Poems of Alexander Pope, Vol. I: *Pastoral Poetry and An Essay on Criticism* (1961), ed. E. Audra and Aubrey Williams, pp. 220-21.

In the light of this it will not appear absurd to treat Pope's translation less as a translation in the ordinary sense of the word than a
Hymn to Nature 'still divinely bright'. It will not be so easy to argue
that if Homer can involve us seriously it must be because he reveals
to us something of human nature that is permanent, a nature 'which
is still the same'. I have no real interest in constructing a doctrine
of General Nature, since the *fact* is so overwhelming; I mean that,
in those places where we are carried away as Pope was carried away,
I will accept any more plausible explanation of it if any can be produced. Since we can still be moved by parts of the *Iliad* that have
moved readers of all times, I do not know what else to say but that we
have much in common down the ages when it comes to the very finest
moments in poetry. So I would argue that, if to have these finest moments we must transcend time and enter into the timeless, then we
might help ourselves by reading Pope where he, too, is presenting us
with General Nature rather than with a Nature known only to men
of his generation. To give some much-needed reassurance, I will at
once admit that Homer's Nature is almost always freer and larger than
Pope's, and I shall mercilessly draw the contrast as much as the
parallel. But Pope had a worthy vision of Man, and if we try to
discover it, we shall not be wasting our time, I firmly believe, even
though we shall sometimes find ourselves sharing in a vision that was
valid for only one or two generations.

Pope, I should say then, felt that whatever else he was bound to
do as a translator, his chief duty was to *bring out* the nature in Homer
at all costs, to concentrate at all costs on what is of permanent value
in Homer and on what is as modern as it is ancient. He did not think
it his duty to make Homer strictly contemporary. His duty was, he
felt, to do for Homer's heroes what he would do for a contemporary
figure who aspired to go down to history as a hero. Pope thought that
he had to assure his readers that underlying the unfamiliar Greek
customs, dress, speech, etc., there was the same essential structure that
an enlightened contemporary could discover behind the extremely thin
façade of Augustan manners. This essential structure, Pope knew
from the incredulity of too many of his contemporaries, especially in
France, was in Homer visible only to the eyes of faith. Therefore
Pope in his translation deliberately *drew in* the lines of Nature that
were not visible on Homer's surface. To take a random instance, I
think we can safely say that in the following passage Pope is putting
in what he took to be part of the essential structure and bringing out

that Nature which was the common ground between Homer and himself and between himself and posterity:

> *Achilles* heard, with Grief and Rage opprest,
> His Heart swell'd high, and labour'd in his Breast.
> Distracting Thoughts by turns his Bosom rul'd,
> Now fir'd by Wrath, and now by Reason cool'd:
> That prompts his Hand to draw the deadly Sword,
> Force thro' the *Greeks*, and pierce their haughty Lord;
> This whispers soft his Vengeance to controul,
> And calm the rising Tempest of his Soul.    (251-58)

When we first read this, we may be pardoned for smiling as we seem to recognize the typical Popeian travesty: the balance and opposition seem all too neat for Homer. And if we turn to Dr Rieu's version, our first impression that Homer has been totally replaced by Pope is only strengthened:

> This cut Achilles to the quick. In his shaggy breast his heart was torn between two courses, whether to draw his sharp sword from his side, thrust his way through the crowd, and kill King Agamemnon, or to control himself and check the angry impulse.[1]

Nevertheless, without much reflection, we may wonder whether the modern translator may not be further from the original than Pope. At any rate we can see at once that both translators are imposing a *contemporary psychology* on Homer's hero. Like Pope, Rieu has rethought the passage and revisualized the scene in modern terms —'thrust his way through the crowd'—but done so in such a way as to make Achilles a figure of less than heroic stature.

If we now turn to the raw material—the inscrutable Greek—we find both a number of formulae, but also a certain amount of balance and antithesis: the former seem to justify Rieu, the latter, Pope. Yet by what right do we suppose that the effect of Homer's formulae was to reduce the stature of Achilles? Here, in the consideration of detail, and in making a subordinate step in an argument, we stumble on the principal question about Homer: what was his conception of the heroic, and what did he think of his heroes? I hope to be contributing material towards an answer to these principal questions as we go along, but my last word comes only at the end of my last chapter. But since

---

[1] *Homer: The Iliad*, translated by E. V. Rieu, p. 28.

the question has been raised, since it *had* to be raised, a preliminary answer has to be given.

Two things seem to be true: Homer admired Achilles, Homer did not approve of him. Achilles is a hero, but not an ideal man. How then are we to represent him? In language and behaviour often petty and coarse, in his deeds more often succeeding by will of the gods than by his own worth? A satisfactory answer could only be given by one who claimed to know how Homer should be translated. The only answer open to one who, unlike Arnold, cannot make this claim is a negative one: it is to keep very close to the letter of the text and thereby to show where the would-be translators are clearly taking decisions on their own responsibility. My answer, then, is to do something less than translation; to creep along near the literal meaning of the Greek:

> That was what Agamemnon said: to the son of Peleus
> Came grief and pain: the heart in his hairy chest felt
> Two-way division, whether to draw his sword from his thigh-side
> And after breaking up the meeting to kill the son of
> Atreus or to put an end to his resentment
> And to tame his temper.

It would be a fraud if I were to pass that off as the kind of thing everybody *must* accept as a starting-point. There is hardly a word in the Greek with a fixed meaning. The bit about the hairy chest is a formula, in the sense that it recurs several times in Homer with very little variation. Presumably it was already a formula before the *Iliad* was composed. Homer's psychological vocabulary defines itself in the course of the poem, but without suggesting any precise terms for us nowadays.

But the most important feature of the text is missed by the creeping method of near-translation. I mean the formal structure. We find two Greek lines given for the inner division, two for the inclination to murder, and one for the peaceful alternative. Also the words for either-or stand at the beginning of lines. These considerations alone should force us to reconsider Pope's version:

> *Achilles* heard, with Grief and Rage opprest,
> His Heart swell'd high, and labour'd in his Breast.
> Distracting Thoughts by turns his Bosom rul'd,
> Now fir'd by Wrath, and now by Reason cool'd:

That prompts his Hand to draw the deadly Sword,
Force thro' the *Greeks*, and pierce their haughty Lord;
This whispers soft his Vengeance to controul,
And calm the rising Tempest of his Soul.          (251-58)

But just as it is clear that Pope has changed the formal structure, regrouping the three parts in a 4-2-2 division, so he has clearly recomposed the scene. In what spirit? What has Nature required? Apparently, a great deal of surface *drama*—Pope uses an abundance of verbs—but, above all, definition in contemporary terms of the elements that constitute the natural soul, the passions in their dynamic relation to Reason.

Pope, then, has made Achilles' soul natural, fully natural. But it is not only natural, it is *noble*, and noble in a sense that perhaps conflicts with Homer's.

This whispers soft his Vengeance to controul,
And calm the rising Tempest of his Soul.

The manner of his couplet suggests a nobility loftier than Homer's. It is too noble for the theme of τιμή affronted. The heroes in Pope become infinitely more capable of listening to Reason than ever Homer's were. If we explore further this topic of the difference between Pope's heroes and Homer's, we soon note that to make up his heroes Pope has gone rather to Milton and to Dryden for their conceptions of the heroic than to Shakespeare for his. To put the point in another way, we may say that, when making heroes talk, Pope preferred *Virgil's* manner to Homer's. Arnold was right in saying,

Virgil is elegant,—'pervadingly elegant,'—even in passages of the highest emotion:

O, ubi campi,
Spercheosque, et virginibus bacchata Lacænis
Taygeta!

Even there Virgil, though of a divine elegance, is still elegant: but Homer is not elegant . . .[1]

[1] *Last Words* (1862), pp. 11-12. His translation of the Virgil passage runs as follows:
Oh for the fields of Thessaly and the streams of Spercheios!
Oh for the hills alive with the dances of the Laconian maidens,
the hills of Taygetus!          (*Georgics*, ii. 486.)

This brings up again a topic I raised in the first chapter when discussing the Victorian ideal of nobility and Arnold's choice of passages to illustrate the grand style. Pope clearly sides with Arnold in admiring Virgil's combination of decorum and rhetoric in the passionate set speeches. Homer, of course, has set speeches, too; the whole of Book I is carried by the set speeches, and they are managed with much art.[1] But in the speeches the speakers are uniquely concerned with their immediate object. In Virgil we get the impression that the speakers have a double consciousness; they speak as though they are also thinking of the impression they are making; they appear to be also aware of what is the seemly way of saying something that otherwise might be said in an unseemly fashion, but with much more force. They mind the p's and q's of noble decorum all the time. Consequently, they replace a vigour we are tempted to call natural (though we know it is art) by a vigour of rhetorical art which we always know to be artificial, a deliberate substitute for simple-minded feeling. In such speeches our consciousness easily leaves the dramatic aspect of what is being said in favour of the beautiful sound of the words.[2]

The point I wish to make here is that in this book Pope in his concern for noble decorum has raised the dignity of the two quarrelling Greeks and disguised their manners if not the matter of their quarrel. I cannot rid myself of the conviction that in this book Homer sees the heroes as occasionally behaving in a very *childish* way. The

---

[1] Pope has some admirable remarks on the speeches in his *Preface*.

[2] This is generally true of the high rhetorical style; cf. T. S. Eliot:

A disadvantage of the rhetorical style appears to be, that a dislocation takes place, through the hypertrophy of the auditory imagination at the expense of the visual and tactile, so that the inner meaning is separated from the surface, and tends to become something occult, or at least without effect upon the reader until fully understood. To extract everything possible from *Paradise Lost*, it would seem necessary to read it in two different ways, first solely for the sound, and second for the sense. The full beauty of his long periods can hardly be enjoyed while we are wrestling with the meaning as well; and for the pleasure of the ear meaning is hardly necessary, except in so far as certain key-words indicate the emotional tone of the passage. Now Shakespeare, or Dante, will bear innumerable readings, but at each reading all the elements of appreciation can be present. There is no interruption between the surface that these poets present to you and the core. While, therefore, I cannot pretend to have penetrated to any 'secret' of these poets, I feel that such appreciation of their work as I am capable of points in the right direction; whereas I cannot feel that my appreciation of Milton leads anywhere outside of the mazes of sound. *Essays and Studies by Members of the English Association*, Vol. XXI (1936), p. 38.

accent of childishness comes out strongly for me in the set speech
Agamemnon makes when Calchas points out his fault and its consequences. I pass the naïvety of the shameless avowal that he prefers
his captive to his lawful spouse, since it is doubtful whether Agamemnon, Homer, or any Greek audience laid much stress on the attachment
of heroes to women. No, let us pass with Agamemnon to the question
of τιμή, to the consideration of the girl as both a symbol and the
substance of the public estimation he claims from his contemporaries,
to the girl not as his girl but his γέρας. 'Get me an equivalent,' he
says in effect, 'and be quick about it.' Then comes the would-be
pathetic appeal, what strikes me as the childish note: 'Look, all of
you, you see my γέρας going away from me.' I can't help hearing the
last word of the Greek as a childish wail:

> λεύσσετε γὰρ τό γε πάντες, ὅ μοι γέρας ἔρχεται ἄλλη.
>
> (120)

This note is suppressed by Pope.

The same point might be made about the tone of the quarrel, all
that justifies the translation 'filthy temper' for the μῆνις of this book.
If Pope felt this, he refused to render it. Instead he makes his heroes
express themselves in a way that preserves the Virgilian seemliness.
He gives them a dignity and poise of language even when what they
are saying is extremely undignified.


So far, though I have not quite said it, I have written as if Homer
had no eye for the dignity of heroic life. He certainly had: one small
episode makes that plain. The decencies of life come out in the
behaviour of the sacrosanct persons Agamemnon sends to fetch away
Achilles' 'piece'. Let me this time reverse the process and give a
fairly literal version before quoting Pope's beautiful recreation of
lines 327 ff.:

> The two men obeyed Agamemnon, though they did not like it,
> Walking beside the barren sea till they came to the hutments
> And the ships of the Myrmidons. They found their master
> Sitting there near his hut and his black ship. And when he
> Saw them both, Achilles was far from pleased. They, full of
> Fear and respect for the king, stood still: they neither
> Told him a thing nor asked any questions. But *he* knew inside him
> What it all meant, and said, 'Welcome, you messengers

Of Zeus and men. Come closer. I don't blame you, I
Blame Agamemnon, who sent you for the girl from Brisa.
Bring the girl out, Patroclus, and let these two men take her
Away. I want them to speak as witnesses for me before the
Blessed immortals, before all mortal men and before the
Brute of a king, whatever day there is once more need of
Me to protect the rest of the army from unbearable
Destruction. He has lost his senses in his rage, he
Cannot bring what has been and will be into connection
And so find how the Achaeans are going to fare in
Fighting alongside their ships.' Those were his words. Patroclus
Did as his dear friend commanded. He brought Bri-
seis, the lovely-cheeked, out of the hut and gave her
To them, and they went away past the ships of the Achaeans.
The woman moved off with them, though she did not like it.

Th'unwilling Heralds act their Lord's Commands;
Pensive they walk along the barren Sands:
Arriv'd, the Heroe in his Tent they find,
With gloomy Aspect, on his Arm reclin'd.
At awful Distance long they silent stand,
Loth to advance, or speak their hard Command;
Decent Confusion! This the Godlike Man
Perceiv'd, and thus with Accent mild began.
With Leave and Honour enter our Abodes,
Ye sacred Ministers of Men and Gods!
I know your Message; by Constraint you came;
Not you, but your Imperious Lord I blame.
*Patroclus* haste, the fair *Briseis* bring;
Conduct my Captive to the haughty King.
But witness, Heralds, and proclaim my Vow,
Witness to Gods above, and Men below!
But first, and loudest, to your Prince declare,
That lawless Tyrant whose Commands you bear;
Unmov'd as Death *Achilles* shall remain,
Tho' prostrate *Greece* should bleed at ev'ry Vein:
The raging Chief in frantick Passion lost,
Blind to himself, and useless to his Host,
Unskill'd to judge the Future by the Past,
In Blood and Slaughter shall repent at last.

*Patroclus* now th'unwilling Beauty brought;
She, in soft Sorrows, and in pensive Thought,
Supported by the Chiefs on either Hand,
In Silence past along the winding Strand.[1]      (426-53)

Pope has smoothed away some characteristic Homeric touches, but he has brought out the spirit, what the passage was written for, the spirit that is still there. Here we can say that Homer himself if he had a perfect command of Augustan English and wished to tell his tale over again to Augustan Englishmen, could not conceivably have hit on a more effective selection and arrangement of words. It is a pity that 'pensive' cannot easily be made to yield to us the meaning it had for Pope. He used it regularly to indicate the silent appreciation by sensitive people of the hell on earth represented by the conditions of war before Troy.

I turn now to the parts of the book which have to do with the gods. Here, to resume my thesis in advance, I shall argue that, because Pope was unable to find an equivalent for the dual stance I described in my previous lecture, the result of his trying to bring out the essential nature of the gods, the attempt to see them as representing the permanently divine, was to assimilate them as far as he could to the *Christian* scheme. The consequence has been that at almost every point in Pope's version Homer's gods disappear and something we may provisionally call *Miltonic* takes their place. These radical changes, however, though in one sense they take us away from a discoverable Homer, and thus in one sense damn Pope's translation, in another sense save it, and make it radically true to Homer. For by these changes Pope brings his gods and men into a harmonious parallel which is analogous to Homer's.

The most striking of Pope's attempts to bring about the parallelism of men and gods is his rewriting of Homer's Zeus and his recreation of Homer's Agamemnon. To put it crudely, Pope has made his Agamemnon resemble a coarser Louis Quatorze rather than an Achaean chieftain, precariously *primus inter pares*. The distinction that Homer took such trouble to draw between Agamemnon and

---

[1] Lines 452-53, in editions after 1715, read:

Past silent as the Heralds held her Hand,
And oft look'd back, slow-moving o'er the Strand.

Achilles, between the rival claims of φέρτερος and καρτερός disappears in Pope's version. Pope's Agamemnon brooks no rival near the throne; he entertains no opposition; his power tends to the absolute, and his authority to the supreme. Something similar happens to Zeus, as will appear in due course.

The first victims of this shift of accent are Homer's wit and Homer's detachment from morality. Pope's Zeus has to be solemn all the time. Pope therefore fails to render the crucial passage where Homer forces us to take in simultaneously his two views of Zeus, his mockery and his reverence. Yet Pope has a consistent attitude; something is conveyed by his deliberate act of criticism. If we place alongside Pope the corresponding passage of Rieu, we shall be forced to make a decision between what the French used to call a *belle infidèle*, that is, a credible substitute for Homer, and a solution that is no solution at all:

> What hast thou ask'd? Ah why should *Jove* engage
> In foreign Contests, and domestic Rage,
> The Gods Complaints, and *Juno*'s fierce Alarms,
> While I, too partial, aid the *Trojan* Arms?
> Go, lest the haughty Partner of my Sway
> With jealous Eyes thy close Access survey;
> But part in Peace, secure thy Pray'r is sped:
> Witness the sacred Honours of our Head,
> The Nod that ratifies the Will Divine,
> The faithful, fix'd, irrevocable Sign;
> This seals thy Suit, and this fulfills thy Vows—
> He spoke, and awful, bends his sable Brows;
> Shakes his Ambrosial Curls, and gives the Nod;
> The Stamp of Fate, and Sanction of the God:
> High Heav'n with trembling the dread Signal took,
> And all *Olympus* to the Centre shook.            (672-87)

Zeus the Cloud-gatherer was much perturbed. 'This is a sorry business!' he exclaimed. 'You will make me fall foul of Here, when she rails at me about it, as she will. Even as things are, she scolds me constantly before the other gods and accuses me of helping the Trojans in this war. However, leave me now, or she may notice us; and I will see the matter through. But first, to reassure you, I will bow my head—and the immortals recog-

nize no surer pledge from me than that. When I promise with a
nod, there can be no deceit, no turning back, no missing of the
mark.'

Zeus, as he finished, bowed his sable brows. The ambrosial
locks rolled forward from the immortal head of the King, and
high Olympus shook. (pp. 36-37.)

A man or god who says, 'I will see you through', cannot bow his
sable brows. He can slop his front hair forwards, perhaps, or pompously bring his face parallel to the ground. But only in mock-epic
can you combine this slangy talk with this (in Rieu's context) theatrical
description of shaking Olympus. All we feel is: 'a roll of shot across a
metal sheet is heard from the wings.' The violence of Pope's departures
from Homer, both the omissions and additions, will serve to measure
the pressure Pope was under. This pressure, however, has always been
severe, for the Greeks as well as for us. Homer does not speak for his
race in his treatment of Zeus. Yet the line that was too shocking for
Pope to translate: 'she is always trying to pick a quarrel with me when
the immortals are gathered together, even without a pretext' is clearly
crucial to the scene that follows. Pope, however, was committed to a
more exalted view of Hera, and continues to Miltonize to save the
faces of the Olympians.

An even more far-reaching change is introduced by Pope when
he makes Zeus speak as though he thought of his decisions in the
spirit of the God of Milton's *Paradise Lost*. For the whole value of
the *Iliad* rests on the *absence* of such convictions. Homer has no such
resources to fall back upon. It is this above all that distinguishes
Homer from the Greek tragedians. So here, for instance, Pope's
tone is quite wrong:

> Say, artful Manager of Heav'n (she cries)
> Who now partakes the Secrets of the Skies?
> Thy *Juno* knows not the Decrees of Fate,
> In vain the Partner of Imperial State.
> What fav'rite Goddess then those Cares divides,
> Which *Jove* in Prudence from his Consort hides?
>     To this the Thund'rer: Seek not thou to find
> The sacred Counsels of Almighty Mind:
> Involv'd in Darkness lies the great Decree,
> Nor can the Depths of Fate be pierc'd by thee.          (698-707)

Homer deliberately avoids all this: Hera is not 'the Partner of Imperial State', nor are the secrets of Zeus represented in Homer as 'Decrees' or 'Depths' of 'Fate'. In Homer, the whole thing, as I explained in the last chapter, is on a plain domestic level. When Zeus loses his temper, Homer says, 'Hera was frightened by this: she did sit down and shut up and mastered her temper. There was a painfully tense silence in heaven. . . .' At least, that is my overwhelming impression: it is a moment of incipient anarchy, a situation that might turn very ugly in a second, a situation parallel to that between Achilles and Agamemnon, when the former feels for his knife.

It is too indecorous for Pope: he effaces Homer here and makes Zeus speak to Hera as the Hebrew God might have addressed Milton's Lucifer:

> Then thus the God: Oh restless Fate of Pride,
> That strives to learn what Heav'n resolves to hide;
> Vain is the Search, presumptuous and abhorr'd,
> Anxious to thee, and odious to thy Lord.
> Let this suffice; th' immutable Decree
> No Force can shake: What *is*, that *ought* to be.
> Goddess submit, nor dare our Will withstand,
> But dread the Pow'r of this avenging Hand;
> Th' united Strength of all the Gods above
> In vain resists th' Omnipotence of *Jove*.
> The Thund'rer spoke, nor durst the Queen reply;
> A rev'rend Horror silenc'd all the Sky.          (726-37)

'What *is*, that *ought* to be' —could there be a greater anachronism than that? It summarizes Pope's whole procedure. That, he felt, was how God ought to speak, must speak, and therefore that is what Homer must have said, or, at least, must have meant to say.

We can see from Pope's Notes that he was quite conscious and deliberate; he knew he was making Homer nobler in English than he was in Greek, and therefore more acceptable to the readers of his translation than he was to readers of the Greek. Pope found the satirical remarks of French commentators impossible to answer. Here is an extract:

> Mr. *Dryden* has translated all this with the utmost Severity upon the Ladies, and spirited the whole with satyrical Additions of his own. But Madam *Dacier* (who has elsewhere animadverted

upon the good Bishop of *Thessalonica*, for his sage Admonitions against the Fair Sex) has not taken the least notice of this general Defection from Complaisance in all the Commentators. She seems willing to give the whole Passage a more important Turn, and incline us to think that *Homer* design'd to represent the Folly and Danger of prying into the Secrets of Providence. 'Tis thrown into that Air in this Translation, not only as it is more noble and instructive in general, but as it is more respectful to to the Ladies in particular . . .[1]

Whether Pope realized that his treatment of the Homeric gods automatically prevented him from adequately translating the *détente* following upon the quarrel between Zeus and Hera is not easy to determine. Pope seems to have understood that Hephaestos was a figure of fun, but not that the whole of Olympus is brought down to his level as the gods turn their council into a party. One thing is certain—that he thought *Dryden* had gone too far in making Olympus ridiculous. We might therefore take this opportunity to compare Pope's version of the close of the book with Dryden's.


I come now to the first instance that led me to propose the hypothesis that a translation might be useful to somebody who could read the poem in the original. For I could make nothing of the Greek of the last part of this book until I first 'heard' it in Dryden's English. By 'make out nothing' I mean I could have said nothing to silence a sceptical friend who challenged me like this: 'I have read this passage in the original twenty times and I can find nothing distinguished about it. Nothing tells me that this is part of one of the world's greatest poems. It isn't even funny. I wish you would have the honesty to confess that you are as much in the dark as I am.' And if we imagine this sceptic to be a man well-read in the commentators on the *Iliad*, he could have gone on to say: 'There isn't one of the commentators who is happy about this passage, and several are clearly ashamed of Homer and wish it could be shown that the lines were inserted by an unworthy successor.'

I freely admit that I find it difficult to enter into Homer's point of view and see his gods in the dual vision that the Greek forces on us once we have caught the hint from Dryden. The step from the sublime

---

[1] *Observations on the First Book* (1715), LI, p. 34.

to the ridiculous may be a short one, but it is very difficult to take, in religious matters. The appreciation of the greatness of this part of the *Iliad* depends on the possibility of entering imaginatively into two states of belief which rarely exist at the same time. On the one hand, we have to adjust ourselves to a world in which there are no sceptics. As *forces*, the Homeric gods just *are*; they *are* in the same way as the sky, the stars, the winds, the sea, are. This is a more meaningful remark for Homer, since in his mind the two sets of beings were really one set. A modern poem begins

> I do not know much about gods; but I think that the river
> Is a strong brown god. . . .

I bring it in here since it is a modern attempt to recreate the permanent reality behind and in Homer's identification of what we call the natural and the supernatural. Only, in my opinion, Eliot in that poem was very successful in bringing out the life of the river

> . . . with its cargo of dead negroes, cows and chicken coops,[1]

but the sense in which that river was a god is far less tangibly evident. Let that pass, for the moment, for one religious view. On the other hand, when we consider the gods as *persons*, Homer might have spoken like Thackeray at the end of *Vanity Fair*:

> Come children, let us
> shut up the box and the puppets, for our play is played out.

For Homer's gods are very much his own inventions, his playthings; like Shakespeare's fairies, they shade off into folk-lore, but when they are placed in a strong light they are seen to be puppets of his own as well as of folk fancy. So we may say that Homer's gods are at the same time the colossal figures of a vigorous and naïve faith and the little folk of decayed religions.

Gods with both the freedoms of fact and the freedoms of fiction are very hard to take. It is easier to throw ourselves into the frame of mind in which we accept one lot of beliefs and refuse the other. It is also one way of coming to appreciate the superior happiness of Homer's peculiar double permissiveness to dwell alternately on each set and tell ourselves the disadvantages of an exclusive adherence to each. Is it a silly, Mark Twain-like observation that we are all glad

---

[1] *The Dry Salvages* (1941), pp. 7 and 11.

that we are not damned to live eternally with Milton's . . . angels, since we could not put up with Milton's God (in any of his moods) for long stretches? That the atmosphere of Milton's Heaven is wanting in necessary dimensions for the free unfolding of our cramped earth-worn spirits? I have just been sampling Lucian's *Dialogues of the Gods* again to test the observation that to regard Homer's gods as merely buffoons, as Lucian does there, is to become a bore, as blasphemy quickly becomes a bore to chronic unbelievers.

Since there is not much scientific rigour in *ex post facto* judgments of the type, 'What was must have been', I'll put it very tentatively that Dryden's success here may be due to a rare concatenation of the man and the moment. At least it strikes me as significant that the mixture of reverence and irreverence that Dryden could compass in 1699 was impossible for Pope only twenty years later, and has not proved recoverable by any subsequent translator. Only an age in which reverence and irreverence were equally balanced could hope to see a good translation of this passage. Perhaps the very defects of the Restoration were a help here. All the same, I do not wish to ruin a good case by pressing it too strongly. Good as Dryden is here, I am not saying that he replaces Homer. But when we have relished Dryden to the full, I think we shall have prepared ourselves to discover something in Homer that we might otherwise have missed.

Dryden, then, I am claiming, makes it possible for us to feel that this is a great moment in a great poem. More than this: if we can feel this as a great moment, we can then bring an indispensable corrective to Matthew Arnold. I like Arnold's insistence on the word 'tonic', and, in general, his choice of the most moving passages in the *Iliad* seems to me fine. Yet, if we follow Arnold, there is a danger of seeing the *Iliad* as a merely or wholly edifying poem. It is also, as I said at the end of the previous chapter, a disreputable poem. A trifle too much of this part in the whole *Iliad* and we could say that Homer thwarts in us a necessary kind of seriousness. Dryden certainly makes Pope and others sound stuffy, but we may well wonder whether he could have succeeded so well with the whole poem as he has done with this part of the First Book.

> The Limping Smith, observ'd the sadden'd Feast;
> And hopping here and there (himself a Jest)
> Put in his Word, that neither might offend;
> To *Jove* obsequious, yet his Mother's Friend.

E

What end in Heav'n will be of civil War,
If Gods of Pleasure will for Mortals jar?
Such Discord but disturbs our Jovial Feast;
One Grain of Bad, embitters all the best.
Mother, tho' wise your self, my Counsel weigh;
'Tis much unsafe my Sire to disobey.
Not only you provoke him to your Cost,
But Mirth is marr'd, and the good Chear is lost.
Tempt not his heavy Hand; for he has Pow'r
To throw you Headlong, from his Heav'nly Tow'r.
But one submissive Word, which you let fall,
Will make him in good Humour with us All.

He said no more but crown'd a Bowl, unbid:
The laughing Nectar overlook'd the Lid:
Then put it to her Hand; and thus pursu'd,
This cursed Quarrel be no more renew'd.
Be, as becomes a Wife, obedient still
Though griev'd, yet subject to her Husband's Will.
I wou'd not see you beaten; yet affraid
Of *Jove's* superiour Force, I dare not aid.
Too well I know him, since that hapless Hour
When I, and all the Gods employ'd our Pow'r
To break your Bonds: Me by the Heel he drew;
And o'er Heav'n's Battlements with Fury threw.
All Day I fell; My Flight at Morn begun,
And ended not but with the setting Sun.
Pitch'd on my Head, at length the *Lemnian*-ground,
Receiv'd my batter'd Skull, the *Sinthians* heal'd my Wound.

At *Vulcan's* homely Mirth his Mother smil'd,
And smiling took the Cup the Clown had fill'd.
The Reconciler Bowl, went round the Board,
Which empty'd, the rude Skinker still restor'd.
Loud Fits of Laughter seiz'd the Guests, to see
The limping God so deft at his new Ministry.
The Feast continu'd till declining Light:
They drank, they laugh'd, they lov'd, and then 'twas Night.
Nor wanted tuneful Harp, nor vocal Quire;
The Muses sung; *Apollo* touch'd the Lyre.

Drunken at last, and drowsy they depart,
Each to his House; Adorn'd with labour'd Art
Of the lame Architect: The thund'ring God
Ev'n he withdrew to rest, and had his Load.
His swimming Head to needful Sleep apply'd;
And *Juno* lay unheeded by his Side.[1]

I hope in another place to show that Dryden was here profiting from a long tradition. He was certainly picking up phrases from many predecessors who had relished this passage before him. He borrowed one to solve a natural difficulty which occurs to everybody who asks: what were the gods laughing at, and what are we to think of their laughter? There must be something amusing in Hephaestos' *manner* as well as the matter of his conciliatory addresses. If so, everything depends on the exact nuance conveyed by one word—ποιπνύοντα— which comes at the end of line 600, and closes the episode. If this word was comic, then Dryden was inspired in taking over 'rude Skinker'; for I assume that in his day this was a surprise word, not the ordinary way of referring to the man who handed round the drinks at a tavern or a coffee-house.

Then there is the consideration: weren't the gods rather easily amused? Was their laughter childish? It is possible to reply, 'No; quite serious people seek relief from serious tension in the first available outlet, however trivial.' Yet, if we see how Homer goes on, and particularly how he closes the book, it is hard not to incline Dryden's way, even if we do not go to Dryden's extreme. The brevity of the last line, 'he went to bed and slept with Hera of the golden throne beside him'; the absence of comment, suggests that Homer ended with at least a smile of malice. I can see no trace of a suggestion that Homer wished us to be impressed by a Heavenly party: he would hardly have had to change a word if he had been describing gnomes or fairies.

To make sure of getting the right tone, Dryden has injected two elements of humour. By making Hephaestos quote Shakespeare, Dryden enables us to enjoy an incongruity without which we cannot see much cause for laughter. (There is virtually no cause in Pope's version.) I do not suppose the following lines are an instance of unconscious reminiscence:

[1] *The First Book of Homer's Ilias* in *Fables* (1700), pp. 217-19, where the paragraphs are separated as here.

> Such Discord but disturbs our Jovial Feast;
> But Mirth is marr'd, and the good Chear is lost.

I take it that Dryden means us to recall another disturbed party:

> Be bright and Joviall among your Guests to Night . . .
> My Royall Lord,
> You do not give the Cheere, the Feast . . .
> Thinke of this good Peeres,
> But as a thing of Custome: 'Tis no other,
> Onely it spoyles the pleasure of the time . . .
> You have displac'd the mirth,
> Broke the good meeting, with most admir'd disorder . . .[1]

A further reinforcement comes when Dryden puts in a line which electrifies the whole scene. He makes the drink itself laugh and, in its eagerness to participate in the spirit of the party, climb up and peep out through the lid over its head:

> The laughing Nectar overlook'd the Lid.

This is a line drawn from the stock which gave us Og rolling home:

> Round as a Globe, and Liqour'd ev'ry chink . . .[2]

But what places Dryden in a class by himself is his command of the 'middle style'. The happy ease of Hephaestos' language is never vulgar: he preserves his dignity while retaining his familiarity. It is this gift which enables Dryden to make us see him as both the 'Limping Smith' and the 'limping God'. It is this ease which makes Pope's 'Architect Divine' sound stilted. Contrast Pope's:

> If you submit, the Thund'rer stands appeas'd;
> The gracious Pow'r is willing to be pleas'd.        (750-51)

with Dryden's:

> But one submissive Word, which you let fall,
> Will make him in good Humour with us All.

Pope's language suits only a Louis Quatorze; Dryden's enables us to see Zeus as both a God and a Father.

---

1 *The Tragedie of Macbeth* in the 1623 Folio edition, Act III, ii and iv.
2 *The Second Part of Absalom and Achitophel* (1682), p. 15.

# FOUR

# Homer's Similes (I): Inanimate Nature

To take a glorious stride right into the centre of our subject, we should turn to the end of the Eighth Book, in the Greek at line 553, and in Pope at line 685; for there we find Homer's most beautiful simile and Pope's best-known piece of descriptive writing. 'This Comparison,' he wrote,[1] is inferior to none in *Homer*. It is the most beautiful Night-piece that can be found in Poetry.' My 'crib' is more than usually impertinent:

> Full of confident hope they camped on the roadways of battle,
> Lit many fires and sat the whole long night-time beside them;
> As when the moon shines clear in the sky, the stars around it
> Stand out prominent when high up no wind is stirring,
> And every rock can be seen and peak and chasm between them,
> And the heavens appear to burst open revealing an infinite distance,
> And every star is clear to the sight, and the shepherd is cheerful:
> So many lights could be seen as the Trojans kindled their fires,
> With Troy in front, the river on one side, the ships on the other.

I shall defer for a moment the annihilating confrontation with Pope, since I wish to begin by discussing *hostile* accounts of Pope's version. So long as the reasons which justified Pope were understood (during the short period which alone deserves the epithet 'Augustan') this passage of his translation might have been chosen to prove that Pope's *Iliad* was a masterpiece. Echoes of its immense reputation as a show-case sample can be found well past the death of Byron. But serious opposition had set in by the 1760s, when to the younger spirits Pope appeared to have done too much here, and the surplus was felt to be merely Pope and not an extended Homer. But the first printed expression of more radical criticism that I have come across is to be found in the

---

[1] *Observations on the Eighth Book* (1716), LI, p. 304.

*Gentleman's Magazine* of August 1785. Cowper's letter, however, gives us convictions he had formed at least twenty years earlier:

> The famous simile at the end of the 8th book, in which the fires kindled in the Trojan camp are compared to the moon and stars in a clear night, may serve as a specimen of what I blame. In Homer it consists of five lines; in Pope, of twelve. I may be told, perhaps, that the translation is nevertheless beautiful, and I do not deny it; but I must beg leave to think that it would have been more beautiful, had it been more compressed. At least I am sure that Homer's close is most to be commended. He says, simply, The shepherd's heart is glad; — a plain assertion, which in Pope is rendered thus:
>
> > 'The conscious swains, rejoicing in the sight,
> > Eye the blue vault, and bless the useful light.'
>
> Whence the word *conscious* seems to be joined with *swain*, merely by right of ancient prescription, and where the blessing is perfectly gratuitous, Homer having mentioned no such matter. But Pope, charmed with the scene that Homer drew, was tempted to a trial to excel his master, and the consequence was, that the simile, which in the original is like a pure drop, of simple lustre, in the copy is like that drop dilated into a bubble, that reflects all the colours of the bow. Alas! to little advantage; for the simplicity, the almost divine simplicity, of Homer is worth more than all the glare and glitter than can be contrived.[1]

Here we have an important landmark in our cultural history: a serious shift in the relation of man and nature has occurred. Cowper is implying that Pope's imagination was *alien* to Homer's Nature, and, to bring out the truly natural, a different vocabulary and a different manner were required. Cowper's own version of this passage powerfully reinforces his criticism:

> As when around the clear bright moon, the stars
> Shine in full splendour, and the winds are hush'd,
> The groves, the mountain-tops, the headland-heights
> Stand all apparent, not a vapour streaks
> The boundless blue, but æther open'd wide
> All glitters, and the shepherd's heart is cheer'd; . . .[2] (643-48)

---

[1] *Op. cit.*, p. 612.
[2] *The Iliad of Homer* (1791), Vol. I, p. 210.

Behind this passage lies a quite different conception of the effect Homer was trying for. Cowper assumes that Homer was lost in wonder at the contemplation of the night sky. Cowper was also moving towards the view that Homer's eye was more singly on the objects of inanimate nature than on the adornment he was thus providing his narrative with. Pope, as we shall see, was more aware that Homer was embellishing the situation of the Trojans at night by a stroke of art.

History was on Cowper's side. Thirteen years after his letter, an English poet looked up at the night sky and saw the very Nature Homer had created in his simile:

> —The sky is overcast
> With a continuous cloud of texture close,
> Heavy and wan, all whitened by the Moon,
> Which through that veil is indistinctly seen,
> A dull, contracted circle, yielding light
> So feebly spread that not a shadow falls,
> Chequering the ground, from rock, plant, tree, or tower.
> At length a pleasant instantaneous gleam
> Startles the pensive traveller as he treads
> His lonesome path, with unobserving eye
> Bent earthwards; he looks up—the clouds are split
> Asunder—and above his head he sees
> The clear moon, and the glory of the heavens.
> There, in a black blue vault she sails along,
> Followed by multitudes of stars, that, small
> And sharp, and bright, along the dark abyss
> Drive as she drives;—how fast they wheel away,
> Yet vanish not!—the wind is in the tree,
> But they are silent;—still they roll along
> Immeasureably distant;—and the vault,
> Built round by those white clouds, enormous clouds,
> Still deepens its unfathomable depth.
> At length the Vision closes; and the mind,
> Not undisturbed by the delight it feels,
> Which slowly settles into peaceful calm,
> Is left to muse upon the solemn scene.[1]

---

[1] Composed January 25th, 1798. First published in *Poems* (1815), Vol. I, pp. 301-302.

Only *one* man, I would admit, could express himself like that in 1798. When we see how far and how fast *Wordsworth* had come on from what he had been in the ten preceding years, we may conjecture that his success was due in part to the power of self-criticism, the power to make out what had been getting in his way when he tried to tell himself what he was seeing when he looked at inanimate nature. Such self-criticism naturally led to the power of saying clearly why Pope would not do for him. So I take it that Wordsworth had formulated his condemnation long before he explicitly attacked Pope's translation in his *Essay Supplementary to the Preface*.[1] He treats this moon simile of Pope's very roughly there, so this might be the right moment to pause and allow ourselves to take in Pope's version:

> The Troops exulting sate in order round,
> And beaming Fires illumin'd all the Ground.
> As when the Moon, refulgent Lamp of Night!
> O'er Heav'ns clear Azure sheds her sacred Light,
> When not a Breath disturbs the deep Serene;
> And not a Cloud o'ercasts the solemn Scene;
> Around her Throne the vivid Planets roll,
> And Stars unnumber'd gild the glowing Pole,
> O'er the dark Trees a yellower Verdure shed,
> And tip with Silver ev'ry Mountain's Head;
> Then shine the Vales, the Rocks in Prospect rise,
> A Flood of Glory bursts from all the Skies:
> The conscious Swains, rejoicing in the Sight,
> Eye the blue Vault, and bless the useful Light.
> So many Flames before proud *Ilion* blaze,
> And lighten glimm'ring *Xanthus* with their Rays.
> The long Reflections of the distant Fires
> Gleam on the Walls, and tremble on the Spires.
> A thousand Piles the dusky Horrors gild,
> And shoot a shady Lustre o'er the Field.          (685-704)

Several curious problems are raised if we compare Wordsworth's poem, which I have given entire, and the Pope extract. They might all be summed up by noticing that Wordsworth gave his poem the same title as Pope gave the passage in the *Iliad*—A Night-Piece. The first has to do with a note dictated by the author to Isabella Fenwick in 1843:

[1] First published in *Poems* (1815), Vol. I, pp. 341-75.

Composed on the road between Nether Stowey and Alfoxden, extempore. I distinctly recollect the very moment when I was struck, as described 'He looks up at the clouds, etc.'

If our poem bears any resemblance to the extempore production of January 25th, 1798, then its marked resemblance to Pope's translation might be an instructive starting-off place for an enquiry into the rôle of literature in the poet's mind when he was contemplating Nature. That the original extempore version *was* close to the finished poem is suggested by an entry his sister, Dorothy, made in a contemporary private journal:

> *January 25th.* Went to Poole's after tea. The sky spread over with one continuous cloud, whitened by the light of the moon, which, though her dim shape was seen, did not throw forth so strong a light as to chequer the earth with shadows. At once the clouds seemed to cleave asunder, and left her in the centre of a black-blue vault. She sailed along, followed by multitudes of stars, small, and bright, and sharp. Their brightness seemed concentrated (half-moon).

It is usually thought that this entry was made by Wordsworth's sister with a written draft of the extempore poem before her. So far as I know, there is no proof that Wordsworth did not here, as on other occasions, take and re-work felicitous phrases from his sister's prose.

Be that as it may, Wordsworth's would-be knock-out blow is concentrated in three sentences of the *Essay*. Pope's lines, he says,

> . . . though he had Homer to guide him, are throughout false and contradictory. . . .[1]
>
> A blind man, in the habit of attending accurately to descriptions casually dropped from the lips of those around him, might easily depict these appearances with more truth.[2]

He concludes of both Pope and Dryden that they

> . . . could habitually think that the visible universe was of so little consequence to a Poet, that it was scarcely necessary for him to cast his eyes upon it. . . .[3]

Wordsworth was no doubt aided to this clarity of consciousness by

---

[1] *Op. cit.*, p. 359.   [2] *Op. cit.*, p. 358.   [3] *Op. cit.*, p. 359.

Coleridge, both in general and in this particular instance. At any rate, Coleridge later wrote:

> In the course of my lectures, I had occasion to point out the almost faultless position and choice of words, in Mr Pope's *original* compositions, particularly in his satires and moral essays, for the purpose of comparing them with his translation of Homer, which, I do not stand alone in regarding as the main source of our pseudo-poetic diction. And this, by the bye, is an additional confirmation of a remark made, I believe, by Sir Joshua Reynolds, that next to the man who formed and elevated the taste of the public, he that corrupted it, is commonly the greatest genius. Among other passages, I analysed sentence by sentence, and almost word by word, the popular lines,
>
> 'As when the moon, resplendent lamp of light,' &c.
> [A most interesting misquotation]
>
> much in the same way as has been since done, in an excellent article on Chalmers's British Poets in the *Quarterly Review* The impression on the audience in general was sudden and evident: and a number of enlightened and highly educated individuals, who at different times afterwards addressed me on the subject, expressed their wonder, that truth so obvious should not have struck them *before*; but at the same time acknowledged (so much had they been accustomed, in reading poetry, to receive pleasure from the separate images and phrases successively, without asking themselves whether the collective meaning was sense or nonsense) that they might in all probability have read the same passage again twenty times with undiminished admiration, and without once reflecting, that
>
> ἄστρα φαεινὴν ἀμφὶ σελήνην
> φαίνετ' ἀριπρεπέα,
>
> (i.e. the stars around, or near the full moon, shine pre-eminently bright) conveys a just and happy image of a moonlight sky: while it is difficult to determine whether in the lines,
>
> 'Around *her throne* the vivid planets *roll*,
> And stars *unnumber'd gild* the *glowing pole*,'
>
> the sense, or the diction be the more absurd.[1]

---

[1] *Biographia Literaria* (1817), Vol. I, pp. 39-40.

Poets are never fair to their predecessors, and in a sense we cannot wish them to be, since we want a succession of good poets who are different from each other, not a uniform stream of tradition-minded imitators. Because of this, we should never use a younger poet to interpret a senior he is attempting to displace. Wordsworth and Coleridge refused to see what Pope was doing here, and thus left it to us to rediscover the lost art of the Augustans. But they have made us unforgettably aware of what Pope was not doing, i.e. Pope was not here questioning himself on his own moon-experiences, and allowing them to suggest new turns or new adjectives. In fact, he has deliberately withdrawn any personal interest in the subject. Our task must therefore be to find out what he was trying for.

A superficial answer can be quickly supplied. His business was not with the moon but with Troy and with the appearance of those thousand fires at a critical moment in the war. In these circumstances the moon could easily become a distraction. Pope, therefore, gives us some good lines on the fires:

> The long Reflections of the distant Fires
> Gleam on the Walls, and tremble on the Spires.

In his imagination he has *seen* those fires and he makes us see them. Nevertheless such an explanation strikes me as itself a distraction. Coleridge raised a far more important question in asking about the poetic diction, and he forces me to formulate a preliminary answer; that *the function of the diction is to annihilate Nature in one sense and to resurrect it in another*. I hope gradually to be able to expound the full meaning of this sentence. For the moment, let us merely ask out of what the diction was composed. As Coleridge remarked, if you listen to the noise and don't ask too many questions, the passage seems composed uniquely of the best ingredients. The moon as a Lamp of Night was a respectable poetic property. May I remind you of part of Milton's recreation of Day Four in World History?

> . . . then form'd the Moon
> Globose, and everie magnitude of Starrs,
> And sowd with Starrs the Heav'n thick as a field:
> Of Light by farr the greater part he took,
> Transplanted from her cloudie Shrine, and plac'd
> In the Suns Orb, made porous to receive
> And drink the liquid Light, firm to retaine

> Her gather'd beams, great Palace now of Light.
> Hither as to thir Fountain other Starrs
> Repairing, in thir gold'n Urns draw Light,
> And hence the Morning Planet guilds hir horns;
> By tincture or reflection they augment
> Thir small peculiar, though from human sight
> So farr remote, with diminution seen.
> First in his East the glorious Lamp was seen,
> Regent of Day, . . .[1]                          (356-71)

*Heav'ns Azure* is also in Milton. You have just heard the conceit of starlight as a gilding agent. It was thence borrowed by Dryden, who in his translation of the *Aeneid* (Book VII, line 188), wrote

> And Night, and all the Stars that guild her Sable Throne . . .

As for *Stars unnumber'd*, which Coleridge objected to, I suppose that comes from Shakespeare's *Julius Caesar* (III.i.63):

> The Skies are painted with unnumbred sparkes,
> They are all Fire, and every one doth shine: . . .

Somewhat too much fun has been made of *conscious Swains*. What he meant can be gathered from *Windsor-Forest*, where Pope is on one of his pet themes: the transformation of idle land into agricultural wealth:

> Succeeding Monarchs heard the Subjects Cries,
> Nor saw displeas'd the peaceful Cottage rise.
> Then gath'ring Flocks on unknown Mountains fed,
> O'er sandy Wilds were yellow Harvests spread,
> The Forests wonder'd at th' unusual Grain,
> And secret Transports touch'd the conscious Swain.
> Fair *Liberty*, *Britannia*'s Goddess, rears
> Her chearful Head, and leads the golden Years.[2]

What led Pope to choose the diction of

> Around her Throne the vivid Planets roll,
> And Stars unnumber'd gild the glowing Pole, . . .

was the strong impression of *Addison's* hymn, which remained so strong that whenever he heard it Samuel Johnson used to raise his hat:

---

[1] *Paradise Lost* (1667), Book VII.   [2] *Windsor-Forest* (1713), p. 4.

*Soon as the Evening Shades prevail,*
*The Moon takes up the wondrous Tale,*
*And nightly to the listning Earth*
*Repeats the Story of her Birth:*
*Whilst all the Stars that round her burn,*
*And all the Planets, in their turn,*
*Confirm the Tidings as they rowl,*
*And Spread the Truth from Pole to Pole.*[1]

Although I suppose, when Wordsworth fixed a title to his poem, that he was recalling one of Pope's Notes, I am forced to conjecture that by the time he came to compose his *Essay*, all memory of the Notes had passed from his mind. The pernicious habit of printing the translation without the Notes had set in during the eighteenth century and has persisted to our day, with the result that the arguments of Wordsworth and Coleridge have met with little opposition. Yet those arguments do grave injustice to Pope, as I now hope to show. For Wordsworth was completely misled and has completely misunderstood Pope if he included Pope the *man* as one for whom the visible universe was a secondary matter. Until I read the Notes, I thought Pope had no eyes for Nature, and so I gave up the effort to make anything of the translations. But when (I must state with bitterness) in late middle age I first used Pope's original edition, I found the Notes abounding in *absolute proof* that Pope had the keenest eye for large and small natural effects, and that he considered possession of a similar eye as one of Homer's greatest gifts. Then, almost in a matter of days, the scales fell from my eyes and I pushed Wordsworth and Coleridge aside and began to appreciate the canons of Augustan art. For it became plain that what I had taken for helpless deficiency was in fact deliberate creative choice. If Pope appreciated Nature in the raw as something separate from Man, he annihilated it in order to construct something greater, a Nature that formed a unity with Human Nature and a Human Nature thought of as something far more important than inanimate nature in the small or in the large.

So I would argue that the first step in understanding Augustan art is to make a distinction between *Nature as Fact* and *Nature as Value*. In an age when few cities were more than large villages, it is a mistake

---

[1] *The Spectator*, Vol. VI (1713), No. 465, Saturday, August 23rd, 1712.

to suppose that the poets were unaware of what actually went on
in the countryside. Their ears and eyes and noses were constantly
assaulted by potent reminders of the brute facts. This assault made it
very clear to the Men of Feeling that to follow Nature could never
mean to follow their noses. They understood that Nature as Value
was something visible only to the inward eye. (That pathetically
crude summary is one of the penalties of undertaking to deal with a
central topic in eight chapters! It will be impossible here to distinguish
this Augustan aspiration from its very similar predecessor and successor. For Wordsworth is only superficially to be divided from the
Augustans, and the deepest longing of the Augustans has its parallel in
what we loosely call Elizabethan Pastoral. What I named a canon of
Augustan art is a canon of all humanist art.) But I must hasten in the
same clumsy way to what immediately follows. Pope's contemporaries
longed to convert the Ideal Invisible Nature into Actual Visible
Nature, and indulged in the fancy that the conditions which convert
Value into Fact once held on earth, and might return. Thus they
persuaded themselves that they caught in Homer glimpses of what the
countryside could become for us, i.e. the setting for the highest possible
life open to mortals.

Pope made no secret of the fact that for him Homer's Nature was
revealed in *The Adventures of Telemachus*. He agreed with the author
of the *Tatler*, No. 156:

> The Story of *Telemachus* is formed altogether in the Spirit of
> *Homer*, and will give an unlearned Reader a Notion of that
> great Poet's Manner of Writing more than any Translation of
> him can possibly do.[1]

For this reason we are not likely to penetrate very far into Pope's
translation if we neglect Fénelon's Fable, which is itself a very fine
piece of civilized writing. To tempt you into sampling it, let me translate a fable within a fable to illustrate how Nature as Fact was turned
into Nature as Value, how brute existence was given human significance and civilized life became possible:[2]

---

[1] *The Lucubrations of Isaac Bickerstaff Esq.*, Vol. III (1711), p. 265.
[2] *Les Avantures de Telemaque* (1734), Livre II, pp. 26-27:
Jupiter s'irrite contre Apollon, le chasse du Ciel, & le précipite sur la terre. Son
char vuide faisoit de lui-même son cours ordinaire, pour donner aux hommes les
jours & les nuits avec le changement régulier des saisons. Apollon dépouillé de tous
ses rayons, fut contraint de se faire Berger, & de garder les troupeaux du Roi

Jupiter was angry with Apollo, drove him from heaven and flung him down upon earth. His empty chariot continued unaided on its usual course, giving mankind its days and nights and the regular change of the seasons. Apollo was stripped of his light and forced to become a shepherd and keep the sheep of King Admetus. He used to play the flute and all the other shepherds gathered under the elm-trees' shade beside a clear spring to hear his songs. Until Apollo came, their lives had been savage and brutal; all they knew was how to look after their sheep, to shear them, to milk their goats and to make various cheeses. The whole countryside was like a frightful desert.

Soon Apollo began to teach the shepherds how to make their lives pleasing to them. He would sing of the flowers that make Spring's crown, the sweet smells that She exhales, the grass that grows where She treads. Then he would sing of lovely Summer nights when the West Wind cools mankind and dew refreshes the earth. In his songs he would speak of the golden fruits with which Autumn rewards men for their labours, and of the repose

---

Adméte. Il jouoit de la flute, & tous les autres Bergers venoient à l'ombre des ormeaux sur le bord d'une claire fontaine écouter ses chansons. Jusques-là ils avoient mené une vie sauvage & brutale; ils ne savoient que conduire leurs brebis, les tondre, traire leur lait, & faire des fromages: toute la campagne étoit comme un désert affreux.

Bientôt Apollon montra à tous les Bergers les Arts qui peuvent rendre leur vie agréable. Il chantoit les fleurs dont le Printems se couronne, les parfums qu'il répand, & la verdure qui naît sous ses pas: puis il chantoit les délicieuses nuits de l'Eté, où les Zéphirs rafraîchissent les hommes, & où la rosée désaltére la terre. Il mêloit aussi dans ses chansons les fruits dorez dont l'Automne récompense les travaux des Laboureurs, & le repos de l'Hyver, pendant lequel la jeunesse folâtre danse auprès du feu. Enfin il représentoit les forêts sombres qui couvrent les montagnes & les creux vallons, où les riviéres par mille détours, semblent se jouër au milieu des riantes prairies. Il apprit ainsi aux Bergers quels sont les charmes de la vie champêtre, quand on sait goûter ce que la simple nature a de gracieux. Bientôt les Bergers avec leurs flutes se virent plus heureux que les Rois, & leurs cabanes attiroient en foule les plaisirs purs qui fuyent les Palais dorez: les jeux, les ris, les graces, suivoient par tout les innocentes Bergéres. Tous les jours étoient des Fêtes. On n'entendoit plus que le gazouillement des oiseaux, ou la douce haleine des Zéphirs, qui se jouoient dans les rameaux des arbres, ou le murmure d'une onde claire qui tomboit de quelque rocher, ou les chansons que les Muses inspiroient aux Bergers qui suivoient Apollon. Ce Dieu leur enseignoit à remporter le prix de la course, & à percer de fléches les daims & les cerfs. Les Dieux mêmes devinrent jaloux des Bergers; cette vie leur parut plus douce que toute leur gloire, & ils rapellérent Apollon dans l'Olympe.

of Winter, when youths dance wild, wanton dances round the
fire. He pictured to them the dark forests which cover the
mountain-sides, and the deep valleys where myriad-meandering
streams play as they pass through laughing meadows.

In this way he taught the shepherds the charms of life in the
country by creating in them a taste for Nature's simplicity and
grace. Soon the shepherds, too, were playing their flutes and
were happier than kings. They attracted to their simple huts a
crowd of pure and uncorrupted pleasures that always run away
from gilded palaces. Wherever the innocent shepherd-lasses went,
they were followed by games, by laughter, and by all the graces.
Every day became a holiday. Now all had ears for the soft voices
of birds, the sweet breath of the West Wind playing in the
branches of the trees, the murmur of clear water falling from a
rock, and for the songs which, inspired by the Muses, the shepherds who followed Apollo began to compose.

Apollo taught them to run races and to hunt the deer. The
gods themselves became envious of the shepherds: the shepherds'
life, they thought, was sweeter than all their glory. So they re-
called Apollo to Olympus.

If we wish to be sure that the best people in the heyday of French
civilization were not dupes of their ideals, we have only to turn to the
end of Book VIII, where this ideal life of happiness in the simplicity
of Nature is described in greater detail. 'So spoiled have we become,'
Telemachus tells himself, 'that we can hardly believe such simplicity
as theirs can be realized. We regard the account of the life of these
people as a mere Fable. They would think ours a nightmare.' The
work, for all its bland gentle geniality, is sternly critical of the actual.
In Book XIV, you will find a former courtier living the simple life
and refusing to return to polite society. The full moral is revealed
towards the end, in Book XXII, where modern society is condemned
root and branch in the name of this ideal simplicity. It is therefore
possible to approach Pope's incorporation or poetical embodiment of
Fénelon with positive appreciation. Yet I shall still contend that
Homer's simplicity is grander than Pope's, and that Shakespeare's
Great Creating Nature is greater than the Ideal Nature of the best
Augustan writers.

We can now explain why Pope turns so often to Virgil's *Pastorals*,
and above all to the *Georgics*, when he is trying to make Homer's

Nature into General Nature. We can also now understand why he drew so often on Milton's Paradise, the unspoiled Nature of the Fourth Book of his epic. Let me give you a small instance that you might easily overlook on a first reading of Pope's translation. It occurs at line 53 of the Seventeenth Book, where Homer purports to be giving us a simile for the death of a young man, but characteristically forgets about the dead hero and concentrates on the arts of the gardener. I must regretfully skip the comparison with Homer, however, and jump to Pope at line 57:

> As the young Olive, in some Sylvan Scene,
> Crown'd by fresh Fountains with eternal Green . . .

That Pope wishes us here to recall Milton's Garden is certain:

> . . . and to the border comes
> Of *Eden*, where delicious Paradise,
> Now nearer, Crowns with her enclosure green,
> As with a rural mound the champain head
> Of a steep wilderness, whose hairie sides
> With thicket overgrown, grottesque and wilde,
> Access deni'd; and over head up grew
> Insuperable highth of loftiest shade,
> Cedar, and Pine, and Firr, and branching Palm,
> A Silvan Scene,[1]

where, we learn from line 229,

> Rose a fresh Fountain, . . .

I hope it is a harmless way of describing the meditations out of which this book arose to say that I dream that Pope sometimes visits me and condescends to discuss my accounts of what went on in his soul. At other times I have a more frightening vision: of Pope walking through my study windows *arm in arm with Homer*. In this vision I can never believe that the blind poet becomes aware of me, and he certainly never speaks. But I hear Pope saying that once again there is creeping into my writing a cockiness, a claim that I know Homer better than he does, and at the same time there peeps out a diabolical

[1] *Paradise Lost*, IV, 131ff.

tendency to separate him from Homer by trying to distinguish Homer's Nature from Pope's General Nature. Pope firmly believes that they are the same, and when he comes to see me, he applies to me a cruel and humiliating argument:

> Pray recall, my dear Sir, your early years at the University, and your eagerness to share in the Secrets of Nature with the young Natural Philosophers who were your Friends. Can you remember applying your better Eye to the tube of the Microscope —I think I have hit on the right Word, eh?—and seeing absolutely nothing when you looked at a minute Particle of Nature? You surely have not forgotten how your Philosopher Friends then laughed, and, when you persisted in your Asseveration that, by G-d, there was nothing to be seen, began to describe what they said, *Any Fool could descry*. Whereupon—pseudopodium by pseudopodium—the wretched *Amoeba* came into view. My dear Mr Mason, I bid you good Day.

Pope would say that in his translation he was doing his duty to the world's greatest poet by making explicit what his keen eye saw was implicit in Homer: he was unfolding beauties no common eye could discern[1] and presenting them in a noble light so that even fools would notice them. He was convinced that his duty was to have the keenest eye for the minutest beauties of inanimate nature because Homer had even sharper eyes. Let me quote you an extract from a single Note, though you will find evidence of this conviction throughout the Notes:

> The Imagination of *Homer* was so vast and so lively, that whatsoever Objects presented themselves before him impress'd their Images so forcibly, that he pour'd them forth in Comparisons equally simple and noble; without forgetting any Circumstance which could instruct the Reader, and make him see those Objects

---

1 Cf. Boileau, *L'art poétique*, Chant III, 369-72:
  La Nature feconde en bizarres portraits,
  Dans chaque ame est marquée à de differens traits.
  Un geste la découvre, un rien la fait paroistre:
  Mais tout esprit n'a pas des yeux pour la connoistre.

  Nature in various Figures does abound;
  And in each mind are diff'rent Humors found:
  A glance, a touch, discovers to the wise;
  But every man has not discerning eyes.

*in the same strong Light*[1] wherein he saw them himself. And in this one of the principal Beauties of Poetry consists.[2]

If you will now turn to line 520 in the Fifth Book and line 637 in Pope, and first allow me to mediate via my creeping 'crib', I think I can make one example (temporarily) do for all:

> But the soldiers had no need of this; they
> Shewed no fear as they faced the expected charge of the Trojans.
> They stood firm and still like clouds which the son of Cronos
> Halts over mountain peaks when the air is calm and unmoving,
> Motionless in the sleep of the North Wind's fury and all wild
> Winds that storm and blow their cold shrill breath to a whistle,
> And scatter and drive off the clouds that cover the mountains
>     with shadows.
> So the Greeks stood firm and still and awaited the Trojans.

> Embodied close, the lab'ring *Grecian* Train
> The fiercest Shock of charging Hosts sustain;
> Unmov'd and silent, the whole War they wait,
> Serenely dreadful, and as fix'd as Fate.
> So when th' embattel'd Clouds in dark Array
> Along the Skies their gloomy Lines display,
> When now the *North* his boist'rous Rage has spent,
> And peaceful sleeps the liquid Element,
> The low-hung Vapors, motionless and still,
> Rest on the Summits of the shaded Hill;
> 'Till the Mass scatters as the Winds arise,
> Dispers'd and broken thro' the ruffled Skies.          (637-48)

Pope clearly *saw* more in this scene than Homer cared to express, and thanks to Pope's Notes, we can be sure that he used his own eyes to help him to translate:

> This Simile contains as proper a Comparison, and as fine a Picture of Nature as any in *Homer*: Yet however it is to be fear'd the Beauty and Propriety of it will not be very obvious to many Readers, because it is the Description of a natural Appearance which they have not had an Opportunity to remark, and

---

[1] My italics.
[2] *Observations on the Second Book* (1715), XXII, p. 19.

which can be observed only in a mountainous Country. It happens frequently in very calm Weather, that the Atmosphere is charg'd with thick Vapors, whose Gravity is such, that they neither rise nor fall, but remain poiz'd in the Air at a certain Height, where they continue frequently for several Days together. In a plain Country this occasions no other visible Appearance, but of an uniform clouded Sky; but in a Hilly Region these Vapors are to be seen covering the Tops and stretch'd along the Sides of the Mountains, the clouded Parts above being terminated and distinguish'd from the clear Parts below by a strait Line running parallel to the Horizon, as far as the Mountains extend.[1]

Pope's imaginary visitation has not extinguished in me the desire to debate. I cannot believe, for instance, that in the pre-scientific age clouds could stand for the inner tension of soldiers' nerves screwed up to face the enemy's charge. *Homer's clouds are, characteristically, indifferent to the Trojan War.* And how awkward for the closeness of the simile is the suggestion that the first breath of wind will disperse them! Pope gets over this by reading war into the clouds:

The whole Compass of Nature cannot afford a nobler and more exact Representation of a numerous Army, drawn up in Line of Battel, and expecting the Charge. The long-extended even front, the Closeness of the Ranks; the Firmness, Order, and Silence of the whole, are all drawn with great Resemblance in this one Comparison. The Poet adds, that this Appearance is while *Boreas* and the other boisterous Winds which disperse and break the Clouds, are laid asleep. This is as exact as it is Poetical; for when the Winds arise, this regular Order is soon dissolv'd. This Circumstance is added to the Description, as an ominous Anticipation of the Flight and Dissipation of the *Greeks*, which soon ensued when *Mars* and *Hector* broke in upon them.[2]

Pope's eye was not only that of a naturalist; he was a painter himself and was habitually on the look-out for the new value that painters had been successfully teaching poets since 1660—the *Picturesque*. Here is Pope's general comment on the whole action of the Tenth Book:

[1] *Observations on the Fifth Book* (1716), XLVIII, p. 98.
[2] *Op. cit.*, pp. 98-99.

I cannot conclude the Notes to this Book without observing, that what seems the principal Beauty of it, and what distinguishes it among all the others, is the Liveliness of its Paintings: The Reader sees the most natural Night-Scene in the World; he is led step by step with the Adventurers, and made the Companion of all their Expectations, and Uncertainties. We see the very Colour of the Sky, know the Time to a Minute, are impatient while the Heroes are arming, our Imagination steals out after them, becomes privy to all their Doubts, and even to the secret Wishes of their Hearts sent up to *Minerva*. We are alarmed at the Approach of *Dolon*, hear his very Footsteps, assist the two Chiefs in pursuing him, and stop just with the Spear that arrests him. We are perfectly acquainted with the Situation of all the Forces, with the Figure in which they lie, with the Disposition of *Rhesus* and the *Thracians*, with the Posture of his Chariot and Horses. The marshy Spot of Ground where *Dolon* is killed, the Tamarisk, or aquatic Plants upon which they hang his Spoils, and the Reeds that are heap'd together to mark the Place, are Circumstances the most Picturesque imaginable. And tho' it must be owned, that the human Figures in this Piece are excellent, and disposed in the properest Actions; I cannot but confess my Opinion, that the chief Beauty of it is in the Prospect, a finer than which was never drawn by any Pencil.[1]

To return now to my thesis that Pope annihilates Nature in one sense in order to resuscitate it in another, let me pick out two similes concerning waves. In the first I shall concentrate on the annihilation of Nature; in the second, I shall dwell on the recreation, the attempt to join Homer up with the rest of the world's great literature and with General Nature. For an example of Pope's failure to carry us with him, I would turn to the Second Book, to lines 207 ff. in the Greek, and to lines 245 ff. in Pope. Here it is plausible to suppose that Homer was using his Greek to give us the noise of the heavy seas on the shore. But if Homer has given him an inch, Pope has taken an ell. He has worked the passage up, but the effect is to transfer our attention from the things to the words. The result is forcible-feeble; weak Dryden—from whom, by the way, Pope has taken 'remurmur'd' and 'rebound':

[1] *Observations on the Tenth Book* (1717), LIV, p. 140.

The Realms of *Mars* remurmur'd all around,
And Echoes to th' *Athenian* Shoars rebound.[1]        (667-68)

(To the assembly
Back with a roar the soldiers rushed from the ships and the
                                                        hutments,
As when a wave of the echoing sea in the noise of its waters
Murmuring, pounds on the long wide beach with thunderous
                                                        rolling.)

With Words like these the Troops *Ulysses* rul'd,
The loudest silenc'd, and the fiercest cool'd.
Back to th' Assembly roll the thronging Train,
Desert the Ships, and pour upon the Plain.
Murm'ring they move, as when old *Ocean* roars,
And heaves huge Surges to the trembling Shores:
The groaning Banks are burst with bellowing Sound,
The Rocks remurmur, and the Deeps rebound.
At length the Tumult sinks, the Noises cease,
And a still Silence lulls the Camp to Peace.        (245-54)

What is characteristic here is the general shape. Whenever he can,
Pope shapes his similes into a *crescendo* and *decrescendo*. Homer seems
to have no settled view of the order of Nature, no fixed attitude towards
the violent phenomena. He respects them as forces outside himself
which exist in their own right. Pope seems like a demiurge recreating
the world by music, magically conducting a natural symphony:
precisely governing and guiding the volume of sound of the natural
phenomena, and blending the various instruments. There is no suggestion of independent life in Nature, since Pope has replaced God;
he is the sole creator of his own natural universe. In his capacity as
creator of a noble and harmonious Whole, he has, as always, assimilated the human figures to match the natural forces: the soldiers *roll*
to the assembly rather than rush; they *pour* upon the plains. To give
dramatic tension to his *tableau*, he has filled out details that are at
best only implicit in the Greek; thus we get the *trembling* Shores, the
*groaning* Banks. What is not so common is that here Pope extends
the simile after it has ceased in Homer, and goes on to speak of the
assembly as if he were still speaking of the waves.

----

1 *The Works of Virgil* (1697), p. 142. The Fourth Book of the Georgics.

I have taken my next wave simile from the Fourth Book, lines
422 ff. in the Greek, lines 478 ff. in Pope. Here, too, you can say that
Pope annihilates Nature; the impression of a real sea to be got from
Homer is lost; the element has been tamed, and, as I said a moment
ago, moves only at Pope's command. But this time I think that we
can clearly see that the negative result comes from the carrying out of
Pope's positive intentions.

(As wave after wave rises up and crashes down on the sea shore,
Stirred into powerful movement when Zephyros works on the

water:

Far out at sea a crest appears, then swells to a wave, which
Sends up a terrible roar as it breaks on the shingled beach, or
Jets as it arches to run up a rock face and spew the foam over
It, so in wave after wave unceasing the Greek battalions
Swept into battle . . .)

As when the Winds, ascending by degrees,
First move the whitening Surface of the Seas,
The Billows float in order to the Shore,
The Wave behind rolls on the Wave before;
Till, with the growing Storm, the Deeps arise,
Foam o'er the Rocks, and thunder to the Skies.
So to the Fight the thick *Battalions* throng,
Shields urg'd on Shields, and Men drove Men along.          (478-85)

The general line of my argument is that Pope in departing from
Homer was being true to his best self, his profoundest positive beliefs,
to forces, in short, that he could not resist without destroying his
integrity. The deepest reasons made Pope disapprove of Homer's
whole manner of writing similes. If we follow Pope's Notes through
chronologically, we shall find him asserting that in his similes Homer
wanted the two elements of the Comparison to correspond closely,
whereas we can see plainly that they do *not* correspond. Eventually
Pope gave Homer up on this point. But the interesting thing is to
ask: why did Pope want close correspondence? We can never bore
deep enough for an answer, since, I think, in a true sense for once,
it is a matter of Pope's world-view: his sense of how things truly held
together in the stars and in the minutest affairs of earth told him that
he could never allow distracting attention to non-human activity.

Pope's couplets, then, are a direct consequence of his profounder convictions; just as Homer's looser syntax reflects a world-view in which there is no one supreme value that puts all other values in a graded hierarchy. Consequently, Homer's eye on Nature is never single, he is never rooted to one stance. But Pope insists that Homer thought as he did. He says in his Notes:[1]

> The Passage naturally bears this Sense. *As when, upon the rising of the Wind, the Waves roll after one another to the Shore; at first there is a distant Motion in the Sea,* . . .

Put like that, Homer would be proceeding in an orderly fashion and beginning at the beginning of a linear action due to the wind. But Homer in fact begins by giving us the whole process, and then goes back far out to sea and starts again. Secondly, Pope says:

> *then they approach to break with Noise on the Strand, and lastly rise swelling over the Rocks,* . . .

But that *lastly* is Pope, not Homer, who allows us to take the last action of the water as an *alternative* to the last but one. Thirdly, and most significantly, Pope thinks his interpretation is justified *by the example of Virgil*:

> What confirms this Exposition is, that *Virgil* has made use of the Simile in the same Sense in the seventh Æneid.

This time it is as important to turn to the text of Virgil:

> fluctus uti primo coepit cum albescere uento,
> paulatim sese tollit mare et altius undas
> erigit, inde imo consurgit ad aethera fundo.     (528-30)

as to its rendering by Dryden:

> Thus when a black-brow'd Gust begins to rise,
> White Foam at first on the curl'd Ocean fries;
> Then roars the Main, the Billows mount the Skies:

for then we see at once that it was Virgil, not Homer, who gave Pope:

> As when the Winds, ascending by degrees,
> First move the whitening Surface of the Seas,

---

[1] *Observations on the Fourth Book* (1715), XXX, p. 16.

and

> Till, with the growing Storm, the Deeps arise,
> Foam o'er the Rocks, and thunder to the Skies.

and that it is Virgil who is responsible for the generalized vocabulary. To take one example: in Virgil the sea merely *sese tollit*, raises itself, in Homer it *raises its crest—κορυφοῦται*. More profoundly, the unity of tone is Virgilian rather than Homeric. Such a passage makes us say that Pope should have translated Virgil, just as we think sometimes that Dryden should have translated Homer.

Since I have been concentrating on the differences between Pope and Homer on this matter of inanimate nature, and since I shall have to reveal further differences when I deal with Animal Nature, it may be as well to emphasize that in some ways Pope was closer to Homer than most of us are. In Chapter One I quoted an undergraduate letter:

> . . . and then in that Rapture and Fire, which carries you away with him, with that wonderfull Force, that no man who has a true Poetical spirit is Master of himself, while he reads him. Homer makes you interested and concern'd before you are aware, all at once; whereas Virgill does it by soft degrees.

Pope repeated the substance of it when as a mature man he published his translation of the *Iliad*:

> It is to the Strength of this amazing Invention we are to attribute that unequal'd Fire and Rapture, which is so forcible in *Homer*, that no Man of a true Poetical Spirit is Master of himself while he reads him. What he writes is of the most animated Nature imaginable; every thing moves, every thing lives, and is put in Action. If a Council be call'd, or a Battel fought, you are not coldly inform'd of what was said or done as from a third Person; the Reader is hurry'd out of himself by the Force of the Poet's Imagination, and turns in one place to a Hearer, in another to a Spectator. The Course of his Verses resembles that of the Army he describes,
>
> Οἱ δ' ἄρ' ἴσαν ὡς εἴ τε πυρὶ χθὼν πᾶσα νέμοιτο·
>
> *They pour along like a Fire that sweeps the whole Earth before it.*
> 'Tis however remarkable that his Fancy, which is every where

vigorous, is not discover'd immediately at the beginning of his Poem in its fullest Splendor: It grows in the Progress both upon himself and others, and becomes on Fire like a Chariot-Wheel, by its own Rapidity. Exact Disposition, just Thought, correct Elocution, polish'd Numbers, may have been found in a thousand; but this Poetical *Fire*, this *Vivida vis animi*, in a very few. Even in Works where all those are imperfect or neglected, this can over-power Criticism, and make us admire even while we dis-approve. Nay, where this appears, tho' attended with Absurdities, it brightens all the Rubbish about it, 'till we see nothing but its own Splendor. This *Fire* is discern'd in *Virgil*, but discern'd as through a Glass, reflected, and more shining than warm, but every where equal and constant: In *Lucan* and *Statius*, it bursts out in sudden, short, and interrupted Flashes: In *Milton*, it glows like a Furnace kept up to an uncommon Fierceness by the Force of Art: In *Shakespear*, it strikes before we are aware, like an accidental Fire from Heaven: But in *Homer*, and in him only, it burns every where clearly, and every where irresistibly.[1]

Pope found such an instance of irresistible energy in the simile of Hector rushing on the Greeks like a rock down a mountain side, in Book XIII, lines 136 ff.:

(Hector was wilder than all as he headed the charge of the
                                            Trojans
And hurled himself at the Greeks, as a stone falls sheer down a
                                           rock face,
Tumbled over the crown of the hill by the force of unending
Winter rain, which swells the torrent and smashes the bonds that
Hold it terribly fast to the mass of the rock. With a leap it
Throws itself high in the air and crashes its way through the
                                           branches
Till it wins a free run to the plain, and there, though still eager,
Ceases to roll. So Hector threatened at first to cut clean
Through to the sea and reach the huts and ships of the Achaeans,
Killing all in his way, but when he came up against their
Close formations, he stopped, and they locked him tight in their
                                           phalanx.)

[1] *The Iliad of Homer.* Translated by Mr Pope (1715). *Preface, Sigs* B2-B3.

Thus breathing Death, in terrible Array,
The close-compacted Legions urg'd their way:
Fierce they drove on, impatient to destroy;
*Troy* charg'd the first, and *Hector* first of *Troy*.
As from some Mountain's craggy Forehead torn,
A Rock's round Fragment flies, with Fury born,
(Which from the stubborn Stone a Torrent rends)
Precipitate the pond'rous Mass descends:
From Steep to Steep the rolling Ruin bounds;
At ev'ry Shock the crackling Wood resounds;
Still gath'ring Force, it smoaks; and, urg'd amain,
Whirls, leaps, and thunders down, impetuous to the Plain:
There stops—So *Hector*: Their whole Force he prov'd,
Resistless when he rag'd, and when he stop'd, unmov'd.

$$(187\text{-}200)$$

We can see what Pope admired in this simile by turning up his Note
on the passage:

This is one of the noblest Simile's in all *Homer*, and the most
justly corresponding in its Circumstances to the thing described.
The furious Descent of *Hector* from the Wall represented by a
Stone that flies from the top of a Rock, the Hero push'd on by the
superior Force of *Jupiter*, as the Stone driven by a Torrent, the
Ruins of the Wall falling after him, all things yielding before
him, the Clamour and Tumult around him, all imag'd in the
violent bounding and leaping of the Stone, the crackling of the
Woods, the Shock, the Noise, the Rapidity, the Irresistibility,
and the Augmentation of Force in its Progress. All these Points
of Likeness make but the first Part of this admirable Simile.
Then the sudden Stop of the Stone when it comes to the Plain,
as of *Hector* at the Phalanx of the *Ajaces* (alluding also to the
natural Situation of the Ground, *Hector* rushing down the
Declivity of the Shore, and being stopp'd on the Level of the
Sea.) And lastly, the Immobility of both when so stopp'd, the
Enemy being as unable to move him back, as he to get forward:
This last Branch of the Comparison is the happiest in the
World, and tho' not hitherto observ'd, is what methinks makes
the principal Beauty and Force of it. . . .

There is yet another Beauty in the Numbers of this Part.
As the Verses themselves make us see, the Sound of them makes

us hear what they represent, in the noble Roughness, Rapidity, and sonorous Cadence that distinguishes them.

'Ρήξας ἀσπέτῳ ὄμβρῳ ἀναιδέος ἔχματα πέτρης, &c.

The Translation, however short it falls of these Beauties, may yet serve to shew the Reader, that there was at least an Endeavour to imitate them.[1]

After this we can hardly accuse Pope of want of sympathetic contact with *Homer*! Pope's sympathy has led characteristically to an enlargement of the imagination. He has filled out details that Homer does not express. By passing through Pope's imagination Homer's simile has once again become tidier and has also received the *crescendo-decrescendo* shape. Homer leaves the two elements of the comparison to go their own way. The rock or huge stone occupies the attention in its own right, and in two respects at least is quite unlike Hector. One is, that it had to be worked upon by much water before it could be detached from the parent rock. The other is, that it came to a stop gradually and without being hemmed in by an opposing obstacle. Pope has given us a piece full of his own surface drama. I doubt whether we can be sure just how far Homer was here attempting to *enact* the meaning or trying for the effect Pope obtains in these lines:

Whirls, leaps, and thunders down, impetuous to the Plain:
There stops—

Experience has shown us where to look when we wish to know on what Pope has rested his convictions. Virgil had also admired this simile and had adapted it to the Latin language to suit *his* Hector, i.e. Turnus:[2]

ac ueluti montis saxum de uertice praeceps
cum ruit auulsum uento, seu turbidus imber
proluit aut annis soluit sublapsa uetustas;
fertur in abruptum magno mons improbus actu
exsultatque solo, silvas armenta uirosque
inuoluens secum ...                    (684-89)

The same experience leads us to expect that it is Dryden's Virgil which has been decisive. Pope has certainly drawn on Dryden here:

[1] *Observations on the Thirteenth Book* (1718), XVIII, pp. 64-65.
[2] *Aeneid*. Book XII.

As when a Fragment, from a Mountain torn
By raging Tempests, or by Torrents born,
Or sapp'd by time, or loosen'd from the Roots,
Prone thro' the Void the Rocky Ruine shoots,
Rowling from Crag to Crag, from Steep to Steep . . .[1]

(991-95)

and his manner in general here resembles Dryden's. Compare, for
instance:

Precipitate the pond'rous Mass descends:

with

They rowl to Sea with unresisted Force,
And down the Rocks precipitate their Course . . .[2]

(12/766-67)

Pope's word 'Resistless' for Hector had been Dryden's word for
Turnus.

So where resistless *Turnus* takes his Course,
The scatter'd Squadrons bend before his force . . .[3]

(12/546-47)

Pope, as he claimed in his Note, had indeed made one special contribution to the simile. He did his best to raise 'the Justness and Sublimity'
of Homer's simile by adding a detail not in the Greek, that the stone in
its descent would accelerate in speed. To express this, Pope constructs
a dynamic curve which rises to the point of maximum acceleration
and halts abruptly when the stone reaches level ground.

[1] *The Works of Virgil* (1697), pp. 607-608.
[2] *Op. cit.* p. 601.          [3] *Op. cit.*, p. 594.

# FIVE

# Homer's Similes (II): Animal Nature

BEFORE coming at once to grips with the problem of animal nature in Homer's similes, I should like to report an imagined comment by Pope on something I said about him in the last chapter. It was to the effect that, while he was pleased with me for pointing out that he was being true to his deepest principles in translating Homer as he did, he thought my language when I spoke of 'boring deep into his centre' unnecessarily pompous, since he had taken trouble himself to express what was at his heart. 'I wish people would stop saying I have a rage for order. What I care most about is to get a Vision of the Whole, and to prevent myself being side-tracked by anything less. So, when I say that the First Law is to Follow Nature, I think always of Nature as a unity, a Whole. Those were my leading Thoughts as a Boy, I maintained them as a Man, and I hold them still as an Immortal Spirit. So will you please open your next chapter by repeating from my *Essay on Criticism*:

> First follow NATURE, and your Judgment frame
> By her just Standard, which is still the same:
> *Unerring Nature*, still divinely bright,
> One *clear*, *unchang'd*, and *Universal* Light,

and follow it up with these lines:

> In Wit, as Nature, what affects our Hearts
> Is not th' Exactness of peculiar Parts;
> 'Tis not a *Lip*, or *Eye*, we Beauty call,
> But the joint Force and full *Result* of all.[1]

I have complied with Pope's request the more gladly because I now wish to carry on the argument I opened in the last chapter. Pope, I shall be contending, also annihilates animal Nature, and his

---

[1] *An Essay on Criticism* (1711), pp. 7 and 16.

motive is also to subordinate it to the presentation and glorification
of the Heroic. Just as the whole point of the *tableau* of the rock
crashing down the slope was to make the reader feel the force and
might of Hector, so all the suggestions of the animal world are to be
subsumed and made subservient to raising the stature of the heroes
and bringing out the specifically heroic virtues. In pursuing this aim,
Pope was led much further away from Homer than he knew. I hope
gradually to expound Homer's interest in animal nature. It resembles
his interest in inanimate nature in that he has no desire to place animals
in a scale of values. An interesting illustration of this occurs in the
Second Book, beginning at line 474, where Homer appears to be
saying that, if you want to measure the manliness of Agamemnon,
better than comparing him with a god is a comparison with a bull!

As easily, however far they stray, as *his* can be picked out by a
skilful
Goatherd from out of a flock in a pasture, all feeding together,
Each chieftain marched off his own men to their separate stations
And ranged them in order for battle. There great Agamemnon,
With a look in his eyes and a mien like Zeus when he hurls down
the thunder,
A waist like the god of war and a chest as stout as Poseidon's,
Stood out huge, as a bull stands out in a herd of cattle:
Tallest and strongest he stands and dwarfs all the gazers around
him;
So on that day Zeus made the son of Atreus look taller,
Head and shoulders above the crowd: and the heroes looked
smaller.

Pope's Note confirms that his departure from Homer here was both
deliberate and (for him) necessary:

> . . . the Simile of *Agamemnon* to a *Bull* just after he has been
> compar'd to *Jove*, *Mars*, and *Neptune*. This, *Eustathius* tells us,
> was blam'd by some Criticks, and Mr. *Hobbes* has left it out in his
> Translation. The Liberty has been taken here to place the hum-
> bler Simile first, reserving the noble one as a more magnificent
> Close of the Description: . . .[1]

---

[1] *Observations on the Second Book* (1715), XXIV, p. 21.

Each Leader now his scatter'd Force conjoins
In close Array, and forms the deep'ning Lines.
Not with more Ease, the skilful Shepherd Swain
Collects his Flock from Thousands on the Plain.
The King of Kings, majestically tall,
Tow'rs o'er his Armies, and outshines them all:
Like some proud Bull that round the Pastures leads
His Subject-Herds, the Monarch of the Meads.
Great as the Gods th' exalted Chief was seen,
His Strength like *Neptune*, and like *Mars* his Mien,
*Jove* o'er his Eyes celestial Glories spread,
And dawning Conquest play'd around his Head.    (560-71)

I hope it is not fanciful to see in Homer's capping the description of
the deification of Agamemnon with the bull simile a feeling that the
former was somewhat literary whereas the latter was comparatively
real, or, even if Homer was not playing off the animal against the
gods, to suppose that the effect intended was to keep the temporary
superiority given for one day to Agamemnon in its proper place. Pope
was anxious to raise Agamemnon permanently to semi-divine stature.
He therefore calls him *King of Kings*, *Great as the Gods*, and says:

> *Jove* o'er his Eyes celestial Glories spread . . .    (570)

Pope, then, seizes every opportunity to use the animal to make the
hero more heroic. When, for example, he has a lion simile to translate,
the lion is made out to be noble, and his movements are described
in terms that would also fit men. Homer thought of lions also as brutes,
and by doing so reminded us that men have, as we say, animal passions.
Homer was also interested in lions independently of their possibilities
for suggesting what human beings are like. Homer liked *all* the natural
goings-on in this part of the animal world. He allows lions to have their
own beauty, whereas the only beauty Pope finds is a beauty he can
transfer to men. Homer embraces all animals indifferently: to him
they are all part of Nature. Pope distinguishes between the genially
natural and what Tennyson called 'Nature red in tooth and claw'.
As Pope's imagination warmed, he came to see the fiercer aspects of
Nature as *unnaturally* fierce.

A striking instance of this occurs in Book XVI, when Achilles
is assembling his troops and Homer compares them to wolves. Homer's

wolves are certainly meant to be fierce, but Homer admires them and
sees in them their own kind of beauty:

> Like wolves that eat raw flesh, in whose hearts is unlimited
> courage,
> That kill a huge antlered stag in the mountains and tear its flesh;
> each
> One's chaps are dark with blood. Then they rush in a pack,
> lapping
> With their thin tongues from the black water of the spring black
> Water from its surface, belching up clotted blood. The
> Courage in their breasts is without a tremble, their
> Bellies are packed tight.                           (156-63)

Pope makes his predominant impression clear in his Note:

> There is scarce any Picture in *Homer* so much in the savage
> and terrible way, as this Comparison of the *Myrmidons* to Wolves:
> It puts one in mind of the Pieces of *Spagnolett*, or *Salvator
> Rosa*: Each Circumstance is made up of Images very strongly
> colour'd, and horridly lively.[1]

> *Achilles* speeds from Tent to Tent, and warms
> His hardy *Myrmidons* to Blood and Arms.
> All breathing Death, around their Chief they stand,
> A grim, terrific, formidable Band:
> Grim as voracious Wolves that seek the Springs
> When scalding Thirst their burning Bowels wrings.
> (When some tall Stag fresh-slaughter'd in the Wood
> Has drench'd their wide, insatiate Throats with Blood)
> To the black Fount they rush a hideous Throng,
> With Paunch distended, and with lolling Tongue,
> Fire fills their Eyes, their black Jaws belch the Gore,
> And gorg'd with Slaughter, still they thirst for more.
>                                        (190-201)

This might do as a description of *Werewolves*! Pope has suppressed
Homer's repeated reference to the wolves' courage, and replaced it
with the alienating touch that cuts him off from Homer's feeling for
the beauty and mystery of animal Nature: 'they rush a hideous Throng'

---

[1] *Observations on the Sixteenth Book* (1718), XIX p. 295.

G

Quite the opposite occurs whenever Pope is concerned with making his hero nobler. As a random sample, I take the moment I referred to some time ago, in Book III, where Menelaos confronts Paris. It will be found in line 21 in the Greek: in Pope it begins at line 35:

> And when Menelaos (whom Ares loves) identified Paris,
> Coming in front of the mass of the fighters and striding out
> > boldly,
> Joy took hold of his heart, as, chancing upon a huge carcass,
> After long hunger, a lion, finding a stag or a wild goat,
> Terribly tears at the flesh, and joy takes hold of *his* heart,
> (Though men in their lusty prime and fast-running deer-hounds
> > beset him:)
> So Menelaos was glad when his eye fell on great Alexandros.

Homer has given us with the *huge carcass* and *after long hunger* what might be called the internal economy of the animal—all that both justifies and gives its special *natural* quality to the desire for food and the joy over the sight of it. Pope has cut all this away, and has spoken of the animal only in terms that might apply to the hero. So we find that Menelaos bounds like a lion and that the lion is a lordly savage:

> Him *Menelaus*, lov'd of *Mars*, espies,
> With Heart elated, and with joyful Eyes:
> So joys a Lion if the branching Deer
> Or Mountain Goat, his bulky Prize, appear;
> In vain the Youths oppose, the Mastives bay,
> The Lordly Savage rends the panting Prey.
> Thus fond of Vengeance, with a furious Bound,
> In clanging Arms he leaps upon the Ground
> From his high Chariot: . . .                  (35-43)

Nowhere in the *Iliad* is Homer's love of the free independent life of animals so apparent as in his treatment of the simile comparing Paris to a stallion, at the close of Book VI (lines 503 ff. in the Greek, 648 ff. in Pope):

> (Paris was no more to be found dawdling about in the staterooms.
> He buckled on lovely pieces of armour with bronze attachments;
> Then dashed through the streets, quite sure of himself and proud
> > of his running,

As a stallion stamping the earth with joy when he breaks from
                                                    the halter
Where they had tied him up to feed, and runs from the manger
Down to the places he loves and swirls the stream water around
                                                    him;
The high-stepper holds up his head then and shakes it free
                                                    from the water,
Tossing his mane, quite sure of himself and proud of his beauty,
Then quickly moves off to the field where he knows the mares are
                                                    feeding.
So Paris, all the King's Son. He looked like King Shiner himself
                                                    as
He moved down the sloping streets of Troy in the blaze of his
                                                    armour:
Fast and sure he ran, and he laughed as he thought of the fighting.)

> But now, no longer deaf to Honour's Call,
> Forth issues *Paris* from the Palace Wall.
> In Brazen Arms that cast a gleamy Ray,
> Swift thro' the Town the Warrior bends his way.
> The wanton Courser thus, with Reins unbound,
> Breaks from his Stall, and beats the trembling Ground;
> Pamper'd and proud, he seeks the wonted Tides,
> And laves, in Height of Blood, his shining Sides;
> His Head now freed, he tosses to the Skies;
> His Mane dishevel'd o'er his Shoulders flies;
> He snuffs the Females in the distant Plain,
> And springs, exulting, to his Fields again.
> With equal Triumph, sprightly, bold and gay,
> In Arms refulgent as the God of Day,
> The Son of *Priam*, glorying in his Might,
> Rush'd forth with *Hector* to the Fields of Fight.          (648-63)

If we ask ourselves why Pope has reduced Homer's joy in the vitality
and spontaneity of the prime of life to the level of *sprightly*, *bold, and
gay*, we must turn to a further tag from his *Essay on Criticism*:

> Be *Homer*'s Works your *Study*, and *Delight*,
> Read them by Day, and meditate by Night,
> Thence form your Judgment, thence your Notions bring,
> And trace the Muses *upward* to their *Spring*;

Still with *It self compar'd*, his *Text* peruse;
And let your *Comment* be the *Mantuan Muse*.[1]

for the now familiar answer is: Pope took his eyes off Homer and
fixed them on Virgil, who translated this passage in the Eleventh Book
of his *Aeneid*. And as Pope re-visualized the scene through Virgil's
eyes, the specifically Homeric way of seeing and the specific turns
of Homeric speech faded away, and the vocabulary and syntax of Virgil
printed themselves on Pope's imagination.

> cingitur ipse furens certatim in proelia Turnus.
> iamque adeo rutilum thoraca indutus aënis
> horrebat squamis surasque incluserat auro,
> tempora nudus adhuc, laterique accinxerat ensem,
> fulgebatque alta decurrens aureus arce
> exsultatque animis et spe iam praecipit hostem:
> qualis ubi abruptis fugit praesepia uinclis
> tandem liber equus, campoque potitus aperto
> aut ille in pastus armentaque tendit equarum
> aut adsuetus aquae perfundi flumine noto
> emicat, arrectisque fremit ceruicibus alte
> luxurians luduntque iubae per colla, per armos.    (486-97)

So, instead of the Homer, which I rendered:

> breaks from the halter
> Where they had tied him up to feed . . .

we get a translation of Virgil's:

> qualis ubi abruptis fugit praesepia uinclis . . .

> with Reins unbound,
> Breaks from his Stall . . .

But more than this, Pope read his Virgil through Dryden. This made
for a greater, made, in fact, the decisive change. For whereas Homer
here loses all that was effeminate in Paris and sees only the stallion,
Dryden read a satirical portrait of wantonness into the horse. For
him, the key line, we might say with very little exaggeration, was
that he

> . . . snuffs the Females in forbidden Grounds . . .

[1] *Op. cit.*, pp. 9-10.

Pope comes so much under the sway of Dryden that he almost took
the passage entirely over:

> Freed from his Keepers, thus with broken Reins,
> The wanton Courser prances o're the Plains:
> Or in the Pride of Youth o're leaps the Mounds;
> And snuffs the Females in forbidden Grounds.
> Or seeks his wat'ring in the well known Flood
> To quench his Thirst, and cool his fiery Blood:
> He swims luxuriant, in the liquid Plain,
> And o're his Shoulder flows his waving Mane:
> He neighs, he snorts, he bears his Head on high;
> Before his ample Chest the frothy Waters fly.[1]     (743-52)

Pope, however, would not have accepted my insinuation that he
was moving progressively away from Homer. He found his *wanton
and pamper'd Courser* in Homer. Here is part of his Note:

> This beautiful Comparison being translated by *Virgil* in the
> eleventh *Æneid*; I shall transcribe the Originals that the Reader
> may have the Pleasure of comparing them. . . .
>
> Tho' nothing can be translated better than this is by *Virgil*, yet
> in *Homer* the Simile seems more perfect, and the Place more
> proper. *Paris* had been indulging his Ease within the Walls of
> his Palace, as the Horse in his Stable, which was not the Case of
> *Turnus*. The Beauty and Wantonness of the Steed agrees more
> exactly with the Character of *Paris* than with the other: And
> the Insinuation of his Love of the Mares has yet a nearer Re-
> semblance. The languishing Flow of that Verse,
>
> εἰωθὼς λούεσθαι ἐϋρρεῖος ποταμοῖο,
>
> . . . finely corresponds with the Ease and Luxuriancy of the pam-
> per'd Courser bathing in the Flood.[2]

Nemesis awaited this piece of self-deception, for when Pope came
to translate the Fifteenth Book, he discovered that this simile was
repeated *verbatim* for that Hector who had reproached Paris in the
Sixth Book. Pope no doubt felt a fool as he stuck to his guns and applied
to Hector Dryden's line:

---

[1] *The Works of Virgil* (1697), p. 560.
[2] *Observations on the Sixth Book* (1716), LIV, pp. 181-82.

He snuffs the Females in the well known Plain,
And springs, exulting, to his Fields again:
Urg'd by the Voice divine, thus *Hector* flew,
Full of the God; and all his Hosts pursue.        (304-307)

I am now ready to put forward what must begin as merely a thesis, to be tested on the text before it can be accepted, but is for me the fruit of the study I have made of all the similes in the *Iliad*. On the other hand, mere thesis it may be, but my conclusions are very like those of every other reader I know of. Firstly, the similes as a whole, and in particular those that draw on Nature, speak to us more immediately than any other parts of the poem. For one who, like me, finds much of the *Iliad* alien, they are precious evidence that human nature has not essentially altered. There is a possibility of continued imaginative contact here. Where, perhaps, I differ from some is in the further contention, that Pope was right to believe that there is *more* in Homer's similes than what strikes us immediately. So my second point is that Homer's similes prepare us for seeing something that is true of the *Iliad* as a whole, and one of the central truths of the poem. Here I am making my transition back to the main line of my whole argument that I propose to resume in the next chapter. It is, first, that, if we are to enjoy Homer's poem, we must share Homer's beliefs to the extent that we can say that we find Homer true to our modern experience. The point of suggesting that we can get through to Homer by means of Pope has all along been to make us ask whether we can do anything analogous ourselves. Can Catullus walk our way? Certainly not, in any obvious sense. That is what is so blighting about our current translations.[1] They are too modern, too merely modern, too modern with what is of least value in us. If, in our effort to get rid of a merely historical Homer, we set up a Homer whose *Iliad* might sound like a thrilling version of fighting in Vietnam or Nigeria, we shall have merely killed Homer for our times, and made the possibility of his survival into better times that much more difficult. My first contention, then, is that we must recreate beliefs which go deeper than what comes easily to us when we ask ourselves, What is Man? What is Nature? And therefore we must look to those rare geniuses among us who

[1] For some justification for (and qualification of) this sweeping remark, see Epilogue.

can see more in Man and more in Nature than we can. For I think that Homer is a greater poet than those we are used to, and that his greatness lies in reserve for men of genius to mediate to us.

I shall by various methods try to bring out what supports these thoughts as I run over different parts of the *Iliad* in my last three chapters. Let me apply them first to the simile we have just been considering. I shall be arguing that we cannot make the Greek come alive if we cannot to some extent put ourselves in Homer's place. Just as Pope could not have attempted translation if he had not thought Homer and Nature *were* the same, so we cannot expect to get very far into this simile unless we can see the modern stallion in the Homeric horse. Secondly, when we study the whole group of these animal similes, we must feel the *unspoken bond* between Homer's animals and Homer's men. For it is because of the strength of this unexpressed continuity of the animal and human world that Homer does not have to work for close *explicit* resemblances in these similes. It is because Pope's Man is cut off from Pope's animals that Pope has to work so hard to give his animals a human mask. Thirdly, I do not think we shall know what English words to bring in to make sense of the Greek with until we have heard what English words are used by people to carry convictions as deep as Homer's. And there you have the axe's edge, the cutting part of my thesis: it is a mistake to suppose we can tell ourselves what we feel about the supreme things in Greek if we have no access to the supreme things in English. The present study of the Greek and Roman classics represents the last gasp of the ideal of those humanists who had no access to anything supreme in their vernaculars or anything that came within reach of the Greek classics. If there is to be a new upsurge of Greek and Latin, it can only come about if we approach the Classics after prolonged study of the great things that come historically between us and the Greeks and Romans.

I sound my general thesis off here because this simile of the stallion offers an instance by which we may test it. First of all, I must go on record as having read the Greek before I opened a story by D. H. Lawrence entitled *St Mawr*.[1] Whether this story would make a reader stare and open his eyes I cannot guess: but that it would set his imagination racing when he returns to Homer I feel almost certain. So let us take his 'gift horse' at once. In that story Lawrence allows

[1] In the volume *St Mawr together with The Princess* (1925) from which all the quotations are taken.

one of the characters to have the very revelation I think Homer can give us—only she has the vision in reverse. She saw the ancient stallion in the modern horse: 'She realised that St Mawr drew his hot breaths in another world from Rico's, from our world. Perhaps the old Greek horses had lived in St Mawr's world. And the old Greek heroes, even Hippolytus, had known it.'[1] The tragedy of our modern life is that, as it were, the more we intensify our powers of vision as we look at the horse, the further away seems the possibility of discovering the continuity that gives us the conviction of Man as a Hero: in this story the character says: 'I don't know one single man who is a proud living animal.'[2]

To find words with which to recreate Homer's stallion, and a hero worthy to be compared with the stallion, we might with advantage adopt the method of this story—or rather, one of its methods —namely, to see the horse as it appears to the different people who stand in different relations to him. When, for instance, in Homer's text we try to take in the phrase ὁ δ' ἀγλαΐηφι πεποιθώς, where the parallel between hero and horse is explicit, the phrase which I rendered 'quite sure of himself and proud of his beauty', we might first note how the professional 'horsey elderly man like an old maid' appraises St Mawr: '. . . he's a powerful, beautiful hackney, clean as a whistle, and eaten up with his own power . . .'[3] for if we look at the story we see that we can only 'take' the visionary perceptions of the two troubled women looking for reality in themselves and their fellow-humans because of the continuity of those perceptions with the phrases of men who knew horse flesh. Lawrence was well aware of the cheapness that ensues when those visions are taken out of the context of saving earth-contact. Here is a perfect anecdote, even if it is only perfect in the sense of *ben trovato*. Dorothy Brett reports in her book, *Lawrence and Brett* (pp. 100-101), that Mrs Lawrence was one day riding on a newly-acquired horse, and that she cried out in her Teutonic enthusiasm: 'Oh, it's wonderful; wonderful to feel his great thighs moving, to feel his powerful legs!' To which her husband is said to have replied, 'Rubbish, Frieda! Don't talk like that. You have been reading my books: you don't feel anything of the sort!'

With this proviso, we can form a fresh contact with Pope's line:

And laves, in Height of Blood, his shining Sides;

[1] *Op. cit.*, p. 26.　　[2] *Op. cit.*, p. 61.　　[3] *Op. cit.*, p. 18.

by letting ourselves see St Mawr and feel him as the American girl in the story saw and felt:

> She laid her hand on his side, and gently stroked him. Then she stroked his shoulder, and then the hard, tense arch of his neck. And she was startled to feel the vivid heat of his life come through to her, through the lacquer of red-gold gloss. So slippery with vivid, hot life!
>
> She paused, as if thinking, while her hand rested on the horse's sun-arched neck. Dimly, in her weary young-woman's soul, an ancient understanding seemed to flood in.[1]

Somehow a 'message' is conveyed not unlike Homer's in the *Iliad*, that 'You had to keep on holding on, in this life, never give way, and never give in . . .'[2], though, at the moment, the 'message' is only the vision, breaking down, or rather, melting away, the walls of her own world, of a great body glowing red with power.

Similarly, when we are considering what is the modern English for ῥίμφα ἑ γοῦνα φέρει which I rendered 'the high-stepper . . . quickly moves off', it is an advantage to start from the way in D. H. Lawrence's story the expert horse-rider views a horse's action—'The bay moved proud and springy, but with perfect good sense, among the stream of riders . . .'[3]—before we consider the richer notation made by the artist *manqué* in the tale: 'St Mawr could go like the wind, but with that luxurious heavy ripple of life which is like nothing else on earth. It seemed to carry one at once into another world, away from the life of the nerves'.[4] We do not come to care much for the person appreciating here, but we do learn to take in fully what he feels for the horse: 'Marvellous the power and life in the creature. There was really a great joy in the motion'.[5]

This is the capacity we need if we are to appreciate Homer: we must be able to marvel at and to joy in the world of nature. So, if I say we must in some sense share Lawrence's beliefs, it would be chiefly in the awe and wonderment that led him to exclaim: 'Marvellous! The marvellous beauty and fascination of natural wild things! The horror of man's unnatural life, his heaped-up civilisation!'[6] for only then shall we be able to discover the connections at a deep level between the animal and the human that are to be found in the *Iliad*. Only

---

[1] *Op. cit.*, p. 19.   [2] *Op. cit.*, p. 20.
[3] *Op. cit.*, p. 29.   [4] *Op. cit.*, p. 46.
[5] *Op. cit.*, p. 45.   [6] *Op. cit.*, p. 151.

when we have a strong whiff of this can we overcome in ourselves the interest that dominated Dryden and Pope, who saw a stallion only as a powerfully *over-sexed* animal.

All this must be taken with tact, of course, and the actual labour of translation is not yet begun. Nevertheless I regard it as more than whimsy to suppose that if Homer savoured Virgil's translation, he might prefer as a warmer, more imaginative approximation these lines from *St Mawr*, even though at this point in the story the horse was merely bluffing:

> He pretended to hear something, the mares two fields away, and he lifted his head and neighed. She knew the powerful, splendid sound so well: like bells made of living membrane. And he looked so noble again, with his head tilted up, listening, and his male eyes looking proudly over the distance, eagerly.[1]

This, at any rate, is the modern experience to which we find Homer true. The imagination of great artists does not seem to have changed over the years. I can fancy Homer saying to himself, 'This matches my experience', when he finds the young author of 1908 writing 'At the bottom men love the brute in man best, like a great shire stallion makes one's heart beat . . .'[2] and at the same time notes how quietly in *St Mawr* (1925) the stallion comes at last to the mare: 'And St Mawr followed at the heels of the boss'[s] long-legged black Texan mare, almost slavishly.'[3]

A point that now comes up for consideration is a consequence of Homer's heroes having these underground connections. It is that no comparisons could hurt them or diminish their stature. Homer had not to fear for his heroes: Pope's heroes, by contrast, are delicate creatures, creatures of Decorum; they cannot bear comparison with three things: the inherently small or insignificant, the socially degrading, and the disgusting. They cannot associate freely or by underground connections with the rest of humanity, to say nothing of the animal or vegetable kingdom.

It would be proper at this point to give one or two examples of 'low' similes in Homer that Pope had to rewrite to make tolerable

---

[1] *Op. cit.*, p. 89.
[2] *The Collected Letters of D. H. Lawrence* (1962), ed. H. T. Moore, p. 34.
[3] *Op. cit.*, p. 154.

to himself and his immediate public. But first I must allude to the *general low tone* of Homer, which made many of Pope's contemporaries prefer Virgil to Homer. The most shocking thing for Pope was that Homer expected his readers to take an interest in matters felt to be beneath the notice of fine gentlemen. The form of my allusion will be to offer an analogy from Henry James's *The Golden Bowl*, which covers the whole topic. The incident I have in mind presents a contrast between a modern descendant of Pope's fine gentleman, the Italian Prince, and Charlotte, the 'natural' American. By being a born American who brings American eyes to Europe but accepts the standards of European civilization, she becomes in fact a civilized peer to the Prince, without losing the natural touch. Charlotte and the Prince go out on a buying 'spree', and visit a not-too-distinguished antique shop in Bloomsbury, where a Jew tries to sell them a golden bowl:

> Charlotte, after the incident, was to be full of impressions, of several of which, later on, she gave her companion—always in the interest of their amusement—the benefit; and one of the impressions had been that the man himself was the greatest curiosity they had looked at. The Prince was to reply to this that he himself hadn't looked at him; as, precisely, in the general connection, Charlotte had more than once, from other days, noted, for his advantage, her consciousness of how, below a certain social plane, he never *saw*. One kind of shopman was just like another to him—which was oddly inconsequent on the part of a mind that, where it did notice, noticed so much. He took throughout, always, the meaner sort for granted—the night of their meanness or whatever name one might give it for him, made all his cats grey. He didn't, no doubt, want to hurt them, but he imaged them no more than if his eyes acted only for the level of his own high head. Her own vision acted for every relation—this he had seen for himself: she remarked beggars, she remembered servants, she recognised cabmen; she had often distinguished beauty, when out with him, in dirty children; she had admired 'type' in faces at hucksters' stalls.[1]

Charlotte, too, we see, was an aristocrat! Nor is *The Golden Bowl* itself remarkable for its rendering of these humble relations! But, if

---

[1] *The Golden Bowl* (1905), p. 75.

we recall the possibility that Homer, too, was writing for the Greek equivalent of gentlemen, we may say that Homer is Charlotte to Pope's Prince.

Since I must select instances of low similes in Homer, I shall pick out first a common type: those Pope felt to be low because the hero was likened to something small or insignificant. Insect similes are an instance, and to give you Pope's general line, I shall quote from a Note on a simile in Book XVI, where the Myrmidons are compared to wasps:

> One may observe, that tho' *Homer* sometimes takes his Similitudes from the meanest and smallest things in Nature, yet he orders it so as by their Appearance to signalize and give Lustre to his greatest Heroes. Here he likens a Body of *Myrmidons* to a Nest of Wasps, not on account of their Strength and Bravery, but of their Heart and Resentment. *Virgil* has imitated these humble Comparisons, as when he compares the Builders of *Carthage* to Bees. *Homer* has carry'd it a little farther in another Place, where he compares the Soldiers to Flies, for their busy Industry and Perseverance about a dead Body; not diminishing his Heroes by the Size of these small Animals, but raising his Comparisons from certain Properties inherent in them, which deserve our Observation.[1]

The classic instance of this type, to which Pope was alluding here, occurs in Book XVII, line 642, where, once again, Pope's note makes commentary superfluous:

> It is literally in the *Greek, she inspir'd the Hero with the Boldness of a Fly.* There is no Impropriety in the Comparison, this Animal being of all others the most persevering in its Attacks, and the most difficult to be beaten off: The Occasion also of the Comparison being the resolute Persistance of *Menelaus* about the dead Body, renders it still the more just. But our present Idea of the Fly is indeed very low, as taken from the Littleness and Insignificancy of this Creature. However, since there is really no Meanness in it, there ought to be none in expressing it; and I have done my best in the Translation to keep up the Dignity of my Author.[2]

[1] *Observations on the Sixteenth Book* (1718), XXVIII, pp. 303-304.
[2] *Observations on the Seventeenth Book* (1720), XXXVI, pp. 59-60.

So low was the idea of the fly, and so desperate the need to raise the author's dignity, that Pope had to devote to rescuing it the following *four* lines:

> So burns the vengeful Hornet (Soul all o'er)
> Repuls'd in vain, and thirsty still of Gore;
> (Bold Son of Air and Heat) on angry Wings
> Untam'd, untir'd, he turns, attacks, and stings.     (642-45)

A similar difficulty arises for Pope whenever Homer betrays (as he so often does) his interest in the detail of manual work. Homer does not distinguish manual occupations into high and low: all the technical processes by which useful and beautiful artefacts are made seem to interest him equally. There is no impression of holding them at a distance. Homer does not appear to condescend as he watches the various skills practised round the farm or in the city. Pope's attitude towards them is concentrated in Note XLI on the Thirteenth Book:

> We ought not to be shock'd at the Frequency of these Similes taken from the Ideas of a rural Life. In early Times, before Politeness had rais'd the Esteem of Arts subservient to Luxury, above those necessary to the Subsistence of Mankind, Agriculture was the Employment of Persons of the greatest Esteem and Distinction: We see in sacred History Princes busy at Sheepshearing; and in the middle Times of the *Roman* Commonwealth, a Dictator taken from the Plough. Wherefore it ought not to be wonder'd that Allusions and Comparisons of this kind are frequently used by ancient heroick Writers, as well to raise, as illustrate their Descriptions. But since these Arts are fallen from their ancient Dignity, and become the Drudgery of the lowest People, the Images of them are likewise sunk into Meanness, and without this Consideration, must appear to common Readers unworthy to have place in Epic Poems. It was perhaps thro' too much Deference to such Tastes, that *Chapman* omitted this Simile in his Translation.[1]

This note did not lead him to suppress the whole of the offending passage—a scene in the winnowing-shed—but a line that may be rendered:

---

[1] *The Iliad of Homer*, Vol. IV (1718), p. 80.

The black beans and chick-peas jump out of the broad wheat-shovel becomes in Pope:

> Light leaps the golden grain, resulting from the ground . . .

This change is so characteristic that it must be thoroughly understood. To make it so, I will hark back to the Second Book (in Homer, 469 ff., in Pope, lines 552 ff.) where the simile concerns *stable flies:*

> (As thousands and thousand of flies that wander unceasing in
> spring time
> In and out of the cowsheds, through stables and up to the
> sheepfolds,
> As the time of the year comes round when milk splashes into
> milk pails,
> So many thousands of Greeks with their long hair dressed for
> the battle,
> Came up against the Trojans and longed to tear them to pieces.

> . . . or thick as Insects play,
> The wandring Nation of a Summer's Day,
> That drawn by milky Steams, at Ev'ning Hours,
> In gather'd Swarms surround the Rural Bow'rs;
> From Pail to Pail with busie Murmur run
> The gilded Legions glitt'ring in the Sun.
> So throng'd, so close, the *Grecian* Squadrons stood
> In radiant Arms, and thirst for *Trojan* Blood.     (552-59)

Pope's Note is explicit:

> The Lowness of this Image in Comparison with those which precede it, will naturally shock a modern Critick, and would scarce be forgiven in a Poet of these Times. The utmost a Translator can do is to heighten the Expression, so as to render the Disparity less observable: which is endeavour'd here, and in other Places. If this be done successfully, the Reader is so far from being offended at a low Idea, that it raises his Surprize to find it grown great in the Poet's Hands, of which we have frequent Instances in *Virgil's Georgicks.*[1]

Pope has been as good as his word: he has replaced Homer by Virgil,

---

[1] *Observations on the Second Book* (1715), XXIV, p. 21.

and has used Dryden's translation. Here is a specimen from Dryden's translation of the Fourth Book of the *Georgics*:

> The winged Nation wanders thro' the Skies,
> And o're the Plains, and shady Forrest flies:
> Then stooping on the Meads and leafy Bow'rs;
> They skim the Floods, and sip the purple Flow'rs.[1]   (73-76)

Just as with inanimate nature, Pope has converted Homer's animal nature to pastoral. The flies that feed on sheep's droppings become *evening insects*: the stables become *Rural Bow'rs*, and, to live up to this elevation, the flies also become heroes in shining armour, *gilded Legions*. As I explained in my last chapter, Homer's countryside has been replaced by that we find in *Les Avantures de Telemaque*. And that Pope was in his own eyes being faithful to Homer we can see from his Preface, where he tells the reader that after Virgil and Milton 'the Archbishop of *Cambray*'s *Telemachus* may give him the truest Idea of the Spirit and Turn of our Author'. Fénelon was what people wanted Homer to be: he gave the perfect evocation of what the century meant by the Golden Age.


The most disobliging simile in Homer, to judge by the number of protests it evoked, occurs in the Eleventh Book (lines 558 ff.), where Ajax after having been compared to a lion is then compared to a donkey. In Dr Rieu's version it goes like this:

> Even so, he was as stubborn as a donkey who gets the better of the boys in charge of him, turns into a field they are passing, and helps himself to the standing crop. So many sticks have been broken on his back that their feeble cudgelling leaves him unconcerned, till at last they drive him out with much ado, but not before he has eaten all he wants.[2]

Since, as we shall see, Pope cannot bring himself to mention such a low word as donkey, he quotes extensively from the French critics who had tried to defend Homer. The general starting-point is given by Boileau, who, says Pope, had laid down the general law:

---

[1] *The Works of Virgil* (1697), p. 124.
[2] *Op. cit.*, p. 212.

> There is nothing (says he) that more disgraces a Composition than the Use of mean and vulgar Words; insomuch that (generally speaking) a mean Thought express'd in noble Terms, is more tolerable than a noble Thought express'd in mean ones.

His defence of Homer was, according to Pope, that the words have a different effect in the original:

> . . . and it may often happen that a Word which is very noble in *Greek*, cannot be render'd in another Tongue but by one which is very mean. Thus the word *Asinus* in *Latin*, and *Ass* in *English*, are the vilest imaginable, but that which signifies the same Animal in *Greek* and *Hebrew*, is of Dignity enough to be employed on the most magnificent Occasions.

Monsieur Dacier, says Pope, tried another line of defence:

> In the time of *Homer* (says that Author) an Ass was not in such Circumstances of Contempt as in ours: The Name of that Animal was not then converted into a Term of Reproach, but it was a Beast upon which Kings and Princes might be seen with Dignity. And it will not be very discreet to ridicule this Comparison, which the holy Scripture has put into the Mouth of *Jacob*, who says in the Benediction of his Children, Issachar *shall be as a strong Ass*.

Pope, however, had too much sense of humour to take these lines. He concludes his survey with this reflection:

> However, upon the whole, a Translator owes so much to the Taste of the Age in which he lives, as not to make too great a Complement to a former; and this induced me to omit the mention of the word *Ass* in the Translation.[1]

Pope not only leaves out the word, but all the associations Homer delighted in. Just as actors shout the lines they do not understand, Pope goes into his most pompous style to stifle the suggestions of meanness:

> As the slow Beast with heavy Strength indu'd,
> In some wide Field by Troops of Boys pursu'd,
> Tho' round his Sides a wooden Tempest rain,
> Crops the tall Harvest, and lays waste the Plain;

---

[1] *Observations on the Eleventh Book* (1717), XL, pp. 210-12.

Thick on his Hide the hollow Blows resound,
The patient Animal maintains his Ground,
Scarce from the Field with all their Efforts chas'd,
And stirs but slowly when he stirs at last.          (683-90)

The Donkey is thus made fit to be compared with the Hero.


I have reserved for the end an example of the unspeakably low, the disgusting; of similes which Pope thought had to be completely transformed. They are a small class, and to anyone who lived exclusively on some of the publications described by Gillian Freeman in *The Undergrowth of Literature*, they would not qualify as disgusting at all. I bring in our modern perspective to correct a tendency in my praise of Homer to make his Nature *universal*. The comparison with Pope certainly forces me to see Homer's nature as a fresh-air thing of great extent in all directions. But in fact Homer's Nature, too, is not real Nature in its totality but is confined to those aspects of nature that would enable us to believe in fighting men as heroes as well as brutes. I have been neglecting the fact that Homer's Nature is the result of sophisticated art. And here I must quickly insert for the beginner one characteristic stroke of art, a device which Homer uses to enhance the dirty doings of his men and gods. I let it pass when I brushed against it in saying in my last chapter that Homer's clouds were characteristically indifferent to the Trojan War. The consideration of this stroke of art will raise the larger question of the function of the similes and their place in the epic as a whole. But I shall return to, and finish off with, my sample of the simile that was too disgusting for Pope to tolerate.

The largest question to be asked of the *Iliad* is: what was it all for? or what is it essentially? Has it one main feature or purpose which enables us to see others as subordinate purposes or parts? For some people, with naïve ideas about great art and a respect for pseudo-history, the question is settled: for them the *Iliad* had a central core and two sets of expendable ornaments, indeed ornaments that do not go happily with what they are supposed to be decorating. A famous moment in our literary history occurred when Mr E. M. Forster stood up in Cambridge, and, like the Frenchman who when asked to name the greatest native lyric poet said: 'Victor Hugo—hélas', asked himself what a novel was, and taught us to reply (a little sadly)

H

'Yes—oh dear yes—the novel tells a story.'[1] The people I have in mind think that the epic, too, tells a story. So their answer to my question about the *Iliad* runs: it tells the story of the battles leading to the destruction of Troy. And if you raise your eyebrows and ask where in the *Iliad* you can find either the beginning or the end of that story, you are put off with various pseudo-historical reconstructions. But let that pass, for my point is that once a narrative of fights is taken to be the essence, then two other things, the speeches and the similes, don't seem to be in place.

It is not altogether fair to say that some eminent men admire Homer's heroes only for what they have in common with James Bond, that much-enduring licensed killer. But if we accepted their invitation to strip away the speeches and the similes, how should we have to characterize Homer's world? If we also threw out the improper episodes, are we not left with the *Boys' Own Homer*, that used to be part of most civilized adolescent lives? I pass rapidly over the speeches now, since I shall be dealing with them at length later, but are they not shocking to our sense of warriors as men of business, grim-chopped figures of the Coriolanus breed? All that boasting, threatening, and mere hot air, when they ought to be silently swinging their murderous tools! (I have even found critics saying what a bore Book I was because it consisted almost entirely of speeches.)

But let us now consider the effect of reading the *Iliad* with only the similes left out. Shouldn't we be bound to think of the author as very much closer to his heroes, as sharing in their limitations and their prejudices? Many people in fact speak of Homer as Achilles' *Goebbels*. Such people like to think of all artists as lackeys or, in modern terms, as PROs—Public Relations Officers, journalists paid to support the lines laid down for them by their bosses. There is plenty of material in the *Iliad* for those to discover who have a keen nose for the crypto-fascist or the supporter of the idle rich. The frustrated socialist looking for working-class brothers in the *Iliad* finds only Thersites. What would a man, fresh from reading Thorstein Veblen's *The Theory of the Leisure Class*, who thought the only social value was productive labour, have to say about most of Homer's warriors and priests? What figure would the heroes cut in any functional society? Restoring the similes puts back into Homer's world many features that we otherwise would never have guessed at. In them we find men doing, and doing

[1] *Aspects of the Novel* (1927), p. 62.

happily, useful things with their hands. Just as there emanates from the narratives of battles a message that the glory of life consists in useless fighting, so we get a silent sermon from many of the similes that the blessed thing is to live in peace and cultivate the domestic affections, and make the farm, the village, the city, better places to live in. There is no polemic between these two sides of the poem. The pacifist Homer votes with certain of his similes for a life that has no place for war or for expensively maintained idle rich.

But people have always felt that there are more eloquent similes than these cameos of peaceful activity. Yet the effect of the greatest Nature similes is, as Pope said, to *steal the Reader away from War and Horror*. I was going on to speak of a *classic* stillness in Homer and to contrast Pope's perpetual efforts to work up Nature into *dynamic tableaux* as *baroque*, when I remembered Dante. As I have more than once hinted, Dante is for me one of the few mediating geniuses who can help us to see the true greatness of Homer. The particular instance that came to me here occurs in the Twenty-Sixth Canto of the *Inferno*. There with great difficulty the dramatic hero scrambles up a steep mountain face and looking down below him sees innumerable flames moving in the air, flames which, he learns later, each envelop one of the Fraudulent. At this moment of tension, strain and horror, Dante writes a simile which I paraphrase since I cannot translate:

> It was like a scene at the end of a summer's day, just at that hour when evening insects dance and dayflies disappear. At the end of such a day when the sun had been lighting the world more generously than in other seasons, a countryman lolls against a slope and looks down into a valley where he has been labouring in the heat of the day and sees innumerable fireflies below him which light up the valley. The whole depth below me was resplendent with flames like those fireflies so that I could see to the bottom.[1]

Dante's scene is one of movement but the effect is to take us away for a moment into a peaceful world far from hell or any moral tension. It is like a peep into the scene on Keats's Urn, a timeless moment. I don't want to deny the resemblances between the two terms of the comparison: after all, Dante was looking down on flames just as the farmer or farm-labourer was looking down on fireflies. Yet the flies and the farmer do not merge into the flames of hell or add to the excitement of

[1] *Inferno*, Canto 26, lines 25-33.

the moment. It is the *contrast* that makes us feel the horror of hell. So I would argue of Homer's similes. They are not embellishments but constituent parts of the poem. They give it a depth and a complexity which raise the *Iliad* above the primitive.

But let us return to our low and disgusting simile, or rather to one of the most beautiful passages in Homer. It occurs at line 361 of Book XXI, just when Hephaistos has set fire to the river, and the river cries out in surrender. This is what Pope regarded as unspeakably low:

> Φῆ πυρὶ καιόμενος, ἀνὰ δ' ἔφλυε καλὰ ῥέεθρα.
> ὡς δὲ λέβης ζεῖ ἔνδον ἐπειγόμενος πυρὶ πολλῷ,
> κνίσην μελδόμενος ἀπαλοτρεφέος σιάλοιο,
> πάντοθεν ἀμβολάδην, ὑπὸ δὲ ξύλα κάγκανα κεῖται,
> ὣς τοῦ καλὰ ῥέεθρα πυρὶ φλέγετο, ζέε δ' ὕδωρ·     (361-65)

(The beautiful river burned and steam went up from the surface
As the water boils in a pot when a fast fierce flame is kindled
And melts the fat from the bones of a soft-fleshed gelded pigling:
The liquid spurts all round and the good fire-logs lie beneath it:
So with the blazing fire the river's fair waters bubbled.)

How abhorrent these images were to gentlemen of Pope's day, both in themselves and in their associations, we may judge from the famous strictures Samuel Johnson made in *The Rambler*, No. 168, on Shakespeare's use of *knife* and *blanket* in the tragedy of *Macbeth*. Shakespeare himself could associate the delicacy of aristocratic manners with the 'low' company of those who behind the scenes prepared the aristocratic meals. *Loves Labour's Lost* closes with a song, the action of which goes forward 'While greasie Ione doth keele the pot'. This was too much for most Frenchmen, as we may see from a glance at a translation of the *Iliad* which was published in Paris in 1681.[1]

---

[1] [De la Valterie] *L'Iliade d'Homere, Nouvelle Traduction*, Preface:

> Pour prévenir neanmoins le dégoût que la délicatesse du tems auroit peutestre donné de ma traduction, j'ay rapproché les mœurs des Anciens, autant qu'il m'a esté permis. Je n'ay osé faire paroistre Achylle, Patrocle, Ulysse, & Ajax dans la Cuisine, & dire toutes les choses que le Poëte ne fait point de difficulté de representer. Je me suis servi de termes generaux, dont nostre Langue s'accommode mieux que de tout ce détail, particulierement à l'égard de certaines choses qui nous paroissent aujourd'huy trop basses, & qui donneroient une idée contraire à celle de l'Auteur, qui ne les consideroit point comme contraires à la raison & à la nature.

To avoid disgusting gentlemen of modern refinement who might have been shocked by a faithful reproduction of Homer's manners, I have in this translation assimilated them as much as I could to our own. I lacked the courage to allow Achilles, Patroclus, Ulysses and Ajax to visit the kitchen, and to say many things that it did not shock Homer to put in their mouths. I have preserved decency by keeping to general terms and by avoiding detailed mention of certain things and actions too low for our taste. Homer thought them compatible with Nature and Good Sense. If I had mentioned them in my translation, the reader might have thought that Homer had no true perception of the one or the other.

Pope, at any rate, averted his eyes from the horrid contents of the hot pot, and gave us this note:

It is impossible to render literally such Passages with any tolerable Beauty. These Ideas can never be made to shine in *English*, some Particularities cannot be preserv'd; but the *Greek* Language gives them Lustre, the Words are noble and musical.

[And to his great credit Pope then quotes the original.]

All therefore that can be expected from a Translator is to preserve the Meaning of the Simile, and embellish it with some Words of Affinity that carry nothing low in the Sense or Sound.[1]

Whether there is any affinity left we may test by opening his version at line 422:

He ceas'd; wide Conflagration blazing round;
The bubbling Waters yield a hissing Sound.
As when the Flames beneath a Caldron rise,
To melt the Fat of some rich Sacrifice,
Amid the fierce Embrace of circling Fires
The Waters foam, the heavy Smoak aspires:
So boils th' imprison'd Flood, forbid to flow,
And choak'd with Vapours, feels his Bottom glow.

(422-29)

The reader who cares for Pope must have been fuming, if he has followed me through this chapter. For whereas it is notorious that

[1] *Observations on the Twenty-First Book* (1720), XX, pp. 290-91.

Pope lavished all his art on the similes, I seem to have gone out of my way, after what now looks like a hollow tribute to the nobility of his grasp of the Whole, to present him always at a disadvantage. Since this was not my intention, I have attempted to redress matters by concocting a speech which I have imagined as delivered by Pope to me. In fairness, though, my imaginary Pope ought to have dealt with me more severely.

'I may be open to censure in my rendering of many types of simile, but to one type I am perfectly adequate, and to the most sublime. The whole world joins me in admiring the one we find at line 146 of the Sixth Book:

οἵη περ φύλλων γενεή, τοίη δὲ καὶ ἀνδρῶν.
φύλλα τὰ μέν τ' ἄνεμος χαμάδις χέει, ἄλλα δέ θ' ὕλη
τηλεθόωσα φύει, ἔαρος δ' ἐπιγίγνεται ὥρῃ·
ὣς ἀνδρῶν γενεὴ ἡ μὲν φύει ἡ δ' ἀπολήγει.

'What could be lower than this rendering?

As green things flower and fade in turn, so it is with men; when
The wind brings last year's leaves to the ground, the trees in the
forest
Flourish anew with green at the height of the following spring. So
When this generation of men shall fade, another one flowers.

'Let me offer you instead the majestic march of a just cadence:[1]

Like Leaves on Trees the Race of Man is found,
Now green in Youth, now with'ring on the Ground,
Another Race the following Spring supplies,
They fall successive, and successive rise;
So Generations in their Course decay,
So flourish these, when those are past away.     (181-86)

[1] Cf. Boileau, L'Art poétique, Chant I, 131-32:

Enfin Malherbe vint, et le premier en France,
Fit sentir dans les vers une juste cadence . . .

Number and Cadence, that have Since been Shown,
To those unpolish'd Writers were unknown.

'There you have a banal Commonplace raised to Nobility. Of course, I had my helps. There was the famous passage in *Ecclesiasticus:*[1]

All flesh waxeth old as a garment:
For the covenant from the beginning is, "Thou shalt die the death".
As of the greene leaves on a thicke tree,
Some fall, and some grow;
So is the generation of flesh and blood,
One commeth to an end, and another is borne.

'I took the hint for the happy use of *successive* from[2] that beautiful passage in the Fourth Book of Milton's *Paradise Lost*, where Adam gently informs Eve that it is bed-time:

> Fair Consort th'hour
> Of night, and all things now retir'd to rest
> Mind us of like repose, since God hath set
> Labour and rest, as day and night to men
> Successive, and the timely dew of sleep
> Now falling with soft slumbrous weight inclines
> Our eye-lids; ...                     (610-16)

'To make my meaning abundantly clear, I now give you some lines that could not have been written before me, which shew how the Homeric commonplace has reverberated down the Roman ages to my latest successor:

> The snow dissolv'd no more is seen,
> The fields, and woods, behold, are green,
> The changing year renews the plain,
> The rivers know their banks again,
> The spritely Nymph and naked Grace
> The mazy dance together trace.
> The changing year's successive plan
> Proclaims mortality to Man.

[1] Chapter 14, verses 17-18.

[2] No doubt with some help from Roscommon: *Horace of the Art of Poetry* (1684), pp. 5-6:

> Words are like Leaves, some wither every year,
> And every year a younger Race succeeds;

Rough Winter's blasts to Spring give way,
Spring yield[s] to Summer['s] sovereign ray,
Then Summer sinks in Autumn's reign,
And Winter chils the World again.
Her losses soon the Moon supplies,
But wretched Man, when once he lies
Where Priam and his sons are laid,
Is naught but Ashes and a Shade. . . .'[1]      (1-16)

[1] Part of Horace: *Odes*, Book IV, 7, translated by Samuel Johnson.

# SIX

# A Conception and a Conviction
# of the Heroic

THIS chapter and the next two are concerned to make possible answers to the questions, what is an epic? and, what is the essence of the *Iliad*? but they constitute three *separate* roads of enquiry. In this chapter I shall be raising what may at first seem an odd sort of question, to ask, namely, what frame of mind do we need to have ready for the *Iliad* to become a permanent possession?—for we do not normally suppose that there is any special pre-condition for taking in a classic and making it permanently our own. But if we do not so suppose, are we not standing in a pre-Kantian relation to our material, such as would not be tolerated in any other field of mental enquiry? If every philosopher who asks himself, what is Truth? finds himself asking, what is Knowing? and enlarging that question to include, what is man's mind capable of in a general way, ought we not to be interested in the question whether successful contact is merely a matter of will and perseverance when we read an acclaimed masterpiece and wish to give an account of its essence? Is it not one more of the grand illusions of our cultural history that the masterpieces of the past are available to us at any time we care to consult them? And is it not an especial illusion of our universities that *every* period of literature is open to profitable study? And if so, should we not imitate the philosophers and raise the question I am here asking of the *Iliad* apropos of all the authors we are supposed to be competent to deal with? These are large questions, and I shall appear arbitrary in pushing open only one door when there are clearly many inviting corridors.

I used to think it a mark of this century that we who are of it find ourselves so habitually preferring the *modern* to the ancient. It was only when I began to study the behaviour of our ancestors near and remote that I first came to see this as a necessary condition of all vitality. It then became for me a rule to regard all past literature as irrelevant, and an interest in it as suspect, a sign of impotence or a sign of fear.

On the other hand, this same attempt to survey mankind's practice showed me that no age has been artistically self-satisfying. To live exclusively off what comes to hand can often mean to live very well —witness the Greeks—but even they kept some of their classics alive, presumably to meet a real need. This led me to ask: what does a man need in order to become truly modern, to become fully himself? and to consider a long list of things that are indispensable for fullness of life. I bring all this up here because of the thought that it is most unlikely that we would succeed in getting much out of a work of the remote past *unless we needed it very badly in the present.*

As soon as I began feeling around this equivocal word 'need', it came over me that I had somehow to make a distinction between *real and fancied needs*, a distinction D. H. Lawrence had in mind when he wrote, 'I think, do you know, I have inside me a sort of answer to the *want* of to-day: to the real, deep want of the English people, not to just what they fancy they want'.[1] And I in turn began to fancy that one of our real needs might be discovered by considering the principal feature of being modern. My first solution was too simple: it was to say that because the present is meaningless standing alone, what we need to bring in is the future or the past. But I retained the general form of this answer, and it seemed to generate some useful small applications. For example, when we live in the present we don't need to learn about Heracleitus, we have him in our bones. Now, to feel the contemporary flux is to feel a need for the opposite. In a sense we don't need Plato: we generate the same desire as his or very similar desires for the lasting, the non-moving, etc. (And in the *Iliad* we can see that *immortal gods* are an absolute necessity for *mortal men.*) But it is not only the timeless and the permanent that we need: it is quite intolerable to live with the doctrine *quot homines tot sententiae*; if we each generate the standards and rules governing all questions of value, they are wanting in something indispensable: authority.

But as soon as we allow such thoughts to develop, the general conditions of these needs begin to sketch themselves. Our needs, we can say, are for paradoxical states: for Another that is still Ourselves. That would be my definition of a classic, of a classic that can enter our lives. It must be alien and it must be familiar. The greatest harm done to me in youth (and I presume to thousands like me) was to bring me up to believe that the Greek classics were merely backward

[1] Letter of February 1st, 1913, from *The Letters of D. H. Lawrence* (1932), p. 105.

extensions of myself; that Homeric heroes were nothing but the public schoolboys of the twelfth century B.C. The beginning of the satisfaction of a true need is to see the Greeks as incurably alien. The next step is to say: yet not hopelessly other. My image of the ideal stance is that of the unburied dead who in Virgil's *Aeneid* are pictured as gazing across the Styx and stretching out their hands in yearning. I have no image for the two-way traffic that then ensues when the past comes back and visits us and the dead awaken. But since I am hastening towards the name of Ezra Pound, I will quote one of his poems:

> See, they return; ah, see the tentative
> Movements, and the slow feet,
> The trouble in the pace and the
>               uncertain
> Wavering!
>
> See, they return, one, and by one,
> With fear, as half-awakened;
> As if the snow should hesitate
> And murmur in the wind,
>                         and half turn back;
> These were the 'Wing'd-with-Awe',
>               Inviolable.
>
> Gods of the winged shoe!
> With them the silver hounds,
>               sniffing the trace of air!
>
> Haie! Haie!
>   These were the swift to harry;
>   These the keen-scented;
>   These were the souls of blood.
>
> Slow on the leash,
>               pallid the leash-men![1]

I should now like to reformulate my opening question like this: what is the blood we must supply to give substance to the pallid texts so that they in turn can give us what we desperately need? For I now have my answer ready: it, too, must be a paradox: that we cannot have the Homeric hero unless we have in some sense

---

[1] *Ripostes of Ezra Pound* (1912). 'The Return', pp. 53-54.

pre-imagined him. We cannot answer the question: what is the *Iliad*? unless we clearly have a conception of the heroic which the poem must both *confirm and transcend*. And as I tried to fill out the thoughts I shall be expounding in this chapter, I found I had to make a distinction between having a *conception* of the heroic and something very different, which I shall call having a *conviction* of the heroic. Similarly, when I turned my mind to the question of the conditions for the creation of a successful epic, I found myself saying that the epic writer must have more than a *subject*, he must have a *theme*: what he writes about must stand in paradoxical relations to the writer—which I must hazily summarize by claiming, for example, as simultaneously true that Flaubert's novel *Madame Bovary* is an objective work of art and that Flaubert was not lying when he said, 'Emma Bovary is me'.

And, to round off these introductory reflections, I found I had on my hands a definition of what is *serious* literature, or at least an answer to the question: what literature is likely to be of *permanent* interest? To be serious is to have distinguished between real and fancied needs, to know what one really feels. I use the phrase in the spirit of Arnold's lines:

> Below the surface-stream, shallow and light,
> Of what we *say* we feel—below the stream,
> As light, of what we *think* we feel—there flows
> With noiseless current strong, obscure and deep,
> The central stream of what we feel indeed; . . .[1]

And the one permanent need is to have revealed to us what our true feelings are, to discover that greater human Nature which the best minds have caught glimpses of in observing and imagining, in looking before and after, in the course of the short creative span during which they could remould the conventional forms of art.

There you have a framework of ideas but, as expressed, it remains something far off. Not one of the ideas bites. I have therefore taken the liberty of proposing an experiment. Its aim is to gain some preliminary experience to see what must be the general lines on which a crucial experiment ought to be designed. For a crucial experiment nothing less than the whole *Iliad* will do. To choose a part of the *Iliad* knowing it to be only a part would be perverse. So for my pilot-

---

[1] *St Paul and Protestantism* (1870), p. 142.

experiment I have gone off to the *Odyssey*. But for this experiment the *Odyssey* is a mere pretext. What I want to try out in the first place is the plausibility of my general argument that success with Homer depends on what we can bring to Homer as much as on what Homer can bring to us, or, in vaguer language, to avoid contention, whether we must in some sense have a conception of an epic before we can discover whether there is such a thing underlying Homer's *Iliad*.

Well, the first difficulty in setting up such a pilot-experiment is to get some starting material. Where, for instance, is our conception of an epic? Have we each got one? How do we become conscious of it? Since answering these questions might involve years of work, I have plunged arbitrarily for an instance. *Ezra Pound*, in his *Cantos*, can be shown to have had a conception of an epic. His decision to translate the opening of the Eleventh Book of the *Odyssey* is in fact the result of a confrontation with the original. He is telling us how much of the Greek 'makes sense' to him. It seemed to me that we might find out what our having a conception is like by seeing how we discover his. The advantage of searching for a conception—something apparently abstract and intellectual—in a translation is that it forces us to see that the answer will have to do as much with *manner* as with matter. And in fact this type of experiment opens up the question of how far the answer must be in terms of *poetry*. I have therefore given a chance to a prose version. I am responding here to a suggestion often made to me that 'verse epic' is now an archaic thing. I feel the force of this sugges- tion, and part of my reasons for trying to make Pope come alive is the following reflection: if Homer's *Iliad* can only be appreciated if treated as poetry, we badly need a mediate term to help us find our way to the poetry in the Greek. As we are not likely to get very much from existing modern verse translations, let us see if we can get on better with Pope.

The pilot-experiment consists of, first, reading the opening lines of *A Draft of XXX Cantos* (1933).[1] Then I recommend the opening pages of the translation of Homer's Eleventh Book of the *Odyssey* by Dr Rieu.[2] The corresponding passage in the version of the *Odyssey*, published by Pope, is of 97 lines.

> And then went down to the ship,
> Set keel to breakers, forth on the godly sea, and

---

[1] Reprinted, with one variant, in *The Cantos of Ezra Pound* (1964).

[2] *Homer, The Odyssey,* translated by E. V. Rieu (1952), Book XI, pp. 175-177.

We set up mast and sail on that swart ship,
Bore sheep aboard her, and our bodies also
Heavy with weeping, and winds from sternward
Bore us out onward with bellying canvas,
Circe's this craft, the trim-coifed goddess.
Then sat we amidships, wind jamming the tiller,
Thus with stretched sail, we went over sea till day's end.
Sun to his slumber, shadows o'er all the ocean,
Came we then to the bounds of deepest water,
To the Kimmerian lands, and peopled cities
Covered with close-webbed mist, unpierced ever
With glitter of sun-rays
Nor with stars stretched, nor looking back from heaven
Swartest night stretched over wretched men there.
The ocean flowing backward, came we then to the place
Aforesaid by Circe.
Here did they rites; Perimedes and Eurylochus,
And drawing sword from my hip
I dug the ell-square pitkin;
Poured we libations unto each the dead,
First mead and then sweet wine, water mixed with white flour.
Then prayed I many a prayer to the sickly death's-heads;
As set in Ithaca, sterile bulls of the best
For sacrifice, heaping the pyre with goods,
A sheep to Tiresias only, black and a bell-sheep.
Dark blood flowed in the fosse,
Souls out of Erebus, cadaverous dead, of brides,
Of youths and of the old who had borne much;
Souls stained with recent tears, girls tender,
Men many, mauled with bronze lance heads,
Battle spoil, bearing yet dreory arms,
These many crowded about me; with shouting,
Pallor upon me, cried to my men for more beasts;
Slaughtered the herds, sheep slain of bronze;
Poured ointment, cried to the gods,
To Pluto the strong, and praised Proserpine;
Unsheathed the narrow sword,
I sat to keep off the impetuous impotent dead,
Till I should hear Tiresias.
But first Elpenor came, our friend Elpenor,

Unburied, cast on the wide earth,
Limbs that we left in the house of Circe,
Unwept, unwrapped in sepulchre, since toils urged other.
Pitiful spirit. And I cried in hurried speech:
'Elpenor, how art thou come to this dark coast?
'Cam'st thou afoot, outstripping seamen?'
         And he in heavy speech:
'Ill fate and abundant wine. I slept in Circe's ingle.
'Going down the long ladder unguarded,
'I fell against the buttress,
'Shattered the nape-nerve, the soul sought Avernus.
'But thou, O King, I bid remember me, unwept, unburied,
'Heap up mine arms, be tomb by sea-bord, and inscribed:
'*A man of no fortune, and with a name to come.*
'And set my oar up, that I swung mid fellows.'

Pound assumes that we know where he takes his passage from.
We must recall that in Homer Odysseus is telling an assembled company
the story of his misadventures on leaving the nymph Circe and following her instructions to visit Hades in order to obtain from the prophet
Tiresias a knowledge of his present and future fortunes. The immediate advantage I hope to derive from using this passage is to arrive
rapidly at a rough notion of what having a conception of the heroic
is like. I hope that the first reading will bring agreement that Pound
has seen Homer as an author chiefly concerned to keep close to the
*things* he writes about. Pound appears to have supposed that Homer was
also principally concerned to make us live through a number of
*actions*. My rule of thumb for finding the translator's conception is to
look for the kind and quality of the insertions and omissions, the places
where the translator is doing more and less than provide the best close
equivalent for the phrases of the original. I find such tell-tale hints
of the translator's conception peeping out in the lines:

         Bore us out onward with bellying canvas,

and

         Then sat we amidships, wind jamming the tiller. . . .

Here Pound is filling out in his own way things which are implied
but not expressed in Homer. Homer says the wind filled the sails,
but he does not say here that it bellied them. The word has a good

Shakespearean vigour—it occurs in *Troilus and Cressida*—and it fits some of Homer's other set descriptions. The word was properly used by Dryden in his translation of the first book of the *Iliad*, where the scene is characteristically sharper and more vigorous:

> Awak'd, with lab'ring Oars they leave the Shore:
> The Pow'r appeas'd, with Winds suffic'd the Sail,
> The bellying Canvass strutted with the Gale . . .[1]

But in this context 'bellying' is inserted to bring Homer nearer to Pound's conception of the heroic action. What that conception was we may see by now taking the other line. 'Jamming the tiller' is an admirable expression to remind us of the language used by real sailors; yet all that Homer says here is that the wind did not divert the boat from its course. Pound, we may say, is making just a shade more of a sailor's yarn out of the *Odyssey* than Homer intended.

But we do not need to press details to obtain this conviction. We have only to compare Pound with any literal prose 'crib' and note how much of Homer Pound has left out, to be convinced that for Pound Homer's Odysseus was too garrulous. Pound's hero is clearly a more Conrad-like figure than Homer's; a tight-lipped mariner and something of a business man. We can imagine that Hemingway would prefer Pound's conception to Homer's. On the other hand, it is clear that whether or not Pound had the Yankee in mind as his ideal hero, the sort of hero Cooper filled his sea-stories with,[2] the resourceful, dependable man, the nautical counterpart of Davy Crockett, Pound also was seeing Odysseus as a figure of the remote past, a genuine primitive. If we look at other elements in the diction of this translation, and especially at the—on the whole attractive—blend of the alliterative line and the hexameter, we become aware that Pound is also seeing his hero through the Wanderer, the Anglo-Saxon much-enduring warrior.

Now, whereas there is something potentially 'tonic' in stressing the likeness between the Greek mariners of Homer's day and the down-to-earth sailors of the great days of American sailing ships, it is the reverse of tonic to meet with the fake archaic of the Wardour Street, Anglo-Saxon Wanderer. Where Pound has the virtues of

---

[1] *The First Book of Homer's Ilias* in *Fables* (1700), p. 213.

[2] I am sorry to learn that apparently there are no modern readers of *The Pilot* (1823), *The Red Rover* (1827), *The Water Witch* (1830), *The Two Admirals* (1842), *Wing-and-Wing* (1842), and *The Sea Lions* (1848).

prose, he is acceptable: it is his 'poetic' style that is intolerable. At the very beginning I am pulled up by

> We set up mast and sail on that swart ship, . . .

If we could believe that Homer had found the paint peculiar, if he had wished to suggest something out of the way on a ship of his day, we could only applaud Pound for digging up this out-of-the-way word 'swart'. But as far as I can make out, Homer meant a ship painted in the regulation colour, and thus was aiming at the very opposite effect from that obtained by Pound. In fact, 'black ship' forms one single concept, since all ships were black: the adjective is lost in the phrase. Pound's 'swart' is as misplaced as it would be if a BBC commentator rising to epic heights at a coronation were to say: 'as her Majesty's coach passes slowly along Whitehall in the pouring rain, a thousand swart umbrellas hide the faces of the civil servants.' Furthermore, by thus using up 'swart' for the commonplace, Pound loses an effect when he comes to describe the darkness of Hades. For the darkness there is totally unlike the lovely dark of a Mediterranean nightscape at sea. It is a horrible, unnatural dark, an impression we do not get from

> Swartest night stretched over wretched men there.

Another characteristic give-away can be found in these lines:

> To the Kimmerian lands, and peopled cities
> Covered with close-webbed mist, . . .

Pound's poetic style is more affected than Homer's. What is the point of 'peopled' here? 'Close-webbed' is what Arnold would call a 'curious thought'. It is unfortunately alien to the notion of mist, and, like 'peopled', contradicts the plain, matter-of-fact expressions used by Homer. And what Pound thought he was doing by inverting the order of subject and verb I cannot imagine.

But again it is not so much the detail of Pound's poeticalities that matter as their general result: which is to kill the impression of real life that Pound secured by the use of prose words. The consequence for me is that the whole passage reads like a hothouse product: it is not a real adventure and it has no unity of style. It looks as though Pound had here been deficient in imagination. Though he had the Greek before him—with a Latin 'crib'—he cannot present such a living Odysseus as Dante contrived, who had never read Homer.

I

Apart from the scraps in a few authors he would read in Latin, Dante had to make his Ulysses up entirely out of his own conception of the heroic. And he had the daring to present his Ulysses exclusively through one speech, the narrative of his last voyage. Here we badly need the pulse of Dante's verse. I am afraid the heroic note may be inaudible in my prose:

'Circe kept me with her for more than a year, not far from the place your hero later named Caieta. But when she let me go, nothing could keep me at home. I have always been fond of Telemachus, I respect my old father, I give my wife the love she deserves and makes her happy. But I was on fire to learn more of what man could be, how good, how bad, and all between. So I left them and put straight out to sea from the shore. I had only the one little ship and its crew, but they stood by me to the end. We saw all the Mediterranean could shew us as far as Spain and Morocco with Sardinia and the other parts the sea washes all round. We were old, slow-movers, by the time we reached the narrows and the boundary-stones Hercules put there to tell men where exploration should stop. Seville was behind us on the right and Ceuta passed us on the left. "*You* are my family now", I told the men. "We have reached the western edge of the world, and you know what we have been through to get so far. There isn't much life left in us. Let us spend its last flicker in one final experiment. There is another hemisphere: let us go after the sun into the uninhabited, unexplored, wilderness of waters. Think, we were not made to live like vegetables. We were born for knowledge and the full exercise of all our powers."

'This small-scale piece of oratory made such an impression on the crew that even if I had changed my mind, I could not have stopped them from pointing the ship towards the unknown. We pulled on the oars till the boat flew like a mad bird. Our course was a steady south-west. Night now saw all the stars of the Antarctic pole, and our own were so low that they never emerged above the level of the sea. Five times the moon had waxed and five times waned since the day we began our foolhardy expedition. Then we made out on the horizon, dimly, a mountain higher than any I had seen before. Land at last! But we had little time for rejoicing. A whirlwind came out from our new-

found-land and struck the prow and turned the seas and our
ship in them three times round in a circle. On the fourth turn
the poop went up, the prow went down, and, to please some
unknown power, the waters shut over our heads.'[1]

There is more than a touch of the Ancient Mariner about Dante's
*Ulysses*. The strangeness of his fate takes our attention away at the end
from the marked features of individual heroism in the earlier part of
the speech. The most surprising feature of Dante's heroic vision I
seem to have obscured in my efforts to find prose equivalents for the
poetry. It is the luxuriant sensuality implied in the exhortation to use
up the last possibility left to the old men of indulging their senses,
their capacity for experience. To make this the centre of the heroic is
to pass out of the classical world into the modern. Dante, then, gives
us a *conviction* of the heroic, and this passage will serve as a touchstone
when we wish to distinguish between a conception of and a conviction of what it means to be a hero. If we cannot in our translations
embody a conviction of the heroic, we are driven to expressing merely
a belittling conception of the heroic, as here by offering a prose 'crib'
I have clipped and cut down Dante's heroic figure, I have drained
away the colour and energy, and in their place have introduced
commonplace elements for which I alone am responsible.


 I make these remarks by way of transition to Dr Rieu's version of
Homer.

'Our first task, when we came down to the sea and reached
our ship, was to run her into the good salt water and put the
mast and sails on board. We then picked up the sheep we found
there, and stowed them in the vessel. After which we ourselves
embarked. And a melancholy crew we were. There was not a
dry cheek in the company. However, Circe of the lovely tresses,
human though she was in speech, proved her powers as a goddess
by sending us the friendly escort of a favourable breeze, which
sprang up from astern and filled the sail of our blue-prowed ship.
All we had to do, after putting the tackle in order fore and aft,
was to sit still, while the wind and the helmsman kept her
straight. With a taut sail she forged ahead all day, till the sun
went down and left her to pick her way through the darkness.

[1] *Inferno*, Canto 26, lines 90-142.

'Thus she brought us to the deep-flowing River of Ocean and the frontiers of the world, where the fog-bound Cimmerians live in the City of Perpetual Mist. When the bright Sun climbs the sky and puts the stars to flight, no ray from him can penetrate to them, nor can he see them as he drops from heaven and sinks once more to earth. For dreadful Night has spread her mantle over the heads of that unhappy folk.

'Here we beached our boat and after disembarking the sheep made our way along the banks of the River of Ocean till we reached the spot that Circe had described. There, while Perimedes and Eurylochus caught hold of the victims, I drew my sharp sword from my side and dug a trench about a cubit long and a cubit wide. Around this trench I poured libations to all the dead, first with mingled honey and milk, then with sweet wine, and last of all with water. Over all this I sprinkled some white barley, and then began my prayers to the helpless ghosts of the dead, promising them that directly I got back to Ithaca I should sacrifice a barren heifer in my palace, the best I had in my possession, and heap the pyre with treasures, and make Teiresias a separate offering of the finest jet-black sheep to be found in my flocks. When I had finished my prayers and invocations to the communities of the dead, I took the sheep and cut their throats over the trench so that the dark blood poured in. And now the souls of the dead who had gone below came swarming up from Erebus—fresh brides, unmarried youths, old men with life's long suffering behind them, tender young girls still nursing this first anguish in their hearts, and a great throng of warriors killed in battle, their spear-wounds gaping yet and all their armour stained with blood. From this multitude of souls, as they fluttered to and fro by the trench, there came a moaning that was horrible to hear. Panic drained the blood from my cheeks. I turned to my comrades and told them quickly to flay the sheep I had slaughtered with my sword and burn them, while they prayed to the gods, to mighty Hades and august Persephone. But I myself sat on guard, bare sword in hand, and prevented any of the feckless ghosts from approaching the blood before I had speech with Teiresias.

'The first soul that came up was that of my own man Elpenor, for he had not yet had his burial in the wide bosom of Earth. So urgent had we felt our other task to be that we had left his corpse unburied and unwept in Circe's house. Now, when I saw him, tears started to my eyes and I was stirred with pity for him.

'I called across to him at once: "Elpenor! How did you come here, under the western gloom? You have been quicker on foot than I in my black ship!"

'I heard him sigh, and then his answer came: "My royal master, Odysseus of the nimble wits, it was the malice of some evil power that was my undoing, and all the wine I swilled before I went to sleep in Circe's palace. For I clean forgot to go to the long ladder and take the right way down, and so fell headlong from the roof. My neck was broken and my soul came down to Hades. And now, since I know that when you leave this kingdom of the dead you will put in with your good ship at the Isle of Aeaea, I beseech you, my prince, by all the absent friends we left behind, by your wife, by the father who supported you as a child, and by Telemachus, your only son, whom you left at home—by all these I beg you to remember me then and not to sail away and forsake me utterly nor leave me there unburied and unwept, or the gods may turn against you when they see my corpse. So burn me there with all my arms, such as they are, and raise a mound for me on the shore of the grey sea, in memory of an unlucky man, to mark the spot for future voyagers. Do this for me, and on my barrow plant the oar I used to pull when I was alive and on the benches with my mates." '[1]

Rieu, too, has no conviction but merely a conception of the heroic. For him Homer is not depicting heroic action but non-heroic actions. His emphasis is on what Odysseus *did*.

There, while Perimedes and Eurylochus caught hold of the victims, I drew my sharp sword from my side and dug a trench about a cubit long and a cubit wide. Around this trench I poured libations to all the dead, first with mingled honey and milk, then with sweet wine, and last of all with water. Over all this I sprinkled some white barley, and then began my prayers to the helpless ghosts of the dead, promising them that directly I got back to Ithaca I should sacrifice a barren heifer in my palace, the best I had in my possession, and heap the pyre with treasures,

<hr />

[1] *Op. cit.*, Book XI, pp. 175-177.

and make Teiresias a separate offering of the finest jet-black sheep to be found in my flocks.

It is remarkable, if we turn to the Greek, to find how close to the original this is. Homer, it appears, has found the equivalent of prose before prose existed. Homer insists with the same clarity and economy on our taking in each individual item of the ritual act. Because here Homer wants nothing else, Rieu's 'deprived' style—if we tidy up his English and lop off a few redundancies such as 'had *in my possession*' —is as adequate as prose could well be.

It is, paradoxically, when Rieu finds Homer too prosaic for him and therefore begins to inject his own idea of the poetical that Homer disappears. But let me first deal with the passages where Rieu achieves bathos rather than pathos. Here, for example: 'After which we ourselves embarked. And a melancholy crew we were. There was not a dry cheek in the company.' It is, of course, very difficult for ex-public school boys to imagine themselves as the Greek and Trojan heroes who weep so copiously. Homer says here they wept 'buckets', or rather, buckets is just what he did not say. He felt no embarrassment about tears such as that which takes this refuge in the facetious. Homer's word is the opposite of an escape from the fact. In his poem the rush of tears calls up vigorous human and vegetable nature, something rich with the gloss of health on it: abundant strength. The effect on me of θαλερὸν κατὰ δάκρυ χέοντες. is: 'wept lusty tears'. This abundant activity of the whole vascular system that we find in all the heroes of antiquity has always pained and shocked the modern Englishman. Rieu says Elpenor sighed: Homer said he howled (οἰμώξας). 'I heard him sigh, and then his answer came' belongs to Tennyson's Arthurian heroes. From bathos it is but a step to the banal. The following banalities do not occur in Homer: '. . . the friendly escort of a favourable breeze'. Homer says that the following wind was a good friend. Nor is Homer responsible for 'With a taut sail she forged ahead all day', or 'left her to pick her way through the darkness'.

One of the striking poeticalities of Rieu's translation is the dash of Omar Khayyám we get here: 'When the bright Sun climbs the sky and puts the stars to flight', which is out of place when what was to be rendered was 'when it proceeds in the direction of the region of the stars', 'ὁπότ' ἂν στείχῃσι πρὸς οὐρανὸν ἀστερόεντα'. 'For dreadful Night has spread her mantle over the heads of that unhappy folk.'

It might be thought that 'dreadful night' was a phrase a translator would leave alone after the author of *The City of Dreadful Night* had done his worst with it. 'Spreading her mantle', if not FitzGerald, is Yeats: 'Had I the heavens' embroidered cloths, . . .' Homer is content to say, 'night was stretched over the poor wretches'. Other signs that the translator found Homer too flat for him are the various attempts to inject *pathos* into the narrative, such as this:

> And now the souls of the dead who had gone below came swarming up from Erebus—fresh brides, unmarried youths, old men with life's long suffering behind them, tender young girls still nursing this first anguish in their hearts,

'Life's long suffering' is the translator's own. Homer merely says they had put up with a lot. As for 'nursing anguish', the conceit is not Homer's.

The consideration of these two translations brings home to us some of the inescapable facts about translation, and about translating Homer. It becomes clear that without the deepest sincerity and the profoundest imagination a modern translation will not seem credible. Clearly, too, the translator must have a *mediate term* in mind between Homer and us. He must believe in a hero who at the same time appears like a modern hero and like what Homer writes about. Homer appeals so easily to boys because for them the question of credibility hardly arises: they do not require the confirmation of the heroic in modern terms. But when we say that Achilles is real, we mean something different. We mean that he stands the test of our experience. To speak of one mediate term, however, is to over-simplify; but mediate terms there must be or . . . *incredulus odi*. Homer becomes distasteful when he does not seem to be in touch with life as we have known it.

The deepest sincerity and the profoundest imagination are also required to communicate the credible hero. We have seen that, where they fail, we get the banal and the spuriously poetic. For this reason we may say with Arnold that Homer's matter cannot be divorced from his manner. For this reason we can say that the task of the translator is almost entirely to find a style, what Milton called an answerable style. For the modern writer's convictions must all be embodied in his style. Yet the same consideration makes it clear that the style cannot be Homer's. For just as there must be mediate terms to recreate the heroic, the answerable style must use the possibilities inherent in English style to convince us. We shall not believe that heroes are being described or themselves speaking in an English translation if they do not sound like the heroes we have enjoyed hearing described or speaking in English poems. For this reason only a great writer could dream of attempting a translation of Homer. If he can't make us believe that heroes are talking and being described in his own writings, he won't stand a chance of convincing us when he attempts Homer. The translator of Homer must command a style before he tackles Homer. Even then he must have the insight to discover how the style has to be adapted and modified to bridge the gap between the present and the past.

Facing these inescapable facts ought to remove some of the prejudices with which we approach Pope's[1] translation:

> Now to the shores we bend, a mournful train,
> Climb the tall bark, and launch into the main:
> At once the mast we rear, at once unbind
> The spacious sheet, and stretch it to the wind:
> Then pale and pensive stand, with cares opprest,
> And solemn horrour saddens every breast.
> A freshning breeze the Magic pow'r supply'd,
> While the wing'd vessel flew along the tyde:
> Our oars we shipp'd: all day the swelling sails
> Full from the guiding pilot catch'd the gales.
>     Now sunk the Sun from his aerial height,
> And o'er the shaded billows rush'd the night:
> When lo! we reach'd old Ocean's utmost bounds,
> Where rocks controul his waves with ever-during mounds.
>     There in a lonely land, and gloomy cells,
> The dusky nation of *Cimmeria* dwells;
> The Sun ne'er views th'uncomfortable seats,
> When radiant he advances, or retreats:
> Unhappy race! whom endless night invades,
> Clouds the dull air, and wraps them round in shades.

---

[1] The reader who exclaims at this point, 'But this is Broome!' is asked to persevere to the end of the chapter, and then to return and ask himself whether he has at any line of the verse met another mind than Pope's.

The ship we moor on these obscure abodes;
Dis-bark the sheep, an offering to the Gods;
And hellward bending, o'er the beach descry
The dolesome passage to th'infernal sky.
The victims, vow'd to each *Tartarean* pow'r,
*Eurylochus* and *Perimedes* bore.

Here open'd Hell, all Hell I here implor'd,
And from the scabbard drew the shining sword;
And trenching the black earth on ev'ry side,
A cavern form'd, a cubit long and wide.
New wine, with honey-temper'd milk, we bring,
Then living waters from the chrystal spring;
O'er these was strow'd the consecrated flour,
And on the surface shone the holy store.

Now the wan shades we hail, th'infernal Gods,
To speed our course, and waft us o'er the floods,
So shall a barren heifer from the stall
Beneath the knife upon your altars fall;
So in our palace, at our safe return
Rich with unnumber'd gifts the Pyle shall burn;
So shall a Ram, the largest of the breed,
Black as these regions, to *Tiresias* bleed.

Thus solemn rites and holy vows we paid
To all the Phantom nations of the dead.
Then dy'd the sheep; a purple torrent flow'd,
And all the cavern smok'd with streaming blood.
When lo! appear'd along the dusky coasts,
Thin, airy shoals of visionary ghosts;
Fair, pensive youths, and soft-enamour'd maids,
And wither'd Elders, pale and wrinkled shades:
Ghastly with wounds the forms of warriors slain
Stalk'd with majestic port, a martial train:
These, and a thousand more swarm'd o'er the ground,
And all the dire assembly shriek'd around.
Astonish'd at the sight, aghast I stood,
And a cold fear ran shivering thro' my blood;
Strait I command the sacrifice to haste,
Strait the flea'd[1] victims to the flames are cast,

---

[1] = flayed.

And mutter'd vows, and mystic song apply'd
To griesly *Pluto*, and his gloomy bride.
    Now swift I wav'd my faulchion o'er the blood;
Back started the pale throngs, and trembling stood.
Round the black trench the gore untasted flows,
'Till awful, from the shades *Tiresias* rose.
    There, wand'ring thro' the gloom I first survey'd,
New to the realms of death, *Elpenor's* shade:
His cold remains all naked to the sky
On distant shores unwept, unburied lye.
Sad at the sight I stand, deep fix'd in woe,
And ere I spoke the tears began to flow.
    O say what angry pow'r *Elpenor* led
To glide in shades, and wander with the dead?
How could thy soul, by realms and seas disjoyn'd,
Out-fly the nimble sail, and leave the lagging wind?
    The Ghost reply'd: To Hell my doom I owe,
Dæmons accurst, dire ministers of woe!
My feet thro' wine unfaithful to their weight,
Betray'd me tumbling from a tow'ry height,
Stagg'ring I reel'd, and as I reel'd I fell,
Lux'd the neck joynt—my soul descends to hell.
But lend me aid, I now conjure thee lend,
By the soft tye and sacred name of friend!
By thy fond consort! by thy father's cares!
By lov'd *Telemachus* his blooming years!
For well I know that soon the heav'nly pow'rs
Will give thee back to day, and *Circe's* shores:
There pious on my cold remains attend,
There call to mind thy poor departed friend.
The tribute of a tear is all I crave,
And the possession of a peaceful grave.
But if unheard, in vain compassion plead,
Revere the Gods, the Gods avenge the dead!
A tomb along the wat'ry margin raise,    ⎫
The tomb with manly arms and trophies grace, ⎬
To shew posterity *Elpenor* was.        ⎭
There high in air, memorial of my name
Fix the smooth oar, and bid me live to fame.    (1-97)

But let us begin at the lowest: Pope, like Pound and Rieu, had, at the lowest, a conception of the heroic. Let us define that before we go on to ask whether he had also a conviction based on vivid experience of mediate terms, what it meant to be a hero in his own day. Comparison with these two modern versions tells us at once what Pope's hero was *not*: Pope's Ulysses is neither a Fenimore Cooper nor an Ernest Hemingway hero. He is an active man, of course, but Pope's eye is not primarily on the bare actions. Pope is concerned rather to catch the hero's feelings: his Ulysses has a soul above mere adventure. To prove that he was being faithful to his original, Pope had only to say: look at Homer's *manner*. But here Pope's difficulties begin. However much more than mere action Homer wished to convey, his choice of words in describing actions is often as simple and direct as Hemingway's. Verbally, Pope knew this: in the letter of 1708 he had written: 'The great Beauty of Homer's Language, as I take it, consists in that noble simplicity, which runs through all his works' . . . The difficulty for Pope was that the mediate terms out of which his sense of the heroic was constructed could not supply the necessary combination of the expression of noble feelings and the performance of simple acts. It was only with the fictions of *Télémaque*, the heroes of the Golden Age, that Pope could believe in such a combination. Thanks to this mediate term, Pope managed to go a long way. Arnold was over-simplifying when he claimed that Pope could not succeed with 'flat' descriptions. And Pope goes a long way in this passage until he comes one dreadful cropper that ruins all. Let us put Pope to the severe test of comparison with Rieu at his best. Here is part of the passage I quoted a moment ago:

> There, while Perimedes and Eurylochus caught hold of the victims, I drew my sharp sword from my side and dug a trench about a cubit long and a cubit wide. Around this trench I poured libations to all the dead, first with mingled honey and milk, then with sweet wine, and last of all with water.

Pope does not shrink from any of these items:

> The victims, vow'd to each *Tartarean* pow'r,
> *Eurylochus* and *Perimedes* bore.
> Here open'd Hell, all Hell I here implor'd,
> And from the scabbard drew the shining sword;

And trenching the black earth on ev'ry side,
A cavern form'd, a cubit long and wide.
New wine, with honey-temper'd milk, we bring, ... (25-31)

There is a slight fictional air about it, a whiff of Fénelon, but it is
nearer the acts than Pound's: 'I dug the ell-square pitkin'; 'pitkin' is a
neologism comparable only to Newman's 'bulkin'! But what are we
to think of Pope's next line?

Then living waters from the chrystal spring ...

Why do we get this freezing touch? I suppose because Pope had felt:
'thus far and no farther can I go in the direction of simplicity. If I go
a step further and keep to the plainness of *water*, I shall fall from the
heroic into the low.' I think Pope's mediate terms imprisoned him
in the decorous. I imagine that at this point he asked himself how
Dryden had handled this topic when he was translating the sacrifice
made by Dido in the Fourth Book of the *Aeneid*:[1]

> Go *Barcè*, call my Sister; let her Care
> The solemn Rites of Sacrifice prepare:
> The Sheep, and all th' attoneing Off'rings bring
> Sprinkling her Body from the Crystal Spring
> With living Drops: ...                    (910-14)

Since, as I have said, and is generally believed, Pope was more
interested in bringing out the humanity of the heroes than in any
other aspect of the heroic, we might expect that his mediate terms
here would contain far more of the directly experienced than they do.
For Pope has boldly substituted his conception of humanity to replace
Homer's, though Pope, no doubt, would have denied that there could
be two conceptions of humanity. He felt sure that in endowing the
figures of the epic with the sensibility of his own more enlightened
readers he was merely giving the permanent and unchanging its
appropriate expression. Consequently, what mattered for Pope, it
would seem, was not that we should see mariners, but representatives
of feeling humanity. So the sailors stand like ghosts, *pale and pensive*.
Yet is Pope really giving us here of his deepest self? The phrase looks
suspiciously like a cliché. If we take the whole line

Then pale and pensive stand, with cares opprest,

[1] *The Works of Virgil* (1697), p. 323.

we cannot help seeing it as a mechanical formula as soon as we find it doing service both for January's Squire (in his version of Chaucer's Tale):

> But anxious cares the pensive squire opprest,[1]

and for Belinda (in the *Rape*):

> But anxious cares the pensive nymph opprest . . .[2]

All these lines, by the way, are derived from Dryden's *Aeneid*. Our line, then, is as much a borrowing as the one about living waters. We can say a little more about it if we extend the line to a couplet:

> Then pale and pensive stand, with cares opprest,
> And solemn horrour saddens every breast.

This certainly suggests that Pope is drawing on the 'pensive' of *Il Penseroso*, which gave him these suggestions for the 'pensive' Eloisa and her cell where

> Black Melancholy sits, and round her throws
> A death-like silence, and a dread repose:
> Her gloomy presence saddens all the scene,
> Shades ev'ry flow'r, and darkens ev'ry green,
> Deepens the murmur of the falling floods,
> And breathes a browner horror on the woods.[3]

All of which is more theatrical than human.

The desire for an understandable modern conception of humanity led Pope almost to rewrite the account of the ghosts:

> When lo! appear'd along the dusky coasts,
> Thin, airy shoals of visionary ghosts . . .

This is as modern as the opening of the 'Elegy':

> What beck'ning ghost, along the moonlight shade
> Invites my steps, and points to yonder glade?
> 'Tis she!—but why that bleeding bosom gor'd,
> Why dimly gleams the visionary sword?[4]

---

1 *The Works of Mr. Alexander Pope* (1717), p. 207. *January and May*, line 392.
2 *Ibid.*, p. 139. *Rape of the Lock*, Canto IV, line 1.
3 *Ibid.*, p. 399. *Eloisa and Abelard*, lines 165-70.
4 *Ibid.*, p. 358. 'Verses to the Memory of an Unfortunate Lady.'

The pull of this prevents Pope going all the way with Homer. Homer's ghosts are mutilated bats, but Pope has assimilated his to Hamlet's Father:

> Ghastly with wounds the forms of warriors slain
> Stalked with majestic port, a martial train . . .

Shakespeare knew the classical conception of the after-life:

>                               . . . the sheeted dead
> Did squeake and gibber in the Roman streets;

but the Ghost in *Hamlet* is a different figure: it moves with *martiall stauke* and is *so Maiesticall*. But Pope's Shakespeare was crossed with his Milton. The ghosts come from Milton's Hell not Homer's Hades, as we may see if we compare

> These, and a thousand more swarm'd o'er the ground,
> And all the dire assembly shriek'd around.

with the assembly of the devils in Pandemonium:

>                               thir summons call'd
> From every Band and squared Regiment
> By place or choice the worthiest; they anon
> With hunderds and with thousands trooping came
> Attended: . . .

> Thick swarm'd, both on the ground and in the air.[1]

One consideration, however, causes me embarrassment. I brushed it aside a moment ago, but if we turn to Pope's treatment of Elpenor, it returns with impressive force. The consideration is that Pope's humanity cannot be labelled modern, if we mean distinctively modern and opposed to Homer's. This consideration can be brought home with almost scientific rigour by observing that Pope's sentiments for Elpenor are as modern as some of those he expresses for the Unfortunate Lady—or, conversely, Pope borrows from the ancients to find adequate expression for his sensibility in a modern case. Simple juxtaposition makes this clear:

> There, wand'ring thro' the gloom I first survey'd,
> New to the realms of death, *Elpenor*'s shade:

---

[1] *Paradise Lost* (1667), I, lines 757-61, 767.

His cold remains all naked to the sky
On distant shores unwept, unburied lye . . .
But lend me aid, I now conjure thee lend,
By the soft tye and sacred name of friend! . . .
There pious on my cold remains attend,
There call to mind thy poor departed friend.
The tribute of a tear is all I crave,
And the possession of a peaceful grave . . .
 What can atone (oh ever-injur'd shade!)
Thy fate unpity'd, and thy rites unpaid?
No friend's complaint, no kind domestic tear
Pleas'd thy pale ghost, or grac'd thy mournful bier;
By foreign hands thy dying eyes were clos'd . . .
Ev'n he, whose soul now melts in mournful lays,
Shall shortly want the gen'rous tear he pays;
Then from his closing eyes thy form shall part,
And the last pang shall tear thee from his heart . . .[1]

These Eloisa-like lines of sentimental reflection are almost identical
with Achilles' lament over Patroclus in Book XXII of the *Iliad*:

Divine *Patroclus*! Death has seal'd his Eyes;
Unwept, unhonour'd, uninterr'd he lies!
Can his dear Image from my Soul depart,
Long as the vital Spirit moves my Heart?
If, in the silent Shades of Hell below,
The Flames of Friends and Lovers cease to glow,
Yet mine shall sacred last; mine, undecay'd,
Burn on thro' Death, and animate my Shade. (483-90)

When Pope's soul felt like melting in mournful lays, he turned to
what he thought was the greater humanity of Virgil and to the movement of Dryden's translation, as we may see from Dryden's version
of a mother lamenting for her son, from Book IX:

And cou'dst thou leave me, cruel, thus alone,
Not one kind Kiss from a departing Son!
No Look, no last adieu before he went,
In an ill-boding Hour to Slaughter sent!

---

[1] *The Works of Mr. Alexander Pope* (1717), 'Verses to the Memory of an Unfortunate Lady', pp. 358-62, lines 47-51, 77-80.

> Cold on the Ground, and pressing foreign Clay,
> To *Latian* Dogs, and Fowls he lies a Prey!
> Nor was I near to close his dying Eyes,
> To wash his Wounds, to weep his Obsequies:
> To call about his Corps his crying Friends[1] . . .   (641-49)

Pope felt for Elpenor what Dryden felt, following Virgil, for Pali-
nurus:

> And now, by Winds and Waves, my lifeless Limbs are tost.
> Which O avert, by yon Etherial Light
> Which I have lost, for this eternal Night:
> Or if by dearer tyes you may be won,
> By your dead Sire, and by your living Son,
> Redeem from this Reproach, my wand'ring Ghost;
> Or with your Navy seek the *Velin* Coast:
> And in a peaceful Grave my Corps compose[2] . . .    (493-500)

Nevertheless, even in the face of all this, I think we can distinguish
a modern element in Pope's tender feelings. If one strand in the
'Elegy' is heavily overlaid with literary reminiscences, it is only one
strand. Notice what the passage I have been using *modulates into*:

> By foreign hands thy decent limbs compos'd,
> By foreign hands thy humble grave adorn'd,
> By strangers honour'd, and by strangers mourn'd!
> What tho' no friends in sable weeds appear,
> Grieve for an hour, perhaps, then mourn a year,
> And bear about the mockery of woe
> To midnight dances, and the publick show?[3]

There we have the authentic modern voice of Pope bursting through,
as it never bursts through, not once, in Pope's translation of Homer.
For here the words—even the reminiscence of *Hamlet*—do not send
us to things via literature: we grapple directly with them and take
Pope's feeling without intermediary. The movement of the last lines
is not dictated by a concern for epic dignity.

Pope's passage, however, has many other literary debts. One is
to Dryden: let me repeat these lines from Pope:

---

[1] *The Works of Virgil* (1697), p. 483.
[2] *Ibid.*, p. 377, Book VI.
[3] *Op. cit.*, pp. 360-61.

A freshning breeze the Magic pow'r supply'd,
While the wing'd vessel flew along the tyde:
Our oars we shipp'd: all day the swelling sails
Full from the guiding pilot catch'd the gales.          (7-10)

To compass this, Pope clearly borrowed from Dryden's *Ceyx and Alcyone:*

> And now a Breeze from Shoar began to blow,
> The Sailors ship their Oars, and cease to row;
> Then hoist their Yards a-trip, and all their Sails
> Let fall, to court the Wind, and catch the Gales . . .[1]

A stranger borrowing is from Philips' *Cyder,* where to illustrate the dangers of excessive drinking, the poet gives us the following anecdote:

> What shall we say
> Of rash *Elpenor,* who in evil Hour
> Dry'd an immeasurable Bowl, and thought
> T'exhale his Surfeit by irriguous Sleep,
> Imprudent? Him, Death's Iron-Sleep opprest,
> Descending careless from his Couch; the Fall
> Luxt his Neck-joint, and spinal Marrow bruis'd.[2]

In seeking light on such a no doubt vast complex of ideas as made up Pope's total conception of the epic we must be cautious in our expectations of what can be derived from considering this snippet of translation. But the preponderance of imitation and borrowing makes two things probable: that much in Pope's conception of the epic was not peculiarly his own, and that much in Homer's epic checked and thwarted his natural impulses as a writer. His attitude to Homer cannot have been *wholly* approving.

---

[1] *Fables* (1700), p. 365, Lines 91-94.
[2] John Philips: *Cyder* (1708), p. 77.

K

# SEVEN

# Being Serious

$P_{OPE}$ was certainly not alone in assimilating the Homeric Hero to the Gentleman, and in admiring the Greek author as a notable instance of the truly Polite. We can, therefore, justified by Pope's own manner, go outside the poem with some hope of finding thereby what is inside it. The difficulty is only to find some compendious way of bringing out the essence of a development that began in the Renaissance and reached full consciousness in the mid-seventeenth century. We could, I think, fairly say that European civilized man discovered himself by looking at the figures he met in the Greek and Roman classics. At first the Classics were thought of as supplying glorious models of how to live, models too high to emulate, but powerful as incitements to rise above the normal and attain to the heroic level. As men became thereby more civilized and surer of their own worth, their attitude to the Classics changed. The shallower sort of fine gentleman, whose politeness was more a matter of being in the height of fashion, was tempted to exalt contemporary refinement at the expense of what was thought the grossness or naïvety of the ancient world. There was much scoffing at the want of gallantry in Virgil's hero, or the lack of pomp in the circumstances of Homer's. Pope's Notes remind us constantly of the century of gibing that preceded his translation of Homer. This gibing had been largely French, and some of it could be seen by English Gentlemen to be merely French parochialism.

But France had also led the way to a saner view: that differences in manners between the present and the classic past were of little significance compared with the grand discovery that present and past —the age of the Roi Soleil and that of Augustus—were united as being twin modes of a timeless civilization. Both these French parties, however, were anxious for visible proof that their present was fully civilized. They were anxious to have modern counterparts of all the ancient virtues. The strange thing, to our eyes, is that the French were not content with having among them a Corneille, a Racine, a Molière, and so many other figures little short of genius; they wanted, to complete their assurance, a modern epic to set against the classical epics. For the prestige of the epic grew rather than diminished in the course of the seventeenth century. A peculiar fact is that the classical epics themselves were a source of embarrassment to them: they did not clearly embody the Ideal. A consequence of the belief that Man had at last fully realized what it was to be Man, that Man now at last really knew what Reason and Truth were, was that seventeenth-century Frenchmen were bound to claim that what they now fully realized had always existed. People thought that the Reason, Truth and Nature they had come to believe in were permanent values outside time, values that could never change and had never changed. They were therefore bound to argue that the great works of the past must have conformed to the standards they had now fully clarified and established in the seventeenth century. The embarrassing thing was that nobody could give an account of the classical epics that showed them as perfectly conforming to these permanent standards.

That this embarrassment had been acute can be seen from a passage in the Earl of Mulgrave's *Essay on Poetry* (1682), which at the same time informs us of the kind of importance men of his day attached to the classical epics. I quote from the edition of 1691:

> *Heroick* Poems have a just pretence
> To be the utmost reach of human Sence,[1]
> A Work of such inestimable Worth,
> There are but *two* the World has yet brought forth,
> *Homer*, and *Virgil*: with what awful sound
> Do those meer words the Ears of Poets wound!
> Just as a *Changeling* seems below the rest
> Of Men, or rather is a two-legg'd Beast,
> So these *Gigantick* Souls amaz'd we find
> As much above the rest of human kind.
> *Natures* whole strength *united*! endless Fame,
> And universal Shouts attend their Name.
> Read *Homer* once, and you can read no more,
> For all things else appear so dull and poor,

[1] Cf. Rapin, *La Comparaison d'Homere et de Virgile* (1686). His opening remark was 'De tous les ouvrages dont l'esprit de l'homme est capable, le Poëme Epique est sans doute le plus accompli'.

Cf. Dryden, who begins the *Dedication of the Aeneis* with: 'A Heroick Poem, truly such, is undoubtedly the greatest Work which the Soul of Man is capable to perform.'

*Verse* will seem *Prose*, yet *often* on him look,
And you will hardly *need* another Book.
Had *Bossu* never writ, the World had still,
Like *Indians*, view'd this wondrous Piece of Skill,
As something of *Divine* the Work admired,
Not hoped to be *Instructed*, but *Inspired;*
But he disclosing sacred *Mysteries,*
Has shewn where all the mighty *Magick* lies,
Describ'd the *Seeds*, and in what order sown,
That have to such a vast proportion grown;
Sure from some *Angel* he the *Secret* knew,
Who through this *Labyrinth* has given the *Clue!*

Le Bossu's treatise on the epic poem (1675) was the century's god-send. Before he wrote nobody knew how to set about criticizing an epic, for the two great classical epics did not seem to have the sort of plan Frenchmen had come to look for and demand from a work of art. After Le Bossu, they looked for no other plan than the one he had laid down for all epic, past, present, and future. He convinced people that, rather than the celebration of the Hero, the aim of an epic was to illustrate the qualities that make a Gentleman. Here is the definition that was accepted for a century as the central truth about Homer and Virgil:

> An Epick Poem is a Discourse invented with Art, to form the Manners by Instructions disguis'd under the Allegory of Action, which is important, and which is related in Verse in a delightfull, probable and wonderfull manner.[1]

What Le Bossu had done was to find a face-saving formula which allowed the age to eat its cake and have it at the same time. The age wanted its conceptions of the nature of art to remain intact while gratifying its need to have the support of the classical heroic poem. The two demands were incompatible, but Le Bossu's formula enabled the age to suppose that the impossible had occurred.

Some evidence of the immense desire of people to believe this impossibility may be gleaned from the fact that Addison, when trying to convert his contemporaries to the view that Milton's *Paradise Lost* was a great poem, set out his exposition and judged the poem under the heads proposed by Le Bossu. In the seventieth *Spectator* Addison

---

[1] John Dennis, *Remarks on . . . Prince Arthur* (1696), p. 1.

applies Le Bossu's principles to the ballad, *Chevy Chase*! In the course
of that paper Addison presented what he thought the valuable kernel
of Le Bossu's treatise:

> The greatest Modern Criticks have laid it down as a Rule,
> That an Heroick Poem should be founded upon some important
> Precept of Morality, adapted to the Constitution of the Country
> in which the Poet writes. *Homer* and *Virgil* have formed their
> Plans in this View. As *Greece* was a Collection of many Govern-
> ments, who suffered very much among themselves, and gave the
> *Persian* Emperor, who was their common Enemy, many Advan-
> tages over them by their mutual Jealousies and Animosities,
> *Homer*, in order to establish among them an Union, which was so
> necessary for their Safety, grounds his Poem upon the Discords
> of the several *Grecian* Princes who were engaged in a Con-
> federacy against an *Asiatick* Prince, and the several Advantages
> which the Enemy gained by such their Discords.[1]

Le Bossu insisted that the epic poet began in the abstract, looked round
for some point of morals, and only after he had found it did he search
for a suitable fable. This line of reasoning is clearly based on thinking
first about the *Aeneid*. He assumed that Virgil began by wishing to
glorify Augustus and the greatness of Rome and the virtues of the new
empire, and cast round for the elements of a tale that would never be
told for its own sake but only for its symbolic value. In the second
place, Le Bossu argued, we cannot reconcile the praise of Homer in
Aristotle and Horace with the shocking simplicity and naïvety of what
we find in his epics unless we suppose that he was also writing allegori-
cally, and that he had a deeper secret meaning which only the wiser
reader would understand.

Now although Le Bossu modestly disclaimed the pretension to be
laying down rules for future epics, he had clearly provided the pedants
with a new set. Once Le Bossu had fallen into *their* hands, Men of
Sense were bound to react against the absurdities of this formula for
writing and judging an epic. Pope may not have been the first, when
in 1713 he inserted a mocking paper into the *Guardian*.[2]

> It is no small Pleasure to me, who am zealous in the Interests
> of Learning, to think I may have the Honour of leading the

---

[1] *The Spectator*, Vol. I (1712), No. 70, Monday, May 21st., 1711, p. 399.
[2] Vol. I (1714), No. 78, June 10th, 1713.

Town into a very new and uncommon Road of Criticism. As that kind of Literature is at present carried on, it consists only in a Knowledge of Mechanick Rules, which contribute to the Structure of different sorts of Poetry, as the Receits of good Houswives do to the making Puddings of Flower, Oranges, Plumbs, or any other Ingredients. It would, methinks, make these my Instructions more easily intelligible to ordinary Readers, if I discoursed of these Matters in the Stile in which Ladies, Learned in OEconomicks dictate to their Pupils for the Improvement of the Kitchin and Larder.

I shall begin with Epick Poetry, because the Criticks agree it is the greatest Work Human Nature is capable of. I know the *French* have already laid down many Mechanical Rules for Compositions of this Sort, but at the same time they cut off almost all Undertakers from the Possibility of ever performing them; for the first Qualification they unanimously require in a Poet, is a *Genius*. I shall here endeavour (for the Benefit of my Countrymen) to make it manifest, that Epick Poems may be made *without a Genius*, nay without Learning or much Reading. . . .

I know it will be objected, that one of the chief Qualifications of an Epick Poet, is to be knowing in all Arts and Sciences. But this ought not to discourage those that have no Learning, as long as Indexes and Dictionaries may be had, which are the Compendium of all Knowledge . . .

Another Quality required is a compleat Skill in Languages. To this I answer, that it is notorious, Persons of no Genius have been oftentimes great Linguists.

But to proceed to the Purpose of this Paper.

A Receit to make an *Epick* Poem.

### For the *Fable*.

*Take out of any old Poem, History-books, Romance, or Legend... those Parts of Story which afford most Scope for long Descriptions: Put these Pieces together, and throw all the Adventures you fancy into one Tale. Then take a Hero, whom you may chuse for the Sound of his Name, and put him into the midst of these Adventures: There let him work, for twelve Books; at the end of which you may take him out, ready prepared to conquer or to marry; it being necessary that the Conclusion of an Epick Poem be fortunate. . . .*

For the Moral and Allegory. *These you may Extract out of the Fable afterwards at your Leisure: Be sure you strain them sufficiently.*

### For the Manners.

*For those of the Hero, take all the best Qualities you can find in all the best celebrated Heroes of Antiquity;*

### For the Machines.

*Take of Deities, Male and Female, as many as you can use. Separate them into two equal parts, and keep* Jupiter *in the middle. . . .*

### For the Language.

*(I mean the* Diction*). Here it will do well to be an Imitator of* Milton, *for you'll find it easier to imitate him in this than any thing else.* Hebraisms and Grecisms *are to be found in him, without the trouble of Learning the Languages. I knew a Painter, who (like our Poet) had no* Genius, *make his Dawbings be thought* Originals *by setting them in the* Smoak: *You may in the same manner give the venerable Air of Antiquity to your Piece,* by *darkening it up and down with* Old English. *With this you may be easily furnished upon any Occasion, by the Dictionary commonly Printed at the end of* Chaucer.

Here, I think, we see the genius of the poet breaking out in the direction of health. This squib, however, is only a squib, merely a pointer. To understand Pope's relation to the epic, we must go the whole way in the direction indicated. What I am arguing, in short, is that Homer did not allow Pope to be fully 'serious'. For this he had to embed his serious convictions in a comic context. To bring out what he cared most for in the epic he had to compose a mock-epic. The mock-epic gave him full release of all his feelings; in the first place, to the feeling that the epic machinery was hopelessly comic and out-of-date. It was impossible to be awed by the supposition that you could save the appearances by invoking Allegory. I think, too, that the longing for an epic, of which I made so much, was the fancied, not the real need, of the age. Imitation epic could never have brought into play the deeper needs of people in the late seventeenth and early eighteenth centuries.

To put these arguments to the test, I have chosen a passage from the *Iliad* which calls attention to itself by its exceptional self-consciousness, a passage which itself asks and attempts to answer our question: what is the underlying conception of the heroic in the *Iliad*? What justifies our taking all the fighting seriously? In a phrase I shall be using in a few moments, it is a passage which *opens the moral* of the poem. After dwelling on its significance in this respect, by taking another passage which parodies it, we may obtain a hint of an answer to the question of questions for us: whether Pope had a theme in translating the *Iliad*, whether he stood in the right relation to his original, whether he was as a translator truly or wholly *serious*.

Let us begin by putting ourselves in the position of a reader who is approaching Homer's *Iliad* for the first time and through the medium of Rieu's translation. When he reaches Book XII, he comes across the following passage:

> Thus did the godlike Sarpedon feel impelled to assault the wall and break through the battlements. He turned to Glaucus, Hippolochus' son. 'Glaucus,' he said, 'why do the Lycians at home distinguish you and me with marks of honour, the best seats at the banquet, the first cut off the joint, and never-empty cups? Why do they all look up to us as gods? And why were we made the lords of that great estate of ours on the banks of Xanthus, with its lovely orchards and its splendid fields of wheat? Does not all this oblige us now to take our places in the Lycian van and fling ourselves into the flames of battle? Only so can we make our Lycian men-at-arms say this about us when they discuss their Kings: "They live on the fat of the land they rule, they drink the mellow vintage wine, but they pay for it in their glory. They are mighty men of war, and where Lycians fight you will see them in the van."
>
> 'Ah, my friend, if after living through this war we could be sure of ageless immortality, I should neither take my place in the front line nor send you out to win honour in the field. But things are not like that. Death has a thousand pitfalls for our feet; and nobody can save himself and cheat him. So in we go, whether we yield the glory to some other man or win it for ourselves.'[1]

[1] *Op. cit.*, p. 229.

Can we imagine that such a reader, with no other access to Homer than
this, would mark the passage in his Penguin and say: this is one of the
things we read Homer for, here we see him rising above his story and
opening more clearly the Moral of the Poem, here Homer justifies
so many accounts of detailed butchery, here we have the faith that
makes us believe in the possibility of the heroic life, this is the permanent
expression of the claims of members of the aristocracy in all ages to be
our lords and rulers, this is the truly memorable, the classic formulation
of the grandeur and the pathos in all heroic action, thanks to this
passage we can become conscious of what a lower-middle class society
inevitably loses in wiping out its upper classes, thanks to this passage
we can dimly see the possibilities of grandeur and pathos in a society
with no high tables and with equal shares of meat and wine for all
who dine in common, since here Homer transcends the structure of
his particular society, the imagined social structure of his Greek and
Trojan warriors, and puts the question: *what price glory?* to us on the
broadest facts of human existence, facts that will never materially
change?

If our reader could comment on those lines without further assistance, he would not need to read this chapter or any of Arnold's
lectures. We, however, might pause here to take in one or two hints
that Arnold threw out in his lectures on translating Homer. Let
*us* begin where he did, with a glance at Chapman's version of those
lines:

So far'd divine *Sarpedons* minde, resolv'd to force his way
Through all the fore-fights, and the wall: yet since he did not see
Others as great as he, in name, as great in minde as he:
He spake to *Glaucus*: *Glaucus*, say, why are we honor'd more
Then other men of *Lycia*, in place? with greater store
Of meats and cups? with goodlier roofes? delightsome gardens?
                                                                walks?
More lands, and better? so much wealth, that Court and countrey
                                                                talks
Of us, and our possessions; and every way we go,
Gaze on us as we were their Gods? this where we dwell, is so:
The shores of *Xanthus* ring of this; and shall not we exceed,
As much in merit, as in noise? Come be we great in deed
As well as looke; shine not in gold, but in the flames of fight;
That so our neat-arm'd *Lycians*, may say; See, these are right

Our Kings, our Rulers; these deserue, to eate, and drinke the
>best;
These governe not ingloriously: these, thus exceed the rest,
Do more then they command to do. O friend, if keeping backe
Would keepe backe age from us, and death; and that we might
>not wracke
In this lifes humane sea at all: but that deferring now
We shund death euer; nor would I, halfe this vaine valour show,
Nor glorifie a folly so, to wishe thee to advance:
But since we must go, though not here; and that, besides the
>chance
Proposd now, there are infinite fates, of other sort in death,
Which (neither to be fled nor scapt) a man must sinke beneath:
Come, trie we, if this sort be ours: and either render thus,
Glorie to others, or make them, resigne the like to us.[1]

In his marginal note Chapman calls this speech one 'never equalled
by any (in this kind) of all that have written', and he has clearly risen
to the height of his feeling. Has Arnold put his finger on the radical
weakness in drawing attention to the retarding effect of the rhymes?
Do we in fact, as we read, lose the separating effect of the *But* which
separates *advance* from all that follows? Is it not a more radical criticism
that the passage lacks dramatic distinction because Chapman interlards
direct speech with commentary? Sarpedon is made by Chapman to
give more of a *lecture* than a speech. Chapman's parallels and antitheses
are too insistent:

>and shall not we exceed,
As much in merit, as in noise? Come be we great in deed
As well as looke; shine not in gold, but in the flames of fight; . . .

I resent the over-explicitness of:

> . . . nor would I, halfe this vaine valour show,
Nor glorifie a folly so, to wish thee to advance: . . .

On the other hand, while it may be true that nowhere in Homer do
we find such an expression as

> . . . and that we might not wracke
In this lifes humane sea at all:

---

[1] *The Whole Works of Homer* (1633), pp. 165-66.

yet I must confess that this is how I could imagine Homer speaking if he had to return to earth as an Elizabethan.

Arnold, I would say, was more inspired in giving us the eighteenth-century anecdote which shows us how the heroic of Homer was linked to the possibilities of a modern hero. Let me, since I wish to put the passage to further use, quote Arnold's own words:

> Robert Wood, whose Essay on the Genius of Homer[1] is mentioned by Goethe[2] as one of the books which fell into his hands when his powers were first developing themselves, and strongly interested him, relates of this passage a striking story. He says that in 1762, at the end of the Seven Years' War, being then Under-Secretary of State, he was directed to wait upon the President of the Council, Lord Granville, a few days before he died, with the preliminary articles of the Treaty of Paris. 'I found him,' he continues, 'so languid, that I proposed postponing my business for another time; but he insisted that I should stay, saying, it could not prolong his life to neglect his duty; and repeating the following passage out of Sarpedon's speech, he dwelt with particular emphasis on the third line, which recalled to his mind the distinguishing part he had taken in public affairs:
>
> ὦ πέπον, εἰ μὲν γὰρ πόλεμον περὶ τόνδε φυγόντε
> αἰεὶ δὴ μέλλοιμεν ἀγήρω τ' ἀθανάτω τε
> ἔσσεσθ', οὔτε κεν αὐτὸς ἐνὶ πρώτοισι μαχοίμην
> οὔτε κε σὲ στέλλοιμι μάχην ἐς κυδιάνειραν·
> νῦν δ' ἔμπης γὰρ κῆρες ἐφεστᾶσιν θανάτοιο
> μυρίαι, ἃς οὐκ ἔστι φυγεῖν βροτὸν οὐδ' ὑπαλύξαι,
> ἴομεν, . . .
>
> His Lordship repeated the last word [let us go] several times with a calm and determinate resignation; and after a serious pause of some minutes, he desired to hear the Treaty read, to which he listened with great attention, and recovered spirits enough to declare the approbation of a dying statesman (I use his own words) "on the most glorious war, and most honourable peace, this nation ever saw".'

I quote this story, first, because it is interesting as exhibiting the English aristocracy at its very height of culture, lofty spirit,

---

[1] (1775), p. vii.

[2] *Aus meinem Leben. Wahrheit und Dichtung.* Book XII.

and greatness, towards the middle of the last century. I quote it, secondly, because it seems to me to illustrate Goethe's saying which I mentioned,[1] that our life, in Homer's view of it, represents a conflict and a hell; and it brings out, too, what there is tonic and fortifying in this doctrine. I quote it, lastly, because it shows that the passage is just one of those in translating which Pope will be at his best, a passage of strong emotion and oratorical movement, not of simple narrative or description.[2]

Before looking at Pope, however, in order to complete the historical chain, I offer the passage first in an 'early Augustan' version, which has the additional interest for us of being as much an Augustan revision of Chapman as an interpretation of Homer:

> Thus to *Glaucus* spake
> Divine *Sarpedon*, since he did not find
> Others as great in Place, as great in Mind.
> Above the rest, why is our Pomp, our Power?
> Our flocks, our herds, and our possessions more?
> Why all the Tributes Land and Sea affords
> Heap'd in great Chargers, load our sumptuous boards?
> Our chearful Guests carowse the sparkling tears
> Of the rich Grape, whilst Musick charms their ears.
> Why as we pass, do those on *Xanthus* shore,
> As Gods behold us, and as Gods adore?
> But that as well in danger, as degree,
> We stand the first; that when our *Lycians* see
> Our brave examples, they admiring say,
> Behold our Gallant Leaders! These are They
> Deserve the Greatness; and un-envied stand:
> Since what they act, transcends what they command.
> Could the declining of this Fate (oh friend)
> Our Date to Immortality extend?

---

[1] In a letter to Schiller, dated December 13th, 1803, Goethe wrote: 'Da wir denn aber, wie ich nun immer deutlicher von Polygnot und Homer lerne, die Hölle eigentlich hier oben vorzustellen haben. . . .' which was translated by Matthew Arnold as follows: 'From Homer and Polygnotus I every day learn more clearly that in our life here above ground we have, properly speaking, to enact Hell.' The German, however, seems to be saying rather that we must think of Hell not as something below ground but here on earth, and Goethe complains in this letter that he was leading a hell of a life.

[2] *On Translating Homer* (1861), pp. 16-18.

Or if Death sought not them, who seek not Death,
Would I advance? Or should my vainer breath
With such a Glorious Folly thee inspire?
But since with Fortune Nature doth conspire,
Since Age, Disease, or some less noble End,
Though not less certain, doth our days attend,
Since 'tis decreed, and to this period lead,
A thousand ways the noblest path we'll tread,
And bravely on, till they, or we, or all,
A common Sacrifice to Honour fall.[1]

I shall not pause to analyse this preliminary stage of the Augustan
attitude. For my immediate purposes it is enough to note that Pope
admired this rendering so much that after composing his own, he
wrote: 'if I have done it with any spirit, it is partly owing to him.'
Yet this, too, is not part of my immediate purpose. I have brought up
Sarpedon's speech to help determine for us what it meant to be really
serious in Pope's idiom. And the use I wish to make of this speech in
Pope's version is not to compare it for seriousness with the preceding
translations, but with another, closely related passage, that I am about
to introduce.


   When Pope had completed *The Rape of the Lock*, one of the criti-
cisms he was most sensitive to was that, in his enjoyment of making
fun of the epic, he had lost sight of the serious purpose that justified
all the fun; that he had, in short, obscured his point, or moral: what
the poem was all to be for. He therefore, to put matters right, composed
a short speech, which I shall be quoting in a moment. Warburton,
Pope's editor, said of it, "A new Character introduced in the subsequent Editions, to open more clearly the MORAL of the Poem."[2]
That this is what Pope intended we can be sure from a marginal note
in Pope's own copy of an attack on his poem written by the critic,
Dennis. Where Dennis complained that Boileau (in his *Lutrin*) had
given a broad hint of his real meaning, but Pope had not, we can see a
note in Pope's hand: *Clarissas Speach*.[3] This is the speech I wish to

   [1] *Poems and Translations,* Written by the Honourable Sir John Denham (1668),
pp. 78-79.
   [2] *The Works of Alexander Pope Esq.* (1751), Vol. I, p. 255.
   [3] For details see the Twickenham Edition of *The Rape of The Lock* (1961), ed.
Geoffrey Tillotson. Appendix D, pp. 368-75.

set alongside Sarpedon's in the version of Homer that Pope first published in 1709:

> Resolv'd alike, Divine *Sarpedon* glows
> With gen'rous Rage, that drives him on the Foes.
> He views the Tow'rs, and meditates their Fall;
> To sure Destruction dooms the *Grecian* Wall;
> Then casting on his Friend an ardent Look,
> Fir'd with the Thirst of Glory, thus he spoke.
> Why boast we, *Glaucus*, our extended Reign,
> Where *Xanthus'* Streams enrich the *Lycian* Plain?
> Our num'rous Herds that range each fruitful Field,
> And Hills where Vines their Purple Harvest yield?
> Our foaming Bowls with gen'rous *Nectar* crown'd,
> Our Feasts enhanc'd with Musick's sprightly Sound?
> Why on those Shores are we with Joy survey'd,
> Admir'd as Heroes, and as Gods obey'd?
> Unless great Acts superior Merit prove,
> And Vindicate the bounteous Pow'rs above:
> 'Tis ours, the Dignity They give, to grace;
> The first in Valour, as the first in Place:
> That while with wondring Eyes our Martial Bands
> Behold our Deeds transcending our Commands,
> Such, they may cry, deserve the Sov'reign State,
> Whom those that Envy dare not Imitate!
> Cou'd all our Care elude the greedy Grave;
> Which claims no less the Fearful than the Brave,
> For Lust of Fame I shou'd not vainly dare
> In fighting Fields, nor urge thy Soul to War.
> But since, alas, ignoble Age must come,
> Disease, and Death's inexorable Doom;
> The Life which others pay, let Us bestow,
> And give to Fame what we to Nature owe;
> Brave, tho' we fall; and honour'd, if we live;
> Or let us Glory gain, or Glory give![1]

> Then grave *Clarissa* graceful wav'd her fan;
> Silence ensu'd, and thus the nymph began.

---

[1] *Poetical Miscellanies: The Sixth Part* (1709), pp. 303-305.

Say why are Beauties prais'd and honour'd most,
The wise man's passion, and the vain man's toast?
Why deck'd with all that land and sea afford,
Why Angels call'd, and Angel-like ador'd?
Why round our Coaches crowd the white glov'd Beaus,
Why bows the side-box from its inmost rows?
How vain are all these glories, all our pains,
Unless good sense preserve what beauty gains:
That men may say, when we the front-box grace,
Behold the first in virtue, as in face!
Oh! if to dance all night, and dress all day,
Charm'd the small-pox, or chas'd old age away;
Who would not scorn what huswife's cares produce,
Or who would learn one earthly thing of use?
To patch, nay ogle, might become a Saint,
Nor could it sure be such a sin to paint.
But since, alas! frail beauty must decay,
Curl'd or uncurl'd, since Locks will turn to grey,
Since painted, or not painted, all shall fade,
And she who scorns a man, must die a maid;
What then remains, but well our pow'r to use,
And keep good humour still whate'er we lose?
And trust me, dear! good humour can prevail,
When airs, and flights, and screams, and scolding fail.
Beauties in vain their pretty eyes may roll;
Charms strike the sight, but merit wins the soul.[1]

Even when so flung out, without time given for meditation, can we not nevertheless at once answer, if asked which of these two passages is the better poetry: surely the second? And if we are asked, which is the more serious, do we not answer with equal readiness: surely the second? We may for a moment find our decision clouded by the solemnity of the first, by the largeness of the issues, their more obviously heroic nature compared with what may strike us as the flippancy of the second and the domestic nature of the issues, yet, when we clear our minds and put the question: which of them is, not the more solemn, but the more serious, does not our instinct for language guide us to the passage from the *Rape*?

When we look at the language of Pope's translation from the

---

[1] *The Works of Mr Alexander Pope* (1717), pp. 148-50.

*Iliad*, we can give another meaning to Arnold's phrase: 'one feels that Homer's thought has passed through a literary and rhetorical crucible and come out highly intellectualized'. Although I am no Bentley, I feel pretty sure that Homer's language itself in this passage of calculated rhetoric has passed through such a crucible. But that is by the way. What I want to look at is the state of Pope's English in the Homer translation. It is English such as no Englishman could have spoken: it is English as *declaimed*. That is bad, but not fatal; yet it prevents our experiencing the passage as fully dramatic utterance. If we press for the 'message', we begin to ask for much more meaning than Pope's language could possibly yield. Pope's style here is not quite like Macaulay's, one in which you cannot tell the truth, but it is a style in which it is very hard to get much *in* per couplet. For instance:

> For Lust of Fame I shou'd not vainly dare
> In fighting Fields, nor urge thy Soul to War.

There is a sort of muffled meaning—but oh, what a small proportion to the huge amount of Noble Solemnity! Surely, the more we challenge the passage for its gold of intellectual energy, the more we receive instead of the other currency, that of stately, but monotonously rigid, feeling?

Only the careful corseting, bracing neatness of phrase prevents sloppiness, adds the tonic that Arnold rightly saw was the saving element in the Greek, and preserves Homer's point that the lament for the harshness of life must end in resolution nevertheless to fight the war with spirit. I feel the presence of steel under Pope's trappings just where for me it is most needed. When we come to

> But since, alas, ignoble Age must come,
> Disease, and Death's inexorable Doom;

(which is Pope's inspired translation of Virgil's great passage in the *Georgics: optima quaeque dies* . . . [3/66], which Dryden had rendered:

> In Youth alone, unhappy Mortals live;
> But, ah! the mighty Bliss is fugitive;
> Discolour'd Sickness, anxious Labours come,
> And Age, and Death's inexorable Doom . . .[1]        (108–11)

—when I reach this point, part of me begins to dread that Pope will be fumbling for more stops in this part of the register. I dread anything

---

[1] *The Works of Virgil* (1697) p. 99. *Georgics*, Book III.

more open and booming (and loose) than 'inexorable Doom'. Will it, I ask myself, be the Milton stop next, or the Addisonian, or the Eloisa stop? It hasn't happened yet, these reflections are the work of infinitesimal time, we are still in the state of what the plastics experts call 'controlled pour'— this, after all, is not Wordsworthian blank verse—but after 'The Life which others pay'—which hasn't declared itself either way—ends with 'let Us bestow', the felicity of the contrast of 'pay' and 'bestow', and the sense that only a poet in full command of his emotions could have placed the distinction just there, restores my confidence, *reconciles* me, at least, to the closing breadth of the summary, to the terms Nature, Fame and Glory. What we have here, then, is not a case of intellect swamping emotion, but the reverse, or almost the reverse. Pope, I think, has not felt the passage deeply—it is all too vague for that—but warmly, as a noble attitude. It was a congenial feeling, but, alas, 'congenial' means 'fatal to its merits as poetry of the highest order'. I hope that I may bring in here the verdict reached in examining the passage from the *Odyssey*: that this style excludes so much of reality, that it sends us to things via literature, that, in short, Pope was here the prisoner of the age's idea of the heroic, the fancied need for decorum.

The passage from the *Rape* shows Pope emerging from that prison. I would not call it a final and clinching argument to say, look how much more is going on in the second passage, but I think that if we tell ourselves how much, we insensibly pass from quantity to quality. To bring out the superior precision, may I go back to the point I made in calling the language of the first passage muffled? The Homeric hero as Pope renders him here never makes us see his precise job as a fighter in the front rank. It is hardly malicious to suggest that he might equally well be describing the actions of one whose fights are confined to the front benches in the House of Lords. The heroic acts are more than Acts of Parliament, but I have an obscure feeling of dissatisfaction with this side of the passage, which is mirrored in an impression I get every time I read over the anecdote Arnold gave us of the application the Dying Minister made of this piece of fighting talk. Was there not a touch of conscious nobility in the reception accorded to Mr Wood? Something for him to put in the future *memoirs* of Earl Granville?

The precision of the passage from the *Rape* is admirable. To sharpen our consciousness of it, let us compare Pope with Gay. Pope is sharper when he writes:

L

> Why round our Coaches crowd the white glov'd Beaus,
> Why bows the side-box from its inmost rows?

Gay took up the point in *The Toilette: A Town Eclogue, 1716*:

> Nor shall Side-Boxes watch my wand'ring Eyes,
> And as they catch the Glance in Rows arise
> With humble Bows; nor White-Glove Beau's incroach
> In Crowds behind to guard me to my Coach.

How felicitous in Pope is that 'inmost'. The fine gentleman bows to the belle as much to be seen bowing by others as to convey his respects. And that even the poor fellows at the back of the box, who were deprived of this chance, nevertheless bowed along with the lucky ones in front and well in the public eye, *and* that Clarissa while receiving the broadside from the bigwigs in front nevertheless had leisure to count her successes among the smaller fry—all that gives a solidity to the picture which anchors us in the real. And all the time we are, as it were, in Clarissa's mind, with another part of our minds we are enjoying her from the outside and laughing at the serious way she takes what are evidently substantial triumphs in her eyes, and while we are thus laughing from two points of view, it comes over us, yes, there is something serious at stake here.

The seriousness is inconceivable out of the comic setting. How dreadfully flat the practical advice would be, coming from the plainest of plain housewives; but from such an obvious coquette, capable also of arguing

> To patch, nay ogle, might become a Saint,

the praise of Huswifery, Use and Sense has piquancy and therefore force. And how this force is enhanced by the epic parody! In the *Rape* we are made to feel at grips with the real, and that by comparison the Homeric world is pageantry and primitive magic. Let us, however, press the claim to seriousness further, and ask which passage better hits off our sense that, as Goethe put it in Arnold's phrase, 'life is a hell and a conflict'. Let us each in our own way appraise

> Oh! if to dance all night, and dress all day . . .

and ask ourselves whether, if this cannot symbolize a desirable goal to us, we are really capable of being serious at all. For I use the word 'desirable' to mean, making a lasting claim on us as representing one of our deepest desires. If, from the midst of our all-too-useful lives, we never raise our heads and long for the equivalent for each of us of dancing all night and dressing all day, must we not grant that we are not serious but beneath serious consideration, like Barnadine in Shakespeare's *Measure for Measure*, unfit to live or die?

I should like to cap Arnold's anecdote about Earl Granville with one reported to Henry James about the American novelist, Howells. We are to imagine this 'rather fatigued . . . compatriot' of James, after a life almost exclusively professional, 'a long, hard strain', in a Puritan community, arriving in a Parisian garden one charming June afternoon and meeting for the first time the human equivalent of the charming June—particularly the female equivalent—and we are to imagine Howells bursting out as follows to a young male friend, as with a rush the sense of the whole scene came over him:

> 'Oh, *you're* young, you're blessedly young—be glad of it; be glad of it and *live*. Live all you can: it's a mistake not to. It doesn't so much matter what you do—but live. This place and these impressions, as well as many of those, for so many days, of So-and-So's and So-and-So's life, that I've been receiving and that have had their abundant message, make it all come over me. I see it now. I haven't done so enough before—and now I'm old; I'm, at any rate, too old for what I see. Oh, I *do* see, at least—I see a lot. It's too late. It has gone past me. I've lost it. It couldn't, no doubt, have been different for me—for one's life takes a form and holds one: one lives as one can. But the point is that *you* have time. That's the great thing. You're, as I say, damn you, so luckily, so happily, so hatefully young. Don't be stupid. Of course I don't dream you *are*, or I shouldn't be saying these awful things to you. Don't, at any rate, make *my* mistake. Live!'[1]

This anecdote, too, is equivocal, and we might have all sorts of reserves about the life that in fact was provoking Howells' outburst. But the point is the professional man's reaction after a dutiful long career, and the other devoted professional noting it as a germ for *The Ambassadors*. We are brought by it to a respect for the late Victorian gentlemen: 'one lives as one can'. It is less dramatic than Goethe's 'Life is a conflict and a hell', but. . . .

[1] *The Notebooks of Henry James* (1947), ed. F. O. Matthiessen and K. B. Murdock, p. 374.

That Pope's lines from the *Rape* do send us to life rather than to literature, send us first to life before they send us to literature, that is the claim I wish to set up after comparing the two passages. Pope presents through Clarissa a more serious notion of how to live than through Sarpedon in the translation from Homer. It is a homely conception of the heroic—consider, for instance, the old Elizabethan horse-sense dismissal of the too choosy woman:

> And she who scorns a man, must die a maid;

—but although it is homely and not at all glorious; we may say of it, remembering who is speaking, what Olivia said of her beauty in *Twelfth Night*: "'Tis in graine sir, 'twill endure winde and weather.' By the time Pope reaches his last line: 'but Merit wins the Soul' I feel more concretely what Clarissa is talking about than what Sarpedon means when he says

> Unless great Acts superior Merit prove. . . .

Which brings me to my final point: that we cannot treat Clarissa's speech as a mere parody. Pope may have sat down one day to parody Homer, but he was so carried away by the seriousness of the theme that he improved on his early effort at translating Homer. He almost improved it out of sight. For what does the Homer translation now do for Clarissa's speech? Its chief function now seems to remove any faint sense of awkwardness about the formal perfection of her speech. It would be otherwise too good for her to have pulled off for herself. It is a pity that Pope did not realize that, if his translation of the *Iliad* as a whole was to become a real classic rivalling Shakespeare, he would have to be as seriously concerned with his epic theme as he was with Clarissa's, and would therefore have had to write in the style of his Clarissa rather than that of his Sarpedon.

# EIGHT

# Hector and Andromache

Supposing that investigations similar to those pursued in the last two chapters brought us to the same conclusions; that Pope was, like Arnold on a certain occasion, not wholly serious in translating Homer; that when he wished to express Homer's humanity, the element in the poem with which he felt the deepest sympathy, he turned, whenever he was given the opportunity, to the Virgil revealed to him by Dryden; supposing all this were established, what would be the upshot for our general assessment of the utility of going to Pope's translation as one means of appreciating the greatness of the Greek original? The question is a little unfair in that the answer would in part depend on what further thoughts were turned up in the attempt to establish the term 'serious'. It might, for instance, have to be conceded that nobody can take Homer in a wholly serious way. It might even emerge that Homer himself could be shown to be an author who did not take himself seriously all the time. I am sure that he did not treat his subject matter with uniform seriousness in every part of the twenty-four books of the *Iliad*. Whether it was a disadvantage to see parts of Homer through Virgil's eyes, is for me still an open question. (G. N. Knauer's lists and the general argument of his study, *Die Aeneis und Homer* (1964), would make matter for a long discussion.) But one of my arguments can even now be made to point in the opposite direction. If Pope could only be deeply serious in the mock-heroic mode, success in that mode could not be achieved without taking the epic element in it with great seriousness.

Since there is no immediate prospect of carrying the discussion to its natural limits, a temporary project may now be introduced, which could be described as at one and the same time the natural next step after the arguments of my last two chapters and a preliminary attempt to lay down the lines of a final conclusion. Just as I tried in earlier chapters to expose what I called the essential structures of the First Book, I shall now attempt to sketch the essential structures of the whole poem, that which makes us feel that what we have, however it got there, now constitutes a whole. From this we may be able to derive a criterion for assessing the success of Pope's version. My conclusion will contain the verdict that there was sufficient similarity between what Homer was offering and what Pope could conceive for a successful translation to be made. Finally, out of a discussion of structure will come a canon for the style; a determination of the proper manner for Homeric matter.

If we ask, then, what, above all, gives Homer's epic its classic status, we might begin by agreeing that if the heroes of the *Iliad* were fairly represented by this, to take a random instance,

> Where e're he does his dreadful Standards bear,
> Horror stalks in the Van, and Slaughter in the Rere.
> Whole Swarths of Enemies his Sword does mow,
> And Limbs of mangled Chiefs his passage strow,
> And Floods of reeking Gore the Field o'reflow:[1]

the poem would not deserve its pre-eminent place in the *genre*. The *Iliad*, that is to say, would not be a great epic if it could be summed up as illustrating the heroic solely in terms of successful man-killing. In so far as its heroes resemble killing machines, the *Iliad* is a bore. It does not matter whether each Greek or Trojan is struck down in a different part of his anatomy; the killing in itself is a bore.

But it is very difficult to count on agreement if we try to say where Homer stands in relation to the killing, and ask whether the greatness of the poem depends on what the author was putting in, or the extent to which he identifies himself with what are often at best merely magnificent brutes. There is still a respectable class of readers who would reject outright or at any rate resent the unfavourable implications of that 'merely'. For them the immortal parts of the poem are the earliest. They think of Homer himself as on the brink of decadence, and they regard his contributions to the poem as 'modern' touches quite out of keeping with the primitive core. That core for them consists of—well, not quite war-reporter's despatches, but of impressions taken from eye-witnesses and worked up by 'bards', who may themselves have been expert combatants, and were certainly uncritically

---

[1] John Oldham: 'The Praise of Homer', in *Some New Pieces Never Before Publisht* (1681), p. 65.

one with the fighters and the mob of admirers celebrating recent victories in real historical combats.

We may distinguish those who thirst for the sight and smell of real bloodshed from another class of readers whose fantasy is essentially adolescent. This is not a very precise term, and I might loosely class these readers by saying that their appetite is not so much for blood as for gore. They are not bothered by the presence of the marvellous and the improbable by everyday standards. They are exhilarated by all the analogies that can be drawn between the heroes of the battlefield and those of the playing fields. Their champion among recent translators is the famous one-time Headmaster of the Perse school, Dr Rouse. In their hands the *Iliad* is always on the verge of being fun, and attention is always given to the slayer rather than the slain. Indeed, for all they care, the dead may be imagined to pick themselves up after a conventional interval and retire hurt to the wings.

Now while the exponents of these two class-views would find it hard to support the verdict that the *Iliad* is one of the world's great poems, they could make an excellent detailed case in favour of their descriptive accounts. If, for instance, 'fun' is a telling way of making a point against one class, 'joy' is surely the author's key word for the fighting; he both communicates that joy and seems himself to share it. And if we recall from the passages discussed earlier in these lectures the simile of the stallion in $Z$ 503-14[1], and concede the volumes it seems to speak on the 'adolescent' side, the representative of the 'primitive core' theory could remind us of the simile in $\Gamma$ 23-28[2], which gave us the detecting of Paris by Menelaus, and in particular the joy felt by the hungry lion sighting its prey:

> ὥς τε λέων ἐχάρη μεγάλῳ ἐπὶ σώματι κύρσας,
> εὑρὼν ἢ ἔλαφον κεραὸν ἢ ἄγριον αἶγα
> πεινάων· μάλα γάρ τε κατεσθίει, εἴ περ ἂν αὐτὸν
> σεύωνται ταχέες τε κύνες θαλεροί τ' αἰζηοί·
> ὣς ἐχάρη Μενέλαος Ἀλέξανδρον θεοειδέα
> ὀφθαλμοῖσιν ἰδών·                                              (23-28)

He could triumphantly point out that there is no thought in Homer of distinguishing the μένος (fiery spirit) of lion and that of man. Consequently, he could argue, the word 'brute' as I used it is out of place. Such a reader would never have accepted the account I gave in my

---

[1] See chapter Five, p. 90.
[2] See chapter Five, p. 90, where the Greek is translated.

first chapter of the episode in Book XXI where Achilles slaughters the suppliant Lycaon. For him this was one of Achilles' finest hours. (I have even read somewhere that the victim comes to see his death as Achilles saw it, and willingly spreads himself out to be butchered.)

Although men of brutal or adolescent imagination easily settle for a limited kind of epic, which could never take a lasting hold on us, it remains true that men with the finest capacities for valuing humanity would force us, if reading Homer could not, to give a more generous account of the fighting hero in the *Iliad*. The poem may not have been written by man-killers, as Dryden called them,[1] for man-killers, yet 'Gods and Fighting Men' is a fair summary of what forms the basis of its artistic success. We must acknowledge that the fighting in the poem heightens and strengthens us, makes the blood run swifter, and deepens our sense of the preciousness of human life. Just as wine is not merely alcohol, the fighting hero is not *merely* a killer. The *Iliad* is both an adult and a civilized poem. Even the most primitive and bestial moments in it are free from the willed nastiness of our modern cults of violence and torture. Death is an ever-present reality, as Achilles is the first to remind us; men 'die indeed', and their death is every bit as serious as that of Mercutio in Shakespeare's *Romeo and Juliet*. And, though Homer seems to favour the Achaeans, the 'enemy' are generally treated with honour and respect. The poem ends with a lament for the Trojan, Hector, not with a glorification of his conqueror, Achilles.

A strict regard for the truth forces us to make a further concession to what I have called the adolescent imagination. The spiritual world — if I may so express one aspect of its life — of our public schools during the latter part of the nineteenth century did bear extraordinary resemblances to the imaginative world of the *Iliad*. And even in our day relevant meanings can still be easily found for some of the feelings that Homer expressed, if we are willing to search back among adolescent memories. For example, the most important, the governing, feeling of the fighting man for the supremacy of κλέος ἄφθιτον (deathless fame) is best understood from the adolescent perspective of some recent athletic triumph. If, for instance, we turn to the passage in Book IX, lines 412-13, where Achilles is explaining his fateful choice:

> εἰ μέν κ' αὖθι μένων Τρώων πόλιν ἀμφιμάχωμαι,
> ὤλετο μέν μοι νόστος, ἀτὰρ κλέος ἄφθιτον ἔσται·

[1] In a passage to which I shall be coming in a moment (p. 165).

which might be rendered in adolescent idiom,

> If I stay now and fight it out around Troy, then bang go
> All my hopes of return, but my glory will last for ever:

we are reminded that, as we saw in the First Book, if to be a supreme fighter is a great satisfaction, to become thereby the most admired person in society is a greater.[1]

It was not, as we have seen, an impossible step from the school pavilion to the legislative assembly. The force of Sarpedon's speech may be compromised by equivocal chords, yet it expresses no mean creed. But we may wonder whether this *credo* is enough to secure a poem immortality. We must freely grant that the fighting virtues constitute the basis of the poem, but the noble structure could not rise without wider views and other values. But if we try to detect in the *Iliad* an author standing aside from his heroes and judging them by his own quite different standards, we soon meet the difficulty faced by Schiller, who only slightly overstated the case when he likened Homer to God: *Wie die Gottheit hinter dem Weltgebäude, so steht er hinter seinem Werk; er ist das Werk, und das Werk ist er . . .*[2] The spirit that broods over the fighting, the mind that asks what it all means, is not so overwhelmingly present in the poem as the spirit that animates the fighting itself. I think that humanity is present in the poem as a spectator of the fighting: Pope's 'pensive' has its Homeric counterpart. But if the spectator is more than a spectator, and becomes something like a judge, then that something more is very . . . discreetly managed.

So discreetly indeed that this line had better be dropped in favour of another. Any answer to the question—what raises Homer's epic above others and gives the poem its classical status?—must take the general form of arguing that the specific fighting virtues are measured by being placed in a context of the other precious qualities that make life worth living. *It is only when the manly is enlarged to include all that makes a man* that we feel the poem is great and likely to last. Now one

---

[1] Turnus expresses this sentiment in a coarser form in the Twelfth Book of the *Aeneid*: 'letumque sinas pro laude pacisci'; as does Dryden in his translation of the Ninth Book:

> The thing call'd Life, with ease I can disclaim;
> And think it over sold to purchase Fame.          (264-65)

[2] *Ueber naive und sentimentalische Dichtung* (1795). 'Homer is everywhere present in and cannot be distinguished from his creation, just as God is only to be found in and through the created universe; both are their creations and their creations are them.'

of the Homeric tests for this extended conception of man is the capacity
to *feel*. We are fortunate in having a worthy touchstone for this
capacity in Shakespeare's *Macbeth*, in the scene during which Macduff
is tested, found honest, and then confronted with the news that his
wife and children had been murdered at Macbeth's orders.

> *Macd*. My children too?
> *Ro*. Wife, Children, Servants, all that could be found.
> *Macd*. And I must be from thence? My wife kil'd too?
> *Rosse*. I have said.
> *Malc*. Be comforted.
> Let's make us Med'cines of our great Revenge,
> To cure this deadly greefe.
> *Macd*. He has no Children. All my pretty ones?
> Did you say All? Oh Hell-Kite! All?
> What, All my pretty Chickens, and their Damme
> At one fell swoope?
> *Malc*. Dispute it like a man.
> *Macd*. I shall do so:
> But I must also feele it as a man,
> I cannot but remember such things were
> That were most precious to me: . . .[1]

In the light of this we may say that we measure the fighting hero
by what it costs him as a man; that if the greatness of the *Iliad* depends
in part on the width of context into which the fighting virtues are
placed, we must also include in the essential structure the relations of
the fighting man to what it is not in the power of man to change.
The hero cannot rise to his full stature until he meets his destiny.[2]
Macduff had a reconciling context for his calamity:

> Did heaven looke on,
> And would not take their part? Sinfull *Macduff*,
> They were all strooke for thee: Naught that I am,
> Not for their owne demerits, but for mine
> Fell slaughter on their soules: Heaven rest them now.

[1] IV, iii.

[2] Cf. Dryden in his translation of the *Aeneid* (12/7-8) about Turnus before his
last struggle:

> He rowz'd his Vigour for the last Debate;
> And rais'd his haughty Soul, to meet his Fate.

*The Works of Virgil* (1697), p. 578.

No one who believes in eternal damnation after this life will allow me to call the Christian world an easy one compared with the Homeric; but if we confine our prospect to this life, what the Homeric heroes had to face was bleaker and more inclined to lower a man's courage than the longer view the dying Christian hero had to think of.

This darker side to the *Iliad* is of the essence. If it were itself the whole essence, we should find the poem tedious, just as it would have been a lesser thing had Homer been a primitive Anglo-Saxon and Achilles a much-suffering Anglo-Saxon warrior. The dark side is necessary to the light side: beside the hero's power to *do* we must have his power to *feel*, to suffer. The *Iliad* would be a lesser poem if the killers were professionals with no other enjoyment than in killing. If they had been like the pests of the feudal system, without any other outlets for their vitality than in petty pilfering and organized raiding of their neighbours, the fighters before Troy could not have become the inspiration of a great poem. If Homer's raw material had been a national degradation of man like the Thirty Years' War in Germany, he could not have worked it up into a classical epic.

If we are to have the roughest conception of the essential structure of the poem, we must be able to see in a summary way all that counterbalances the joy and vitality in the fighting. The *Sixth Book* with its alternating emphasis might have been designed to give in a concentrated form a pattern of the essential structure of the whole. If we ever get an insight into Homer's mind, it comes as we follow Hector through his chain of interviews. This behaviour is framed, as it were, by the formidable appearance of Diomedes at one end, and the descent of Paris from Troy at the other, as he goes like a stallion racing to the water, laughing into battle. The climax, the parting of Hector and Andromache, is one of those scenes that are both typically Greek and universal in their power to touch the heart. The scene moves us more as we look back on it from the end of the poem when Hector has been killed. It grips us, of course, even more when we look outside the poem and the dreadful forebodings become true, and Andromache and her son fall into the enemy's hands. Because the *Iliad* would not be the *Iliad* without this scene, we may fairly take it as a good place to go to if we wish to get a perspective on the essential structure of the poem.

In the Dedication Dryden wrote in 1693, introducing a miscellany of poems, among which was his translation of the episode in the Sixth

Book of the *Iliad*, where Hector and Andromache unwittingly or half-wittingly part for ever, there are two remarks which, in the light of what follows, will gather additional interest. The first was that Homer was inferior to Virgil when it came to dealing with the unmanly passions; the second, that Homer was garrulous where he ought to be dramatic. I shall take up the latter point first, but, before settling down to argument, I should like to present the whole passage. In a more ambitious study of the *Iliad* it would be necessary, among many other things, to include a chapter on the last book to correspond to the chapter on the Sixth, for everybody seems to agree that these two books answer and balance each other both in content and in form. In discussing the Twenty-Fourth Book I should make much of a translation of the lamentations over Hector's dead body written by *Congreve*[1] and included in this very Miscellany of Dryden's, which goes by the name of *Examen Poeticum*, a swarm of poems. Congreve is the 'friend' Dryden refers to in this passage from his Dedication (my quotation begins where he has just mentioned their two Homer versions):

> Both the Subjects are pathetical; and I am sure my Friend has added to the Tenderness which he found in the Original; and, without Flattery, surpass'd his Author. Yet I must needs say this in reference to *Homer*, that he is much more capable of exciting the Manly Passions, than those of Grief and Pity. To cause Admiration, is indeed the proper and adequate design of an Epick Poem: And in that he has Excell'd even *Virgil*. Yet, without presuming to Arraign our Master, I may venture to affirm, that he is somewhat too Talkative, and more than somewhat too digressive. This is so manifest, that it cannot be deny'd, in that little parcel which I have Translated, perhaps too literally: There *Andromache* in the midst of her Concernment, and Fright for *Hector*, runs off her Biass, to tell him a Story of her Pedigree, and of the lamentable Death of her Father, her Mother, and her Seven Brothers. The Devil was in *Hector*, if he knew not all this matter, as well as she who told it him; for she had been his Bed-fellow for many Years together: And if he knew it, then it must be confess'd, that *Homer* in this long digression, has rather given us his own Character, than that of the Fair Lady whom he Paints. His Dear Friends the Commentators, who never fail

---

[1] See p. 190, where part of the translation is printed.

him at a pinch, will needs excuse him, by making the present
Sorrow of *Andromache*, to occasion the remembrance of all the
past: But others think that she had enough to do with that
Grief which now oppress'd her, without running for assistance
to her Family. *Virgil*, I am confident, wou'd have omitted such
a work of supererrogation. But *Virgil* had the Gift of expressing
much in little, and sometimes in silence: For though he yielded
much to *Homer* in Invention, he more Excell'd him in his
Admirable Judgment. He drew the Passion of *Dido* for *Eneas*,
in the most lively and most natural Colours that are imaginable:
*Homer* was ambitious enough of moving pity; for he has attempted
twice on the same subject of *Hector*'s death: First, when *Priam*,
and *Hecuba* beheld his Corps, which was drag'd after the Chariot
of *Achilles*; and then in the Lamentation which was made over
him, when his Body was redeem'd by *Priam*; and the same
Persons again bewail his death with a Chorus of others to help
the cry. But if this last excite Compassion in you, as I doubt not
but it will, you are more oblig'd to the Translatour than the Poet.
For *Homer*, as I observ'd before, can move rage better than he
can pity: He stirs up the irascible appetite, as our Philosophers
call it, he provokes to Murther, and the destruction of God's
Images; he forms and equips those ungodly Man-killers, whom
we Poets, when we flatter them, call Heroes; a race of Men
who can never enjoy quiet in themselves, 'till they have taken it
from all the World. This is *Homer*'s Commendation, and such
as it is, the Lovers of Peace, or at least of more moderate Heroism,
will never Envy him.

It is very difficult, when Dryden is trailing his coat so energetically,
to resist following the trail; but let me first quote the passage where
Dryden is so sure that Homer is being garrulous, in Dryden's own
version:

> Eternal Sorrow and perpetual Tears
> Began my Youth, and will conclude my Years:
> I have no Parents, Friends, nor Brothers left;
> By stern *Achilles* all of Life bereft.
> Then when the Walls of *Thebes* he o'rethrew,
> His fatal Hand my Royal Father slew;
> He slew *Aëtion*, but despoil'd him not;
> Nor in his hate the Funeral Rites forgot;

Arm'd as he was he sent him whole below;
And reverenc'd thus the Manes of his Foe:
A Tomb he rais'd; the Mountain Nymphs around,
Enclos'd with planted Elms the Holy Ground.

My sev'n brave *Brothers* in one fatal Day
To Death's dark Mansions took the mournful way:
Slain by the same *Achilles*, while they keep
The bellowing Oxen and the bleating Sheep.
My Mother, who the Royal Scepter sway'd,
Was Captive to the cruel Victor made:
And hither led: but hence redeem'd with Gold,
Her Native Country did again behold.
And but beheld: for soon *Diana*'s Dart
In an unhappy Chace transfix'd her Heart.[1]

How downright may a general critical remark be and still be true?
Can the only positive remark of this sort be: that literary criticism
does not permit the knock-down argument? At any rate, when
Dryden says that Homer is too talkative, too digressive, he is going
too far in adding: *This is so manifest, that it cannot be deny'd.* It not
only can be denied, it will be, and I hope with some plausibility. The
moral I draw is that whenever we find ourselves about to make a
sweeping general assertion, we ought to ask ourselves whether we
have not somewhere *assumed* something that needed to be *proved.*
Dryden, I suppose, was assuming that the laws governing Homer's
art were closer to those governing drama than the facts warrant us in
claiming. Moreover, Dryden was assuming that Homer's art was
governed by the same concern for the *decorum* of rhetoric as Virgil's.
For what appear as digressions once we have made these false assumptions all acquire point and a clear function once we recognize
those assumptions to be unwarranted. Each item we then see is
making a necessary contribution. First, Homer wishes us to feel that
the unusual urgency of Andromache has a good cause: her situation
must be seen to be out of the ordinary. When *we* contemplate the trio
of husband, wife and child, we are apt to say to ourselves: see the
archetypal situation: there we have the Family complete! But a Greek
family was not so shorn down to these bare elements. A bereaved
member of this trio could fall back and be absorbed in the larger normal

[1] *Op. cit.*, pp. 460-62.

family of 'Parents, Friends [and] Brothers'. Andromache is saying
with force what she sums up in the lines that immediately follow the
passage I quoted:

> But thou, my *Hector*, art thy self alone,
> My Parents, Brothers, and my Lord in one. . . .

Many commentators have remarked that it is a fine stroke to make
Achilles appear as the Doom of her family, since we know he is
going to complete her ruin by depriving her of her husband. And in
this connection, the religious respect felt by Achilles for her father's
dead body is going to have its effect when we contrast it with Achilles'
want of respect for Hector's corpse. A truly Homeric touch is that
he has imaginative room for a piece of fancy which makes us believe
that somewhere in the world there *was* a hero's tomb enclosed by
planted elms. It bears no relation to any serious time scheme—at
least I take the elms as *magically appearing*, and do not ask where the
Mountain Nymphs collected the seeds. Finally, this story of exceptional hardship was needed to make Andromache's behaviour tolerable
and pardonable. Even so, we may read a polite rebuke when she
proposes an alternate strategy to the War Leader, and Hector replies:

> Return, and to divert thy thoughts at home,
> There task thy Maids, and exercise the Loom,
> Employ'd in Works that Womankind become.
> The Toils of War, and Feats of Chivalry
> Belong to Men, and most of all to me.
> At this, for new Replies he did not stay,
> But lac'd his Crested Helm, and strode away . . .[1]

But Dryden was right, I feel, to assume that Homer was also
writing for all times and all civilised societies, and that Homer was
asserting the bond of common nature in stressing the natural ties
that bind the little family of three, not forgetting the nurse. Before
Andromache was allowed to speak, Homer brought on the child
carried on the nurse's breast, like a star in beauty, so that for all his
sorrow, Hector smiled at him without speaking. Before Hector can
tell us what is in his mind, what this natural tie means to him,
Andromache makes her plea that without Hector she could not live.

[1] *Op. cit.*, p. 468.

She has to be shown as a figure of some weight and power in order that
Hector by replying effectively may show himself great:

> Spirits are not finely touch'd,
> But to fine issues.

Hector at last speaks out and gives us the clue to the *Iliad* as he
expounds what it costs to be a fighting man. We learn that he is a
human being. There are certain public responsibilities that he puts
before the most sacred family ties, but as a man he knows that he
cares more and will suffer more for the loss of his little family than
for the whole of fallen Troy. It is not the greatest of human emotions,
but it is the perfect counterpart to his public heroism.

Equally confined to the limitations of the heroic is Hector's
prayer for his son. The boy must grow up to be a killer too, and bring
home, to rejoice his mother's heart, the bloody spoils of his first kill.
Does not this bring out all the more the humanity of the scene where
the boy is only a baby and frightened by the horsehair on Hector's
helmet? Has anybody failed to feel the supreme humanity of the
laughter it causes in the parents? There is no drop in the intensity of
grief. Hector feels sorrow for his wife and tries to comfort her with the
soldiers' philosophy: 'it will come when it will come and not before'.
But Andromache will not be comforted. As soon as she re-enters the
man-killer's (ἀνδροφόνοιο) house, she sets up the wail in which all the
members of the household participate, the ritual keening over the dead.
She thus darkens the whole *Iliad* until we meet her again in Book
XXII, when, ironically enough, she is the last to hear the real
keening, but was obeying Hector's counsel to be diligent about the
house, and had just given orders for the hero's bath water to be
heated. There Homer allows himself one of his rare personal inter-
ventions in this pathetic comment:

> νηπίη, οὐδ' ἐνόησεν ὅ μιν μάλα τῆλε λοετρῶν
> χερσὶν Ἀχιλλῆος δάμασε γλαυκῶπις Ἀθήνη.[1]        (445-46)

If we now attempt to sum up what this scene means to us, we must
go some way with Dryden, and concede that a fine but lesser scene

---

[1] *ΙΛΙΑΔΟΣ Χ,*

The poor dear did not know he was far from his bath, tamed
At Athene's orders, the green-grey-eyed, by the hands of Achilles.

—that between Aeneas and Dido in the Fourth Book of Virgil's
*Aeneid*—comes across to us more fully, is more available, owing to our
closer relation to the Latin language, than this broader, saner and, in
Arnold's phrase, more 'tonic' moment in the Trojan War. This, then,
is eminently a scene where we could do with some help, though not a
scene where we are quite helpless. We are not contemplating vacuity
even if we have to approach the scene from a modern prose 'crib'.
Some of its features would be agreed on at once; for instance, that the
principal figures include ordinary humanity while filling out the special
relation of exceptional responsibility they found themselves in as
leaders of their community. (They are a little like the Adam and
Eve of the Fourth Book of Milton's *Paradise Lost*.)

Following up Matthew Arnold's clue of the close relation of
matter and manner, we can see as two cardinal features of the scene,
extreme simplicity and grandeur. Can we respond to both pulls at the
same time? We, I should say, are more likely to go for the domestic
note. I happen to have at home a drawing by a Swiss artist who made a
picture of a soldier of the last war taking leave of his wife. It is quite
possible to see in it some of the truth of the suffering involved when
private and public claims clash. But it would be quite impossible to
imagine the modern Swiss couple breaking into grand oration. The
transition in Homer from simplicity to grandeur is, I should say,
something we have no parallel for. Yet it is not so clear-cut as this:
Homer's simplicity has more than a touch of grandeur and his
grandeur of simplicity. Homer's figures are at the centre of humanity
and expand outwards to the extremes of the heroic and the extremes of
simplicity. We do not habitually occupy that centre, and never, if we do
visit it, can we move easily in both directions as Homer invites us to do.

Do we also have trouble in passing through the hero's code to get
at his humanity? Certainly, if I thought Homer himself were totally
implicated, I should hate some moments, just as I hate a corresponding
scene in Shakespeare's *Coriolanus*, where the hero's mother is behaving,
not like Homer's Andromache, who has no taste for blood, but like
the Andromache Hector was projecting as he imagined his son's
first military success.

> To a cruell Warre I sent him, from whence he return'd his
> browes bound with Oake. I tell thee Daughter, I sprang not
> more in joy at first hearing he was a Man-child, then now in
> first seeing he had proved himselfe a man.

M

This is bearable, but the mother immediately goes on to make all this vivid:

> Me thinkes I see him stampe thus, and call thus,
> Come on you Cowards, you were got in feare
> Though you were borne in Rome; his bloody brow
> With his mail'd hand, then wiping, forth he goes
> Like to a Harvest man, that task'd to mowe
> Or all, or loose his hyre.

This is too much for the wife:

> *Virg.* His bloody Brow? Oh Iupiter, no blood.
> *Volum.* Away you Foole; it more becomes a man
> Then gilt his Trophe. The brests of *Hecuba*
> When she did suckle *Hector*, look'd not lovelier
> Then *Hectors* forhead, when it spit forth blood
> At Grecian sword.[1]

Dryden is not likely to be a great help since, as we have seen, he fathered his own want of tenderness on Homer. Indeed I should not have brought him in here if Pope had not taken so much of him over into his own version. Dryden was too concerned to see the baby as a Royal Child with an imperial future. Consequently, he overlooked Homer's insistent point that it was a real baby and yet someone of importance to the Great Man, though in itself an innocent, even foolish, thing. Homer, Heaven knows, is sparing enough in the *Iliad* of affectionate words for children, but here he piles them on:

$$\mathring{a}\tau a\lambda\acute{a}\phi\rho ova,\ \nu\acute{\eta}\pi\iota ov\ a\mathring{v}\tau\omega\varsigma,$$
$$\text{'}E\kappa\tau o\rho\acute{\iota}\delta\eta\nu\ \mathring{a}\gamma a\pi\eta\tau\acute{o}\nu, \qquad\qquad (400\text{-}01)$$

—and closes this caressing language with the phrase 'like a beautiful star', which Dryden hardens into

> Who, like the Morning Star, his beams display'd.

(What a world away from Macduff's 'all my pretty chickens'!) From such a false start it was impossible to recover the human touch. In Homer, Andromache calls her son by an affectionate diminutive $\nu\eta\pi\acute{\iota}a\chi ov$; in Dryden, she addresses Hector as if he were a step-father:

---

[1] *The Tragedie of Coriolanus* (1623), I, iii.

Nor dost thou pity, with a Parent's mind,
This helpless Orphan whom thou leav'st behind . . .

Dryden's creative powers show up better in the orations:

Not *Troy* it self, tho' built by Hands Divine,
Nor *Priam*, nor his People, nor his Line,
My Mother, nor my *Brothers* of Renown,
Whose Valour yet defends th' unhappy Town,
Not these, nor all their Fates which I foresee,
Are half of that concern I have for thee.
I see, I see thee in that fatal Hour,
Subjected to the Victor's cruel Pow'r:
Led hence a Slave to some insulting Sword:
Forlorn and trembling at a Foreign Lord.
A spectacle in *Argos*, at the Loom,
Gracing with *Trojan* Fights, a *Grecian* Room;
Or from deep Wells, the living Stream to take,
And on thy weary Shoulders bring it back.
While, groaning under this laborious Life,
They insolently call thee *Hector's* Wife.
Upbraid thy *Bondage* with thy Husband's name;
And from my Glory propagate thy Shame.
This when they say, thy Sorrows will encrease ⎫
With anxious thoughts of former Happiness; ⎬
That he is dead who cou'd thy wrongs redress. ⎭
But I opprest with Iron Sleep before,
Shall hear thy unavailing Cries no more.[1]

This is magnificent, but it is fatally severed from the underlying pathos,
as we may see even in the Penguin version:

Ah, may the earth lie deep on my dead body before I hear the
screams you utter as they drag you off!'[2]

Dryden here recalls Johnson's classic verdict:

He is therefore, with all his variety of excellence, not often
pathetick; and had so little sensibility of the power of effusions
purely natural, that he did not esteem them in others. Simplicity

---

[1] *Examen Poeticum*, pp. 464-465.
[2] E. V. Rieu: *The Iliad*, Book VI, p. 129.

gave him no pleasure ... I am not certain whether it was not rather the difficulty which he found in exhibiting the genuine operations of the heart, than a servile submission to an injudicious audience, that filled his plays with false magnificence.[1]

I must not forget, that Mr. *Dryden* has formerly translated this admirable Episode, and with so much Success, as to leave me at least no hopes of improving or equalling it.[2]

Pope's actual subservience to Dryden is very puzzling when we consider that both intellectually and emotionally he had freed himself from Dryden's disabilities. Firstly, we can see from Pope's notes that he had fully assimilated the message which Boileau extracted from Longinus, that the truly simple, and only that, could produce the sublime. Moreover, we can see from Pope's Preface to the *Iliad* that he had understood how truly Longinian was Homer's sublime:

'Tis a great Secret in Writing to know when to be plain, and when poetical and figurative; and it is what *Homer* will teach us if we will but follow modestly in his Footsteps. Where his Diction is bold and lofty, let us raise ours as high as we can; but where his is plain and humble, we ought not to be deterr'd from imitating him by the fear of incurring the Censure of a meer *English* Critick. Nothing that belongs to *Homer* seems to have been more commonly mistaken than the just Pitch of his Style: Some of his Translators having swell'd into Fustian in a proud Confidence of the *Sublime*; others sunk into Flatness in a cold and timorous Notion of *Simplicity*. Methinks I see these different Followers of *Homer*, some sweating and straining after him by violent Leaps and Bounds, (the certain Signs of false Mettle) others slowly and servilely creeping in his Train, while the Poet himself is all the time proceeding with an unaffected and equal Majesty before them. However of the two Extreams one could sooner pardon Frenzy than Frigidity: No Author is to be envy'd for such Commendations as he may gain by that Character of Style, which his Friends must agree together to call *Simplicity*, and the rest of the World will call *Dulness*. There is a *graceful* and *dignify'd* Simplicity, as well as a *bald* and

---

1 *The Lives of the most eminent English Poets* (1790), pp. 182-83.
2 *Observations on the Sixth Book* (1716), XXXVII, p. 174.

*sordid* one, which differ as much from each other as the Air of a *plain* Man from that of a *Sloven*: 'Tis one thing to be tricked up, and another not to be dress'd at all. Simplicity is the Mean between Ostentation and Rusticity.

This pure and noble Simplicity is no where in such Perfection as in the *Scripture* and our Author.[1]

Secondly, Pope differed from Dryden in thinking Homer capable of expressing tenderness:

*Homer* undoubtedly shines most upon the great Subjects, in raising our Admiration or Terror: Pity, and the softer Passions, are not so much of the Nature of his Poem, which is formed upon Anger and the Violence of Ambition. But we have cause to think his Genius was no less capable of touching the Heart with Tenderness, than of firing it with Glory, from the few Sketches he has left us of his Excellency that way too. In the present Episode of the Parting of *Hector* and *Andromache*, he assembled all that Love, Grief, and Compassion could inspire. . . .[2]

Thirdly, and most impressively, whereas in his treatment of the similes Pope tended to regard domestic feelings as inherently low, here nothing inhibits him from entering fully into the smallest details, as we may see from this note:

There never was a finer Piece of Painting than this. *Hector* extends his Arms to embrace his Child; the Child affrighted at the glittering of his Helmet and the shaking of the Plume, shrinks backward to the Breast of his Nurse; *Hector* unbraces his Helmet, lays it on the Ground, takes the Infant in his Arms lifts him towards Heaven, and offers a Prayer for him to the Gods: then returns him to the Mother *Andromache*, who receives him with a Smile of Pleasure, but at the same instant the Fears for her Husband make her burst into Tears. All these are but small Circumstances, but so artfully chosen, that every Reader immediately feels the force of them, and represents the whole in the utmost Liveliness to his Imagination. This alone might be a Confutation of that false Criticism some have fallen into, who affirm that a Poet ought only to collect the great and noble

---

[1] *The Iliad of Homer* (1715), Preface $H_1$—$H_3$.
[2] *Observations on the Sixth Book* (1716), XXXVII, p. 173.

Particulars in his Paintings. But it is in the Images of Things as in the Characters of Persons; where a small Action, or even a small Circumstance of an Action, lets us more into the Knowledge and Comprehension of them, than the material and principal Parts themselves. As we find this in a History, so we do in a Picture, where sometimes a small Motion or Turning of a Finger will express the Character and Action of the Figure more than all the other Parts of the Design. *Longinus* indeed blames an Author's insisting too much on trivial Circumstances; but in the same Place extols *Homer* as 'the Poet who best knew how to make use of important and beautiful Circumstances, and to avoid the mean and superfluous ones'. There is a vast difference betwixt a *small* Circumstance and a *trivial* one, and the smallest become important if they are well chosen, and not confused.[1]

Why, then, we ask with astonishment, does Pope versify '*Hector* unbraces his Helmet, lays it on the Ground' in this pompous couplet:

> The glitt'ring Terrors from his Brows unbound,
> And plac'd the beaming Helmet on the Ground . . . ?
>
> (600-01)

The answer seems to be that in his concern to be *nobly* simple Pope confined his style to a kind of stately majesty which acted like stilts and prevented him from touching the ground of common humanity. He falls into this tone from his first mention of Hector in this episode: whereas Homer felt no need to say more than the bare name, Pope opens pompously:

> Meantime the Guardian of the *Trojan* State,
> Great *Hector* enter'd at the *Scæan* Gate.        (296-97)

To maintain this note, Pope found himself obliged to magnify the artistically beautiful home of Priam into

> *Priam*'s stately Courts
> Rais'd on arch'd Columns of stupendous Frame; . . .
>
> (304-05)

a 'pompous Structure' which recalls Milton's Pandemonium:

---

[1] *Observations on the Sixth Book* (1716), XLVIII, pp. 178-79.

> like a Temple, where *Pilasters* round
> Were set, and Doric pillars overlaid
> With Golden Architrave;

and the bridge over Chaos:

>                         at sight
> Of that stupendious Bridge his joy encreas'd.

But even this false start cannot explain why Pope followed Dryden instead of writing in his own tender vein. All that Pope could contribute was, to borrow a word from plane geometry, to 'produce' his figures in the direction of sentiment rather than passion, mostly by giving explicit or explanatory expanding notes in the text of the translation. When Hector in Homer smiles at his son but does not speak, Pope supplies a comment:

> smil'd, and pleas'd resign'd
> To tender Passions all his mighty Mind: . . .   (504-505)

Homer merely says 'meanwhile Andromache wept', but Pope gives us these details:

> Her Bosom labour'd with a boding Sigh,
> And the big Tear stood trembling in her Eye.   (508-509)

Pope's worst offence is to make the hero a simultaneous commentator on his own feelings:

> Yet come it will, the Day decreed by Fates;
> (How my Heart trembles while my Tongue relates!)
>                            (570-71)

I gladly leave you to confirm the details of this sad subservience, and I must reserve my explanation of it for some other occasion. Let me therefore give one final instance. Where I found Dryden most misguided was in thinking he could make good his deficiencies by supplying Homer with *point*. I have already given one instance:

> Eternal Sorrow and perpetual Tears
> Began my Youth, and will conclude my Years: . . .

Here is another:

> Thy Wife and Son are in thy Ruin lost:
> This is a Husband's and a Father's Post.

If you compare Dryden and Pope you will see that Pope admired these turns so much that he confined his own efforts as a translator to writing elegant variations on them.

In only one place does Pope go beyond imitation to rivalry, and this is all the more creditable since it is a case of Pope surpassing Dryden at his best. I have already quoted a part of Dryden's version, but to enable the difference to be caught at one go, I will give, first, the Dryden, and follow it with the Pope:

> My Wife and Mistress, drive thy fears away;
> Nor give so bad an Omen to the Day:
> Think not it lies in any *Grecian*'s Pow'r,
> To take my Life before the fatal Hour.
> When that arrives, nor good nor bad can fly
> Th' irrevocable Doom of Destiny.
> Return, and to divert thy thoughts at home,
> There task thy Maids, and exercise the Loom,
> Employ'd in Works that Womankind become.
> The Toils of War, and Feats of Chivalry
> Belong to Men, and most of all to me.[1]

> *Andromache*! my Soul's far better Part,
> Why with untimely Sorrows heaves thy Heart?
> No hostile Hand can antedate my Doom,
> Till Fate condemns me to the silent Tomb.
> Fix'd is the Term to all the Race of Earth,
> And such the hard Condition of our Birth.
> No Force can then resist, no Flight can save,
> All sink alike, the Fearful and the Brave.
> No more—but hasten to thy Tasks at home,
> There guide the Spindle, and direct the Loom:
> Me Glory summons to the martial Scene,
> The Field of Combate is the Sphere for Men.
> Where Heroes war, the foremost Place I claim,
> The first in Danger as the first in Fame.          (624-37)

It is striking to note that this piece is leaning so heavily on lines that come from Sarpedon's speech. When we hear

> All sink alike, the Fearful and the Brave. . . .

[1] *Op. cit.*, pp. 467-68.

we cannot help recalling

> Cou'd all our Care elude the greedy Grave,
> Which claims no less the Fearful than the Brave,

and in the same way

> The first in Danger as the first in Fame. . . .

now appears twice-borrowed, but comes to us here no doubt from the same passage:

> 'Tis ours, the Dignity They give, to grace;
> The first in Valour, as the first in Place . . .

I mention these details to recall the verdict on the Sarpedon speech. Hector's words are not great verse: they would not figure in a largish anthology of Pope's and Dryden's best passages. Some people would say that this was inevitable just because the two poets are translating. My view is that if they had felt their subject more intimately and wholeheartedly, they would have written as well in their translations of this passage as in their freer creations.

This is a sour note to end on, and tactically so inept that I feel obliged to make a brief final remark. No introduction to the *Iliad* can be easy. I have found it so hard myself to gain a foothold that I could not pretend that it is a territory for rapid invasion. It therefore seemed to me necessary to show that my proposed remedies are far from doing *all* that we could wish towards increasing our reading and penetrating power. But they can do *something*. We do approach Homer through Pope, and we can come closer the more aware we are of the respects in which Pope is unhelpful. A sympathetic reading of Pope's version leads us straight to what matters most in Homer: his humanity. This is the clue I would place in the hands of the translator I look for to carry us on the crest of his creative imagination further into the mysterious Greek than anyone has yet got.

If there must be a last word to an open-ended discussion, I should like to close with this passage from Matthew Arnold's *Last Words*, which has been with me constantly from the start:

It is for the future translator that one must work. The successful translator of Homer will have (or he cannot succeed) that true sense for his subject, and that disinterested love of it, which are, both of them, so rare in literature, and so precious; he will not be led off by any false scent; he will have an eye for the real matter, and, where he thinks he may find any indication of this, no hint will be too slight for him, no shade will be too fine, no imperfections will turn him aside,—he will go before his adviser's thought, and help it out with his own. This is the sort of student that a critic of Homer should always have in his thoughts; but students of this sort are indeed rare.

# EPILOGUE

## I

# Some Versions of the *Iliad*[1]

SINCE publishers must have a large public in view before they issue
books in paperbacks, the translations of the *Iliad* now on sale in this
form are presumably giving public satisfaction. The sales of the
Penguin version (E. V. Rieu) might alone answer for it. I suspect,
however, that a superficial enquiry would immediately show that the
two terms, 'public' and 'satisfaction', cover so many different things
that the relative worth of these translations could not be measured by
the simple test of comparing the number of copies sold. Short recom-
mendations can, however, be given to some of the numerically significant publics for whom the *Iliad* is 'required' reading. If you have a
weak hold on the original and wish to use a 'crib' instead of carefully
construing the Greek, none of these translations is safe: examiners
will always catch you out. If the knowledge of the *Iliad* you require
could be equally well supplied by a digest, the 'potted' version by I. A.
Richards will save you the trouble of following out the leisurely
breadth and particularity of Homer. This version is suitable for the
reader who habitually skips.

The tests I have applied to these versions may seem pointless, for I
have considered what may be non-existent requirements and have

---

[1] Reprinted from *The Cambridge Quarterly*, Vol. 1, No. 1, Winter 1965-66,
where the following books were reviewed:

1. *The Iliad* translated by W. H. D. Rouse. A Mentor Classic, The New
   American Library, 1950. (First published 1938.)
2. *The Iliad* translated by E. V. Rieu. Penguin Books, 1966. (First published
   1950.)
3. *The Iliad* translated by A. H. Chase and W. G. Perry, Jr. Bantam Books,
   1961.
4. *The Iliad of Homer* shortened and in a new translation by I. A. Richards.
   Norton Library, W. W. Norton & Co. Inc., 1950.
5. *The Iliad of Homer* translated by Richmond Lattimore. Phoenix Books,
   University of Chicago Press, and Routledge & Kegan Paul, Ltd., 1951.
6. *The Iliad* translated by S. O. Andrew and M. J. Oakley. Everyman's Library,
   Dent, 1955.

kept in mind what may be a numerically insignificant public. I have in fact asked only one question: to what extent do these translations make it possible for the *Iliad* to be assimilated into the *living* culture of English-speaking people? That many questions are begged by this formulation I am well aware. First of all, that the *Iliad* itself is alive. 'Connais-tu rien de plus embêtant que l'*Iliade*?' Paul Valéry, I suspect, was not the only distinguished man of letters in this century for whom Homer's one-time 'classics' are now extinct. The many modern attempts to pass the epic off as anything but what it is tell the same story. If what the reader requires is a 'grand adventure story' or a war 'thriller', he could do a great deal better with other works. The *Iliad* cannot stand such competition.

Some things, however, can be fairly stated without claiming to have full possession either of the sense in which it may be said that the *Iliad* is alive or that in which anybody is culturally alive today. At least, the *conditions* for assimilation into living culture are, to my mind, beyond dispute. There must be a degree of concern amounting to passion both on the part of the translator and of the reader before an alien body can be assimilated. The foreign book must be deeply required. Both translator and reader must come to self-expression, self-completion, self-transcendence through the act of assimilating.

That a work cannot become a 'world classic' in any other way is not so immediately obvious. Mr Eliot used to imply that he possessed his Dante as he possessed his Shakespeare. Is it obviously true that we cannot really possess a foreign author in the original until he has been assimilated by translation into the vernacular? I have to step carefully here, for while I believe that it is so, I quite see the illusion under which those people suffer who claim that there is no need to learn Greek or any other foreign language since 'we now have the classics in translation'. Some kinds of successful translation do supersede the originals. FitzGerald's *Rubáiyát* has been assimilated, whereas the original may be alive or dead for all we care. But most translations are a second-best and are rarely consulted by those with access to the originals. Good teachers of modern languages often advocate the suspension of the translation habit in favour of passive immersion in the foreign medium. (The advantages, for instance, of being denied all dictionaries save Larousse when first reading French originals are undeniable.) Nevertheless when we push to the extreme limits of critical reading and attempt the judgments that are total judgments of ourselves, translation is essential. Every word of the alien original must have made contact with all the relevant words of our own tongue. Without this, the Englishman who offers critical verdicts on foreign masterpieces often becomes a mere ape of the foreign critics.

My argument requires that we convert 'often' to 'always', but when I think of the rare but real success of some of our contemporary students of foreign literature—such as that of my distinguished namesake with Rilke—I have to confess to lack of the superior knowledge that would enable me to place them in the disobliging category my argument requires. Is the case any less implausible when the *Iliad* is the issue? The case is clearly different. Nobody can know enough of the Greek that Homer spoke to be in intimate possession of his poem. Therefore to read the original at all worthily is to fill out with hints and guesses. The leap the imagination must take is into creative translation. Successful translation is therefore the condition for knowledge. Hence the ultimate validating authority is the translator's not the scholar's. This view runs counter to all the assumptions made in the last hundred years or so. Matthew Arnold, for instance, takes it for granted that scholars have complete possession of their authors, that the cultivated learned are the body, '*quem penes arbitrium est et ius et norma loquendi*' ('in whose hands lies the judgment, the right and the rule of speech') (Loeb), when the question to be answered is: in what sense is it true to say that Homer's *Iliad* is alive? I consider that some present-day Homeric scholars are fortunate in not being exposed to scrutiny. Nobody asks for proof of the intimacy of their possession of the classics. A cynic might argue that the classics *must* be extinct if lifelong intimacy with the originals results in the miserable efforts at 'appreciation' that some of the learned produce.

To present the facts fairly, however, we must recall the limits we cannot get beyond in our attempts to possess Shakespeare. Yet who save a *chevalier de l'industrie shakspérienne* would see in these limits a barrier to Shakespeare's assimilation into living culture? Clearly the death of one kind of life is the condition for a lasting afterlife. It is therefore a monstrous deflection of interest to attempt, as most scholars do, to resurrect the corpse of the *Iliad* while neglecting its immortal soul. Indeed it might become a principal function of modern translations to force the learned to attend to the lasting value of the *Iliad*. This might happen if the goal of translating were to create a new Greek-reading public. Our Greek scholars badly need an audience used to the critical discussion of literary masterpieces in our own literature. The critics of our literature need almost as badly to acquire half as much Greek as Matthew Arnold enjoyed. Therefore in a world where leisure is ceasing to be the privilege of a very few, the acquisition of a smattering of Greek should be one of the first results of the stimulus of a good translation. For though a good translation is one that satisfies a reader with no access to the original, its full effect is only obtained on those who are thereby enabled to read the original with fresh eyes.

A further implication of my formulation of the standard for a test of these translations is that we should abandon a false, Alexandrian, notion of culture. Assimilation into a living culture is not a disinterested pursuit, not the stocking of a museum with pieces visited once a year. Living culture is a desperate business, to be carried on rather in the spirit of Marvell's

> And tear our Pleasures with rough strife
> Thorough the Iron gates of Life.

We can never expect to be so constituted that the *Iliad* will become for us what much of the Bible in English was for our ancestors. It can never be assimilated as a living whole. The classics do not lie down together like lambs but like beasts in a jungle. The accumulated experiences of mankind have an automatic exclusive action. The amount of the past that can become the present in a living culture is progressively limited. We assimilate only what we badly need. It therefore seems to me something of a pious superstition nowadays to offer a version of the whole *Iliad*. What translators should attempt are the glowing centres where life is abundant and abundantly apparent. For this reason I think it a fair method of sampling these versions to consider only the set speeches of the *Iliad*. Take away the speeches and very little is left of the poem. If the speeches are not well translated there will be no point in taking further samples. For if we cannot believe in the speeches we cannot construct the action, the inner action which gives the 'story' element its point. Speech at the points of extreme tension and speech that causes the mind to extend to the limits of the action, these are the places that must be got right if the life in the *Iliad* is to pass into our own. But to give a public meaning to all the words I have used, a sample must be produced of what assimilation into a living culture is like.

> The beauty of Israel is slaine upon thy high places:
> How are the mightie fallen!

Tell it not in Gath,
Publish it not in the streetes of Askelon;
Lest the daughters of the Philistines rejoyce,
Lest the daughters of the uncircumcised triumph.
Yee mountaines of Gilboa, let there bee no dewe,
Neither let there be raine, upon you, nor fields of offerings:
For there the shield of the mightie is vilely cast away,
The shield of Saul, as though hee had not beene annointed with oile.
From the blood of the slaine,
From the fat of the mightie,
The bow of Jonathan turned not backe;
And the sword of Saul returned not emptie.
Saul and Jonathan were lovely and pleasant in their lives,
And in their death they were not divided:
They were swifter then Eagles,
They were stronger then Lions.
Yee daughters of Israel, weepe over Saul,
Who clothed you in scarlet, with other delights,
Who put on ornaments of golde upon your apparell.
How are the mightie fallen in the midst of the battell!
O Jonathan, thou wast slaine in thine high places.
I am distressed for thee, my brother Jonathan:
Very pleasant hast thou beene to me:
Thy love to mee was wonderfull,
Passing the love of women.
How are the mightie fallen,
And the weapons of warr perished!

Among the many felicities of this passage everyone, I take it, would count its success in bringing the remote near. That success, I take it, was obtained by an addition to the original of something only English could bring. I can detect nothing of it in the Latin:

Considera Israel pro his qui mortui sunt super excelsa tua vulnerati,
Inclyti, Israel, super montes tuos interfecti sunt:
quo modo ceciderunt fortes?

or in the French:

Montagne de Guilboah, que la rosée, et la,
pluye ne tombent jamais sur vous,
ni sur les champs qui y sont haut élevez!

parce que c'est là qu'a été jetée le bouclier
des hommes forts,
& le bouclier de Saül, comme s'il n'eût point
été oint d'huile.

The English version has enabled us to enter into the heroic mode. We are put into the presence of something that we take hold of and that takes hold of us.

Although Homer's *Iliad* is a metrical poem, the success of this prose translation of Hebrew poetry suggests that prose might be able to rise to the heights required to carry us imaginatively into the passion of a similarly formal Greek threnody. I therefore take as my test passage one of the lamentations over the dead body of Hector that gather up the accumulated feeling of the work.

(1) My husband, you have perished out of life, still young, and left me a widow in the house! The boy is only a baby, your son and my son, doomed father, doomed mother! and he I think will never grow up to manhood; long before that our city will be utterly laid waste!

(2) For you, her guardian, have perished, you that watched over her and kept her loyal wives and little babies safe. They will be carried off soon in the hollow ships, and I with them. And you, my child, will go with me to labour somewhere at a menial task under a heartless master's eye; or some Achaean will seize you by the arm and hurl you from the walls to a cruel death,

(3) in his anger because Hector slew his brother or father or son, for very many of the Achaeans at Hector's hands bit the vast earth with their teeth. Your father was not gentle in dreadful combat.

(4) Therefore the people sorrow for him throughout the city. More than all thought is the sorrow you have left to your parents, Hector, and to me still more, for you did not stretch out your arms to me as you lay dying or say words I might have lived with night and day.

I have set out the texts in this way to make the obvious point: that these passages are all alike. The reader may further judge of their similarity by attempting to say where one translator begins and the

other ends in the following piece, which I have concocted exclusively
from these same four prose versions:

> Zeus-born son of Laertes, Odysseus of many wiles, let us go,
> for I do not think we shall achieve our errand this time. Bad
> as the news is, we must at once report it to the Danaans, who
> still sit waiting for it. For Achilles has worked up his anger.
> Hard-hearted man! Nor does he care for the love with which
> his comrades honoured him above others beside the ships. The
> inhumanity of it! A man will take blood-price from one who has
> killed his brother or his own son, and the slayer remains there
> among the people when he has paid a large forfeit; the other
> controls his heart and temper after accepting the price. But you,
> Achilles, are implacable, you have made your heart hard because
> of one girl only. Now we offer you seven of the best and a great
> deal more into the bargain. Be more welcoming and keep in
> mind that we are under your roof. We were picked from the
> whole Danaan army and we would be your nearest and dearest
> friends beyond all others among the Achaeans.

If these passages are faithful translations we can say of the *Iliad*
that it is dull, banal, undramatic and undistinguished. There is nothing
memorable in phrasing or movement to hold the attention. We are
kept at an immense distance from the passion of Andromache. If
Homer's qualities are the reverse of these, then we can say that the
travesty is a direct consequence of the principles of translation adopted.
The radical mistake lies in a literalist fallacy. The versions all put
flat words where Homer put simple words. By 'flat', I mean words
that have only a dictionary relation to the Greek. All their faults
were noted and exposed by Cowper in his classic formulation of the
problem of translation:

> There are minutiae in every language, which transfused into
> another will spoil the version. Such extreme fidelity is in fact
> unfaithful; such close resemblance takes away all likeness. The
> original is elegant, easy, natural; the copy is clumsy, constrained,
> unnatural. To what is this owing? To the adoption of terms not
> congenial to your purpose, and of a context such as no man
> writing an original work would make use of. Homer is every-
> thing that a poet should be. A translation of Homer so made,
> will be everything that a translation of Homer should not be;

N

because it will be written in no language under heaven;—it
will be English, and it will be Greek; and therefore it will be
neither. He is the man, whoever he be—(I do not pretend to be
that man myself); he is the man best qualified as a translator
of Homer, who has drenched, and steeped, and soaked himself in
the effusions of his genius, till he has imbibed their colour to the
bone; and who, when he is thus dyed through and through,
distinguishing between what is essentially Greek, and what may
be habited in English, rejects the former, and is faithful to the
latter, as far as the purposes of fine poetry will permit, and no
further: this, I think, may be easily proved. Homer is everywhere
remarkable either for ease, dignity, or energy of expression; for
grandeur of conception, and a majestic flow of numbers. If we
copy him so closely as to make every one of these excellent
properties of his absolutely unattainable—which will certainly
be the effect of too close a copy,—instead of translating we
murder him . . . an English manner must *differ* from a Greek
one, in order to be graceful, and for this there is no remedy.

My verdict on these translations is as depressing as could be: they
do not transmit any of the qualities that make the *Iliad* distinguished
or deserving of our attention: they do not incite me to take up Greek
grammar and dictionary: nobody with a smattering of Greek could
find a use for them. Consequently, though they do have slight distinguishing marks—Rieu is the most banal and vulgar, Rouse boyishly
facetious, etc.—they must be condemned *en bloc* as not performing the
function of assimilating into living culture what is still there to be
represented in modern English. Are the prospects for verse translation
any brighter? They were once thought to be. Johnson's praise of
Pope's version is well known: 'a poetical wonder', a 'performance
which no age or nation can pretend to equal'. The reader may be
exhilarated to learn that Johnson's claim has been refuted. 'The
finest translation of Homer ever made into the English language' first
appeared in 1951 and was issued in paperback form in 1961. This
refuting verdict is a practitioner's and a fellow-professor's, and was
supported by that of another practitioner, Robert Fitzgerald, in the
*Kenyon Review*: 'The feat is so decisive that it is reasonable to foresee
a century or so in which nobody will try again to put the *Iliad* in
English verse.'

To show that these views are demonstrably absurd will call for peculiar evidence, and I must therefore put on record some odd facts before quoting the test passage from *The Iliad of Homer* by Richmond Lattimore. Many years ago I had while lecturing on the poetry of Pope to handle his neglected translation of the *Iliad* before an audience without even a smattering of Greek. To bring out the creative achievement, I found I needed something to contrast with Pope's verse, and, for the reasons given above, contrast with the prose versions then available seemed too crass. I therefore composed some versions of Homeric similes. Since I had no other obligation than to serve Pope, I was not called upon to fix my principles or to discipline myself to one manner. A few snippets will serve if the reader will take my assurance both that they are a fair sample of the many bits I included and that I give them here untouched from my original lecture scripts. First then, an effort to be literal and straightforward:

As thousands and thousands of flies that wander unceasing in
                                                       spring time
in and out of the cowsheds, through stables and up to the sheep-
                                                              folds
as the time of the year comes round when milk splashes into milk
                                                             pails,
so many thousands of Greeks with their long hair dressed for
                                                        the battle
came up against the Trojans and longed to tear them to pieces.

The reader will judge of my surprise when, in the course of reading for this survey, I discovered Professor Lattimore's version:

Like the multitudinous nations of swarming insects
who drive hither and thither about the stalls of the sheepfold
in the season of spring when the milk splashes in the milk pails:
in such numbers the flowing-haired Achaians stood up
through the plain against the Trojans, hearts burning to break
    them.                                    (Book II, lines 469-73, p. 88)

That this was a general resemblance I found when I went over the other similes I had 'rendered'. Here is a passage where I allowed myself to be less literal in an effort to be more faithful:

                    The men round the Two named Aias
seemed like a cloud a goatherd sees as he stands on a high rock
looking out over the sea: the West Wind blows it towards him:

blacker than pitch it seems as it blows in nearer and nearer,
drawing together and gathering out of the sky and the water
wind, rain and darkness. He shivers and moves his goats into
                                                    shelter.
So like a thick black cloud round the Two was the close-packed
                                                    phalanx
of young men active to kill and be killed as a thrust should
                                                    decide it:
a dark mass broken with light as they shifted their shields and
                                                    their lances.

Professor Lattimore is consistent in rendering it as follows:

These were armed, and about them went a cloud of foot-soldiers.
As from his watching place a goatherd watches a cloud move
on its way over the sea before the drive of the west wind;
far away though he be he watches it, blacker than pitch is,
moving across the sea and piling the storm before it,
and as he sees it he shivers and drives his flocks to a cavern;
so about the two Aiantes moved the battalions,
close-compacted of strong and god-supported young fighters,
black, and jagged with spear and shield, to the terror of battle.
                        (Book IV, lines 274-82, p. 120)

Finally, resisting the temptation to smuggle into print an unpublished
'gem', I give a bit which has no special point:

And when Menelaos (whom Ares loves) identified Paris
coming in front of the mass of the fighters and striding out boldly,
joy took hold of his heart, as, chancing upon a huge carcass,
after long hunger, a lion, finding a stag or a wild goat,
terribly tears at the flesh, and joy takes hold of *his* heart,
(though men in their lusty prime and fast-running deer-hounds
                                                    beset him)
so Menelaos was glad when his eye fell on great Alexandros.

which Professor Lattimore turned as follows:

Now as soon as Menelaos the warlike caught sight of him
making his way with long strides out in front of the army,
he was glad, like a lion who comes on a mighty carcass,
in his hunger chancing upon the body of a horned stag

or wild goat; who eats it eagerly, although against him
are hastening the hounds in their speed and the stalwart young
men:
thus Menelaos was happy finding godlike Alexandros
there in front of his eyes . . .
(Book III, lines 21-28, pp. 100-101)

The point of these comparisons is not '*pereant qui ante nos nostra
dixerunt*' ('The Devil take those who have anticipated our best
things'), but to ask the reader's permission to say something from my
introspective knowledge rather than to comment on the professor's
verse. First, as to the oddity of the degree of resemblance. I deduce
from this that if the paperback publishers had approached half a dozen
academics engaged in the task of 'mediating' Homer to a Greekless
audience, there might have been a similar uniformity of verse translations as there is of prose. But the odder thing is that of my own efforts
I can say with authority they were never meant to be either verse or
translations. I couldn't write a line of poetry if I tried. My bits were
announced as 'creeping translation', a device for funking the task I
have no idea how to set about. They do *not* make on me the effect the
original has. On the contrary, in every respect in which the lines of
the *Iliad* strike me as having clear poetic characteristics, my versions
are the ludicrous opposite. In self-defence I can say that I did not
urge my imagination to leap since I did not know where to land.
I know at what low pressure my bits were put together and how easy
a task the translator has if he so evades his real job.

Professor Lattimore's version, however, seems to me more readable
and less offensive than any of the prose versions:

'My husband, you were lost young from life, and have left me
a widow in your house, and the boy is only a baby
who was born to you and me, the unhappy. I think he will never
come of age, for before then head to heel this city
will be sacked, for you, its defender, are gone, you who guarded
the city, and the grave wives, and the innocent children,
wives who before long must go away in the hollow ships,
and among them I shall also go, and you, my child, follow
where I go, and there do much hard work that is unworthy
of you, drudgery for a hard master; or else some Achaian
will take you by hand and hurl you from the tower into horrible
death, in anger because Hektor once killed his brother,

or his father, or his son; there were so many Achaians
whose teeth bit the vast earth, beaten down by the hands of
Hektor.
Your father was no merciful man in the horror of battle.
Therefore your people are grieving for you all through the city,
Hektor, and you left for your parents mourning and sorrow
beyond words, but for me passing all others is left the bitterness
and the pain, for you did not die in bed, and stretch your arms
to me,
nor tell me some last intimate word that I could remember
always, all the nights and days of my weeping for you.'
(Book XXIV, lines 725-45, pp. 494-95)

Inadequate as this is to meet the test, it is at least within hailing
distance of credible speech, unlike the version by S. O. Andrew and
M. J. Oakley:

Ah! husband of mine! how young from life thou art pass'd,
And thy wife thou leavest a widow, thy son but a babe,
Whom surely we bore to our sorrow, never to grow
To his manhood's prime . . .

And undistinguished as the movement is, it has not the trivialising
effect of the prattling ballads of Robert Graves:

Ah, Hector, fallen young and strong,
Your widow mourns you in this song:
Despaired because our only son,
This little, ill-starred, prattling one
Can never grow to man's estate
Before old Troy has met her fate.

And, finally, it brings home to us that the problem of translating the
great speeches is what it always was: how to be simple without being
flat, how to be grand while remaining simple.[1]

---

[1] In the light of Dryden's remarks (see page 164), it may be of interest to see how
Congreve rendered the passage:

*Andromache* alone, no Notes cou'd find,
*No Musick wild enough for her distracted Mind;*
Her Grief, long smother'd, now from silence broke,
And thus (close pressing his pale Cheeks) she spoke.

### Andromache's *Lamentation*

O my lost Husband! let me ever mourn
Thy early Fate, and too untimely Urn:
In the full Pride of Youth thy Glories fade,
And thou in ashes must with them be laid.

    Why is my Heart thus miserably torn!
Why am I thus distress'd! why thus forlorn!
Am I that wretched thing, a *Widow* left?
Why do I live, who am of Life bereft!
Yet I were blest, were I alone undone;
Alas, my Child! where can an Infant run?
Unhappy Orphan! thou in Woes art nurst;
Why were you born?—I am with blessings curst!
For long e're thou shalt be to Manhood grown,
Wide Desolation will lay waste this Town:
Who is there now, that can Protection give,
Since *He*, who was her strength, no more doth live?
Who, of her Rev'rend Matrons, will have care?
Who, save her Children from the Rage of War?
For *He* to *all* Father and Husband was,
And all are *Orphans* now, and *Widows* by his loss.
Soon will the *Grecians*, now, insulting come
And bear us Captives to their distant home;
I, with my Child, must the same Fortune share,
And all alike, be Pris'ners of the War;
'Mongst base-born Wretches, he, his Lot must have,
And be to some inhuman Lord, a Slave.
Else some avenging *Greek*, with Fury fill'd,
Or for an only Son, or Father kill'd
By *Hector*'s hand, on him will vent his Rage,
And, with *his Blood*, his thirsty grief asswage;
For many fell by his relentless hand,
Biting that ground, which, with their *Blood* was stain'd.

Fierce was thy Father (O my Child) in War,
And never did his Foe in *Battel* spare;
Thence come these suff'rings, which, so much have cost,
Much woe to all, but sure, to me the most.
I saw him not, when in the pangs of Death,
Nor did my Lips receive his latest breath;
Why held he not to me his dying hand?
And why receiv'd not I his last Command?
Something he wou'd have said, had I been there,
Which I shou'd still in sad remembrance bear;
For I cou'd never, never words forget,
Which, Night and Day, I wou'd with Tears repeat.

    She spake, and wept afresh, when all around,
A gen'ral *Sigh*, diffus'd a mournful sound.

                    (*Examen Poeticum*, pp. 219-222)

# Incredible Speech:
# The *Odyssey* of Homer[1]

To anyone who has acquired a taste for the poetry of Pope, to anybody with a taste for English poetry, the possibility of possessing parts at least of the poem known as the *Odyssey* and commonly attributed to Homer is given as immediately as to Keats a key was given through the very inferior version by Chapman. Thanks to Pope we who search for the epics by way of translations can look beyond our noses and see that Homer has an indefinite future among us as exhibiting not only what humanity has been but what it once again might become. Pope's version has this success because it is on the right lines and concentrates on the main things: to make it apparent that, as a critic of our day has put it, Homer *'esprime valori eterni con parole di eternità'*.

The effect of reading Pope is, furthermore, to help us resist temptations to prefer a part of the *Odyssey* to the whole. To listen to some people you would think that the poem existed solely to provide a framework for the hero's long narrative in Books IX-XII of his marvellous adventures by sea and land. For others the poem clearly ends half-way through when Odysseus kisses his native soil in Book XIII. 'Obviously the tale was the thing,' said the pseudonymous T. E. Shaw, and in so saying defined his limitations. For then he is forced to the eccentric conclusion, 'Perhaps the tedious delay of the climax through ten books may be a poor bard's means of prolonging his host's hospitality'.

But what above all comes over us if we approach the epic through Pope is that the deep vein of great humanity in Homer is always cropping out in passages by which men's hearts have never ceased to be touched, from Homer's days to ours. Very often these supreme touches come to us in direct speech, and here Pope has grasped and shown us the chief problem and task of a translator as being to find

---

[1] Reprinted from *The New York Review of Books*, May 9th, 1968.

*credible speech.* The decorum of the Homeric personages is very hard to define, and even harder to match. The personages neither orate nor converse; they strike a note that includes ornate speech and occasionally the most brutally direct word order and economy, but they have an accent all their own and their credibility as heroes depends on our getting it exactly right. The most sublime moments fail to come across if there is anything slightly 'off', as, for me, here:

> Be content, good friend, die also thou! why lamentest thou
> thyself on this wise? Patroclus, too, died, who was a far better
> than thou!
>
> (Matthew Arnold)

On hearing this I find Achilles disappearing and the whole *Iliad* going up in smoke.

Finally, Pope summed up the problem of translating the epics once and for all in his famous *Preface*, where he wrote:

> It is not to be doubted that the *Fire* of the Poem is what a Translator should principally regard, as it is most likely to expire in his managing: However it is his safest way to be content with preserving this to his utmost in the Whole, without endeavouring to be more than he finds his Author is, in any particular Place. 'Tis a great Secret in Writing to know when to be plain, and when poetical and figurative: and it is what *Homer* will teach us if we will but follow modestly in his Footsteps. Where his Diction is bold and lofty, let us raise ours as high as we can; but where his is plain and humble, we ought not to be deterr'd from imitating him by the fear of incurring the Censure of a meer *English* Critick. Nothing that belongs to *Homer* seems to have been more commonly mistaken than the just Pitch of his Style: Some of his Translators having swell'd into Fustian in a proud Confidence of the *Sublime*; others sunk into Flatness in a cold and timorous Notion of *Simplicity*. Methinks I see these different Followers of *Homer*, some sweating and straining after him by violent leaps and Bounds, (the certain Signs of false Mettle) others slowly and servilely creeping in his Train, while the Poet himself is all the time proceeding with an unaffected and equal Majesty before them. However of the two Extreams one could sooner pardon Frenzy than Frigidity: No Author is to be envy'd for such Commendations as he may gain by that

Character of Style, which his Friends must agree together to call *Simplicity*, and the rest of the World will call *Dulness*. There is a *graceful* and *dignify'd* Simplicity, as well as a *bald* and *sordid* one, which differ as much from each other as the Air of a *plain* Man from that of a *Sloven*: 'Tis one thing to be tricked up, and another not to be dress'd at all. Simplicity is the Mean between Ostentation and Rusticity.

The truth of all these propositions is already settled for many minds, and by plausible exemplification and argument the number might helpfully be increased of those who regard Pope's *Odyssey*, with all its faults and mediocrities, as the standard English translation and the one that does most justice to the poetical merits of the original, and so the truest to its essential spirit. But to some American critics the mirror on the wall gave a different answer in 1961, when Robert Fitzgerald's verse translation of the *Odyssey* received the Bollingen Award for the best translation of a poem into English. Tribute as various as this from Moses Hadas: 'Surely the best and truest *Odyssey* in the English language' and from William Arrowsmith this: 'At last we have an *Odyssey* worthy of the original' was capped by Bernard Knox, who wrote: 'The longfelt need for a poetic translation of the *Odyssey* has been filled and it is safe to say that this will be the standard English version for a long time to come.' Even if I were not already inclined to do so, the warmth of these remarks, made by men with whom it would be an honour to be allowed to debate, would impel me to raise the question whether this version of Fitzgerald's is such as both to show up Pope's as inferior and to be a test for any subsequent verse translation of the *Odyssey*.

The general test for a modern verse translation of the *Odyssey*, once made clear by Pope, has been made clearer by the success of several modern prose translations. The prose versions by 'T. E. Shaw' and E. V. Rieu reminded or informed readers that the *Odyssey* can be used to provide some of the low-level pleasures of the novel. Readers noted with surprise that you could go on and on in these versions with never a pause for thought or backward comparisons. At the same time they observed the absence of any potent touches that might justify the view that the *Odyssey* had other merits than those of the-novel-of-the-year. Because of these versions, earlier critics who had referred to the style of the original as 'sublime' or 'majestic', were thought to be too stuffy or pompous to be taken seriously, and the enthusiasm of Keats for Chapman was put down to self-intoxication on the part of both translator and reader.

Yet, if we can learn anything from Pope, a similar 'lift' is the very feature by which we should know that a modern verse translation had begun to justify itself. I do not think that any modern translation could expect to rise *every* time Homer rises, but if it rose once or twice in one or other of the twenty or so places in the *Odyssey* where generation after generation has found Homer rising, then a modern poetic translation would have come into being. No real poet who respected both Homer and himself would dream of attempting the whole epic until he had done one of the great passages in such a way that competent critics told him he had added to the poetry of the *English* language.

To apply the test in a fair way we need a passage that is a genuine outcropping of the vein of humanity, not a piece that could have been tacked on where it is or put in at any other place. If the passage contains direct speech it must satisfy the criteria I mentioned when reviewing some versions of the *Iliad* in *The Cambridge Quarterly* (Vol. I, No. 1, Winter 1965-66). The speech must be such that, without it, we should be unable to construct the action, the inner action which gives the 'story' element its point. It must be speech at a point of extreme tension, and speech that causes the mind to extend to the furthest limits of the action. In that review I was thinking principally of how in the *Iliad* the laments over Hector's body sent the mind travelling back over the whole action of the poem, with the disturbing reflection that the last words of the poem are being given to Hector rather than Achilles. A similar passage is Sarpedon's speech to Glaucus in Book XIX, which Matthew Arnold used to such good effect in characterizing the translations of Pope and Chapman. The scene where Hector parts from Andromache perfectly illustrates what I mean by the outcropping of humanity. I make these specifications because, if the translation passes the test here, it will certainly pass elsewhere, and, if it cannot pass the test here, it will not be worth bothering with.

I have chosen the silent interview between Odysseus and Penelope in Book XXIII for a further reason. If pressed to give a general account of successful translation from Homer I should always leave the emphasis on the degree to which the author has to invent his original. In a short review there is no space to refute the common delusion that there is a public Homer, 'out there' so to speak, an agreed text whose meaning is shared by all who know Greek. I have therefore taken a passage which has always pulled readers up, and forced them to do some of the work of interpretation for themselves. What the difficulties are will emerge from the discussion below, but their general nature is set out beautifully by Pope in a note introducing the whole book. (These notes of Pope will come as a revelation to those who have hitherto had to use nineteenth-century and modern editions of Pope's translations. Not only do they contain some wonderful English prose, they expound Pope's critical creed. They are the one thing in the new edition[1] that the ordinary reader will feel unmixed gratitude for.)

> This book contains the Discovery of *Ulysses* to *Penelope*. Monsieur *Rapin* is very severe upon some parts of it; whose objections I shall here recite.
>
> The discovery of *Ulysses* to his Queen was the most favourable occasion imaginable for the Poet to give us some of the nicest touches of his art; but as he has manag'd it, it has nothing but faint and weak surprizes, cold and languishing astonishments, and very little of that delicacy and exquisiteness which ought to express a conjugal tenderness: He leaves his wife too long in doubt and distrust, and she is too cautious and circumspect; the formalities she observes in being fully assur'd, and her care to act with security, are set down in number and measure, lest she should fall into any mistake; and this particularity makes the story dull, in a place that so much requires briskness and liveliness. Ought not the secret instinct of her love to have inspir'd her with other sentiments? and should not her heart have told her, what her eyes could not? Love is penetrating, and whispers more to us than the senses can convey; but *Homer* understood not this Philosophy: *Virgil*, who makes *Dido* foresee that *Æneas* designs to leave her, would have made better advantage of this favourable opportunity.
>
> The strength of this objection consists chiefly in the long incredulity of *Penelope*, and the slowness she uses to make an undeniable discovery: This *Rapin* judges to be contrary to the passion of love, and consequently that the Poet writes unnaturally.
>
> There is somewhat of the *Frenchman* in this Criticism: *Homer*

---

[1] *Translations of Homer*: The *Iliad* and the *Odyssey* (Volumes VII-X in the Twickenham edition of the poems of Alexander Pope, ed. Maynard Mack, Methuen, 1967.

in his opinion wants vivacity; and if *Rapin* had been to have drawn *Ulysses*, we had seen him all transport and ecstasy. But where there is most fancy, there is often the least judgment. *Penelope* thought *Ulysses* to be dead; he had been absent twenty years; and thro' absence and his present disguise, he was another person from that *Ulysses* whom she knew, when he sail'd to Troy; so that he was become an absolute stranger. From this observation we may appeal to the Reader's judgment, if *Penelope*, without full conviction, ought to be persuaded that this person was the real *Ulysses*? And how could she be convinc'd, but by asking many questions, and descending to particularities, which must necessarily occasion delay in the discovery? If indeed *Ulysses* and *Penelope* had met after a shorter absence, when one view would have assured her that he was her real husband, then too much transport could not have been express'd by the Poet; but this is not the case, she is first to know her husband, before she could or ought express her fondness for his return, otherwise she might be in danger of misplacing it upon an impostor: But she is no sooner convinced that *Ulysses* is actually returned, but she receives him with as much fondness as can be expressed, or as *Rapin* could require.

*While yet he speaks, her pow'rs of life decay,*
*She sickens, trembles, falls, and faints away:*
*At length recov'ring, to his arms she flew,*
*And strain'd him close, as to his breast she grew.*

'Till this moment the discovery was not evidently made, and her passion would have been unseasonable; but this is no sooner done, but she falls into an agony of affection. If she had here appear'd cool and indifferent, there had been weight in *Rapin's* objections.

'T. E. Shaw', for example, who had made up his mind that Penelope was a 'sly cattish wife', found her speaking *sarcastically* to the Old Nurse:

Penelopê responded: 'Even your storied wisdom, mother dear, hardly equips you to interpret the designs of the eternal Gods. Howbeit let us away to my son, for I would see the suitors lying in death; and their slayer.'

Robert Fitzgerald is softer, and more natural, here:

> Penélopê said: 'Nurse dear, though you have your wits about you, still it is hard not to be taken in by the immortals. Let us join my son, though, and see the dead and that strange one who killed them.'

He, however, has taken a bold step and perhaps in the wrong direction in putting in the one adjective that it may have been the whole point of this little scene to withhold. There is no warrant for 'strange' in the mere words of Homer. We, however, ourselves supply some such word as we wonder what Penelope will finally decide to do. 'T. E. Shaw' went on:

> She was going down as she spoke, her heart in a turmoil of debate whether to keep her distance while she examined her dear lord, or go straight up at once to kiss his head and clasp his hand. So when at length she came in across the stone threshold it was to take a seat in the firelight facing Odysseus, but over against the further wall.

Prose can be less distinguished than this, as we are reminded by E. V. Rieu:

> As she spoke she left her room and made her way downstairs, a prey to indecision . . .

but it is poor enough to make us regret that T. E. Lawrence did not feel challenged by Homer to write better. Nor can this of Fitzgerald be called much superior:

> She turned then to descend the stair, her heart in tumult. Had she better keep her distance and question him, her husband? Should she run up to him, take his hands, kiss him now? Crossing the door-sill she sat down at once in firelight, against the nearest wall, across the room from the lord Odysseus.

Only those who are very familiar with Fitzgerald's version as a whole would point out here as characteristic a suggestion of kittenish waywardness in 'should she run up to him . . .?', but the Fitzgerald 'fan' might not accept my further general impression that his is the first version to make the Butlerian thesis plausible that the Homer of the *Odyssey* was a woman.

I am assuming that our eyes at this point are meant to be looking centrally at the *megaron* and that we now turn to Odysseus:

> He sat at the base of a tall pillar, waiting with dropping eyelids to hear his stately consort cry out when she caught sight of him.

Lawrence is so poor that Rieu by contrast seems to have all the quietness of Homer:

> . . . Odysseus, who was sitting by one of the great columns with his eyes on the ground, waiting to see whether his good wife would say anything to him when she saw him.

Fitzgerald seems to have taken this passage in the same spirit:

> There leaning against a pillar, sat the man and never lifted up his eyes, but only waited for what his wife would say when she had seen him.

Now comes the point of the scene. The original is unfortunately hard to construe and the versions may not have exactly the same substratum. Here is 'T. E. Shaw':

> But she sat there in a long silence, with bewildered heart. One moment she would look and see him in his face; and the next moment fail to see him there, by reason of the foul rags he wore . . .

Fitzgerald has risen above this:

> And she, for a long time, sat deathly still in wonderment— for sometimes as she gazed she found him—yes, clearly—like her husband, but sometimes blood and rags were all she saw.

The translation tails off slightly where Mr Fitzgerald's prose faintly suggests a lame iambic pentameter. I use this apparently perverse language, not for the usual purpose, to denigrate the verse pretension; I am appealing to the verdict of the ear that if that organ is allowed to take the lead we are bothered by the typographical layout, which suggests a 'blank verse' metric. The reminders of blank verse in the translation are usually places where Mr Fitzgerald has failed to sustain his staple, which is prose as good as, and sometimes slightly better than, the average of current prose translationese.

The typographical liberty I have taken with Mr Fitzgerald's text will, I hope, serve to make a point in reply to those who regard the staple as consummate *verse*. But such admirers might well ask me whether my ear is so thick that I hear *only* prose in this selected passage! And I would gladly testify that it is just the slight differences from prose that make the translation as a whole such a fluid medium that I can find no passages of stodge or tedium. But it would be unfair to a reader who does not know it to leave this translation there. For it is as distinguished for its poeticalities as for its prose. Many of these are such as to bring a smile of pleasure to a reader with the Greek text before him. They all suggest that Mr Fitzgerald enjoyed translating Homer; they give us a strong impression of a personality so *ondoyant et divers* that we never want to leave his company. Although I judge that his translation never rises, as the best parts of Pope's do, it has a strong *prima facie* case to be the one version we need if we have no Greek to protect us from the merely Augustan poeticalities of Pope.

I hope I have now rigged up a rough-and-ready *experimentum crucis*, a test that will settle the matter for those with only a mild interest in Homer and will compel those more deeply involved to use exact and clear language in setting out their comparative findings. If so, it is time to introduce our central figure.

To many people it will seem ludicrous to speak of 'introducing' Richmond Lattimore,[1] for his other translations have made his name a household word in academic America. His version of the *Iliad* in particular is there taken to be an established classic—though these two words have been so abused that all that is now intended by the phrase may be that the version passes muster with several colleagues in the academic world and is 'recommended reading' for a vast captive audience of undergraduates. On this topic Bernard Knox appears to be a man of one formula, for in the article from which I took the pre-prepared 'blurb' for Fitzgerald's *Odyssey*, I found this comment: '. . . the *Iliad*, by Richmond Lattimore, whose translation, using contemporary English and a rhythmic approximation of Homer's own line, has established itself as the classic translation for our age and I suspect for a long time to come.' Must Mr Fitzgerald's version now make way for Professor Lattimore's or is Lattimore's version so inferior to Fitzgerald's as to be a luxury, without any true *raison d'être*?

---

[1] *The Odyssey of Homer*, translated with an introduction by Richmond Lattimore. Harper & Row, 1968.

*Circumspect Penelope said to her in answer:*
'*Dear nurse, it would be hard for you to baffle the purposes*
*of the everlasting gods, although you are very clever.*
*Still, I will go to see my son, so that I can look on*
*these men who courted me lying dead, and the man who killed them.*'
*She spoke, and came down from the chamber, her heart pondering*
*much, whether to keep away and question her dear husband,*
*or to go up to him and kiss his head, taking his hands.*
*But then, when she came in and stepped over the stone threshold,*
*she sat across from him in the firelight, facing Odysseus,*
*by the opposite wall, while he was seated by the tall pillar,*
*looking downward, and waiting to find out if his majestic*
*wife would have anything to say to him, now that she saw him.*
*She sat a long time in silence, and her heart was wondering.*
*Sometimes she would look at him, with her eyes full upon him,*
*and again would fail to know him in the foul clothing he wore.*

(p. 337)

The impact of this passage, in this particular context, where I have introduced so many breakwaters, may not be great, but anyone who had conscientiously read without interruption all the twenty-three books to this point might well be pardoned if he likened the experience to that of some poor rat forced to wade up to the whiskers through an endless morass of chewed tram tickets. It is a minor annoyance to have things like this:

*looking downward, and waiting to find out if his majestic*

printed as if they were composed lines of poetry; the major *grief* is the tastelessness of the words that painstakingly drain away the distinction of the poem. Heaven knows what a ridiculous noise I make in my head when I open my Homer at this passage but I seem to hear by comparison the music of the spheres. But the contrast is not, I suspect, essentially bound up with what we call 'sound': it is chiefly relief at discovering that there is nothing *Homeric* about all that gives offence in this version. Nothing in my not very learned contact with the Greek words leads me to doubt that I am meeting with a superior mind, the mind of one who thought grandly (on occasions) of the human race, however unable in general to blink the 'miserable condition of humanity'. T. E. Lawrence was convinced of the opposite:

o

My version is fustian: but so is Homer, I think. . . . A great man could make a great poem or a great novel out of its material . . . but a translator can only expose the fraud. . . . What's really wrong with the *Odyssey* is Homer.

The point I am attempting to make here was made long ago by another would-be translator of an epic, John Dryden:

If I cannot Copy his Harmonious Numbers, how shall I imitate his noble Flights, where his Thoughts and Words are equally sublime? . . . What Modern Language, or what Poet can express the Majestick Beauty of this one Verse, amongst a thousand others? . . . For my part, I am lost in the admiration of it: I contemn the World, when I think on it, and my self when I Translate it.

My report, then, is both that

> *the case presents*
> *No adjunct to the Muse's diadem*

and more attention to art was needed and less to matter, since the matter is of no interest to, does not even exist for, lovers of literature without the manner.

To all who would sustain a very high estimate of these two versions as poems, I would offer a challenge to say: are they *significantly* superior to this?—and I would ask for similar comparisons to set the three versions up against one another as wholes.

> *Cautious Penelope answered:*
> '*Dear nurse, it's difficult indeed to comprehend the ways*
> *Of the eternal gods, no matter how wise you are.*
> *But let's go down to my son and see the dead wooers*
> *Along with the man who killed them.*'
> *With this she left*
> *Her room and went downstairs, fiercely debating*
> *Within her heart whether she should keep her distance*
> *From her own dear husband and ask him some questions, or go*
> *Right up and clasp him, kissing his head and hands.*
> *But when she went in across the stone threshold, she sat down*
> *In the firelight close by the wall across from Odysseus,*

*Who sat by a massive pillar with his eyes on the ground*
*Waiting to see if his noble wife would speak*
*When she saw him. Long and silently she sat there, utterly*
*Spellbound. At times she would look him straight in the face*
*And still not know who he was in those rags he had on.*

(Ennis Rees, 1960)

Must the verdict then be that in the sixth decade of the twentieth century the U.S.A. saw *three* translating poets, each great enough to consign Pope's *Odyssey* to oblivion? I must say, though, that in my opinion a man who can believe that can believe anything.

But can ten or more years' work, the composition of 359 pages of verse, with at least thirty-five long lines to the page, be dismissed on the strength of one quotation and a cloudy image of the effect of reading the translation from cover to cover? Dismissal cannot occur until all the steps in the argument are agreed on and accepted as valid. Is it true, for instance, that a translation of Homer must be damned unless 'the Fire of the Poem' is preserved? Is it true that 'the chief problem and task of a translator' of these epics is 'to find credible speech'? The present attempt to set up an ineluctable clinch fails if the reader finds the great figures talking like real heroes in other parts of the translation. Nothing is left of the reviewer's claim to have done his work with scrupulous care if the chosen passage does not represent the poet's *virtues* as well as his deficiencies. It would not have been difficult to find worse passages, but my general impression of Professor Lattimore's version was of a uniform level of performance, and therefore it would not have been helpful to cap my earlier remark about Achilles disappearing by asking what happens to Agamemnon here:

*So there is nothing more deadly or more vile than a woman*
*who stores her mind with acts that are of such sort, as this one*
*did when she thought of this act of dishonor, and plotted*
*the murder of her lawful husband. See, I had been thinking*
*that I would be welcome to my children and thralls of my household*
*when I came home, but she with thoughts surpassingly grisly*
*splashed the shame on herself and the rest of her sex, on women*
*still to come, even on the one whose acts are virtuous.*

(p. 179)

I should have liked to make the verdict turn on one of the most heart-touching moments in Homer's poem, where Odysseus confronts and is confronted by Nausikaa. So many people have found this one of the passages that make the poem a classic that it would be fair to say that, if the poetry of the original is not in some way matched in the translation here, the version cannot be passed as *existing* let alone as deserving praise. But at this place in the book I found Professor Lattimore's poetry actually *repulsive*. As a child and an adolescent the taste of the material from which tram and bus tickets were then made was not repulsive to me (unlike highly flavoured chewing gums) but monotonous in the long run and saliva-absorbent. As a hardened reader, whose critical writing first saw print in 1927, I have had to chew the literary equivalent of much devitalized cellulose and have so learned to distinguish the respectably mediocre from the ever-living and the completely dead. The following seems to me therefore a lapse from Professor Lattimore's *norm*:

> *Only the daughter of Alkinoös stood fast, for Athene*
> *put courage into her heart, and took the fear from her body,*
> *and she stood her ground and faced him, and now Odysseus debated*
> *whether to supplicate the well-favored girl by clasping*
> *her knees, or stand off where he was and in words of blandishment*
> *ask if she would show him the city, and lend him clothing.*
> *Then in the division of his heart this way seemed best to him,*
> *to stand well off and supplicate in words of blandishment,*
> *for fear that, if he clasped her knees, the girl might be angry.*
> *So blandishingly and full of craft he began to address her:*
> *'I am at your knees, O queen. But are you mortal or goddess?*
> *If indeed you are one of the gods who hold wide heaven,*
> *then I must find in you the nearest likeness to Artemis*
> *the daughter of great Zeus, for beauty, figure, and stature.*
> *But if you are one among those mortals who live in this country,*
> *three times blessed are your father and the lady your mother . . .'*
>
> (p. 106)

And lest the reader suspect me of being too narrow-minded an admirer of Pope, I will offer as a relevant comparison a piece of free translation by Chaucer:

> *So longe he walketh in this wildernesse,*
> *Til at the laste he mette an hunteresse.*

*A bowe in hande and arwes hadde she;*
*Hire clothes cutted were unto the kne.*
*But she was yit the fayreste creature*
*That evere was yformed by Nature;*
*And Eneas and Achates she grette,*
*And thus she to hem spak, whan she hem mette;*
*'Saw ye,' quod she, 'as ye han walked wyde,*
*Any of my sustren walke yow besyde*
*With any wilde bor or other best,*
*That they han hunted to, in this forest,*
*Ytukked up, with arwes in hire cas?'*
*'Nay, sothly, lady,' quod this Eneas:*
*'But by thy beaute, as it thynketh me,*
*Thow myghtest nevere erthly woman be,*
*But Phebus syster art thow, as I gesse.*
*And, if so be that thow be a goddesse,*
*Have mercy on oure labour and oure wo.'*
*'I n'am no goddesse, sothly,' quod she tho;*
*'For maydens walken in this contre here,*
*With arwes and with bowe, in this manere.*
*This is the reyne of Libie, there ye ben,*
*Of which that Dido lady is and queen'* . . .

Here, it seems to me, we have a real meeting, and the hero manages
successfully to 'supplicate the well-favored girl' 'in words of blandish-
ment', and we can believe in the people speaking because of the poetry
they speak. This is the music of fairyland, and, no doubt, much of
Virgil has gone—including, possibly, Virgil's own feeling for this
passage of Homer—to pay the piper.

Yet that infelicitous speech puts an immediate extinguisher on our
imagination can be seen by comparing Chaucer's goddess with one of
Professor Lattimore's; Kalypso (*anglicé*: Calypso):

*'You are so naughty, and you will have your own way in all things.*
*See how you have spoken to me and reason with me.*
*Earth be my witness in this, and the wide heaven above us,*
*and the dripping water of the Styx, which oath is the biggest*
*and most formidable oath among the blessed immortals,*
*that this is no other painful trial I am planning against you,*
*but I am thinking and planning for you just as I would do it*

*for my own self, if such needs as yours were to come upon me;*
*for the mind in me is reasonable, and I have no spirit*
*of iron anger inside my heart. It is full of pity.'*
  *So she spoke, a shining goddess . . .*                    (p. 93)

The goddess *cannot* shine if she speaks like that: *incredulus odi.*

# Index

## of Quotations, Allusions and Translations

## NOTE TO THE INDEX

Under the entry for 'FITZGERALD, Robert Stuart' there are two references to an article in *The Kenyon Review* (Autumn 1952). The passages I have in mind are these:

*On Lattimore* (p. 699)

The reason that Mr Lattimore's Iliad seems to me such a big event is that it brings Homer back from the prose where he has been getting submerged for the past several generations and restores him to his proper element, which is poetry and magnificence. If some of the prose has been brought along in the process, that was to be expected, and in any case it has been transformed.

The feat is so decisive that it is reasonable to foresee a century or so in which nobody will try again to put the Iliad into English verse. Taste may change greatly, but it looks to me as if Mr Lattimore's version would survive at least as long as Pope's for in its way it is quite as solidly distinguished.

*On modern translations* (p. 702)

I have deliberated a good deal—for what my deliberation is worth—before praising this Iliad, because I think one of the worst things that people who know Greek or Latin poetry can do is to give unguarded welcome to translations that are not true works of art. The generosity with which professional classicists sometimes embrace inferior translating—the slapdash and flashy kind as well as the worthy industrious kind—not only discredits them but, what is more serious, discredits the perfected works that they are supposed to cherish.